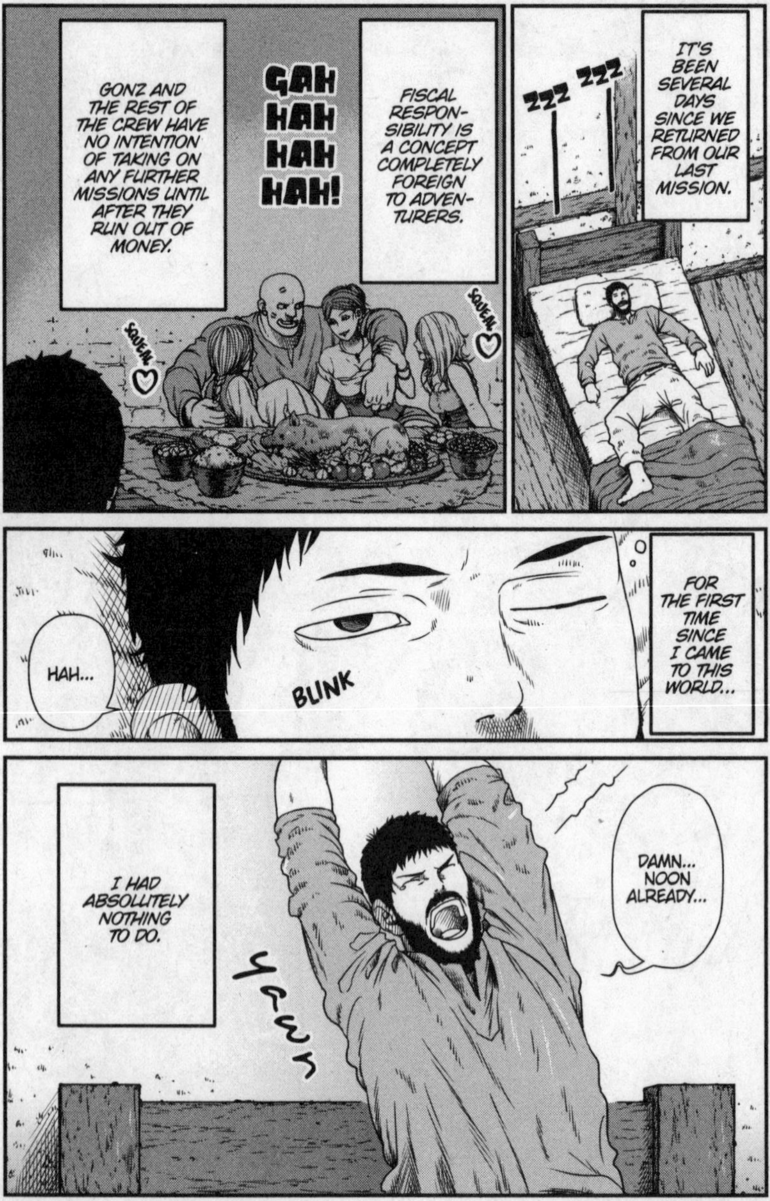
ZZZ ZZZ
IT'S BEEN SEVERAL DAYS SINCE WE RETURNED FROM OUR LAST MISSION.
FISCAL RESPONSIBILITY IS A CONCEPT COMPLETELY FOREIGN TO ADVENTURERS.
GAH HAH HAH HAH!
SQUEAL
GONZ AND THE REST OF THE CREW HAVE NO INTENTION OF TAKING ON ANY FURTHER MISSIONS UNTIL AFTER THEY RUN OUT OF MONEY.
SQUEAL
FOR THE FIRST TIME SINCE I CAME TO THIS WORLD...
BLINK
HAH...
DAMN... NOON ALREADY...
I HAD ABSOLUTELY NOTHING TO DO.
YAWN

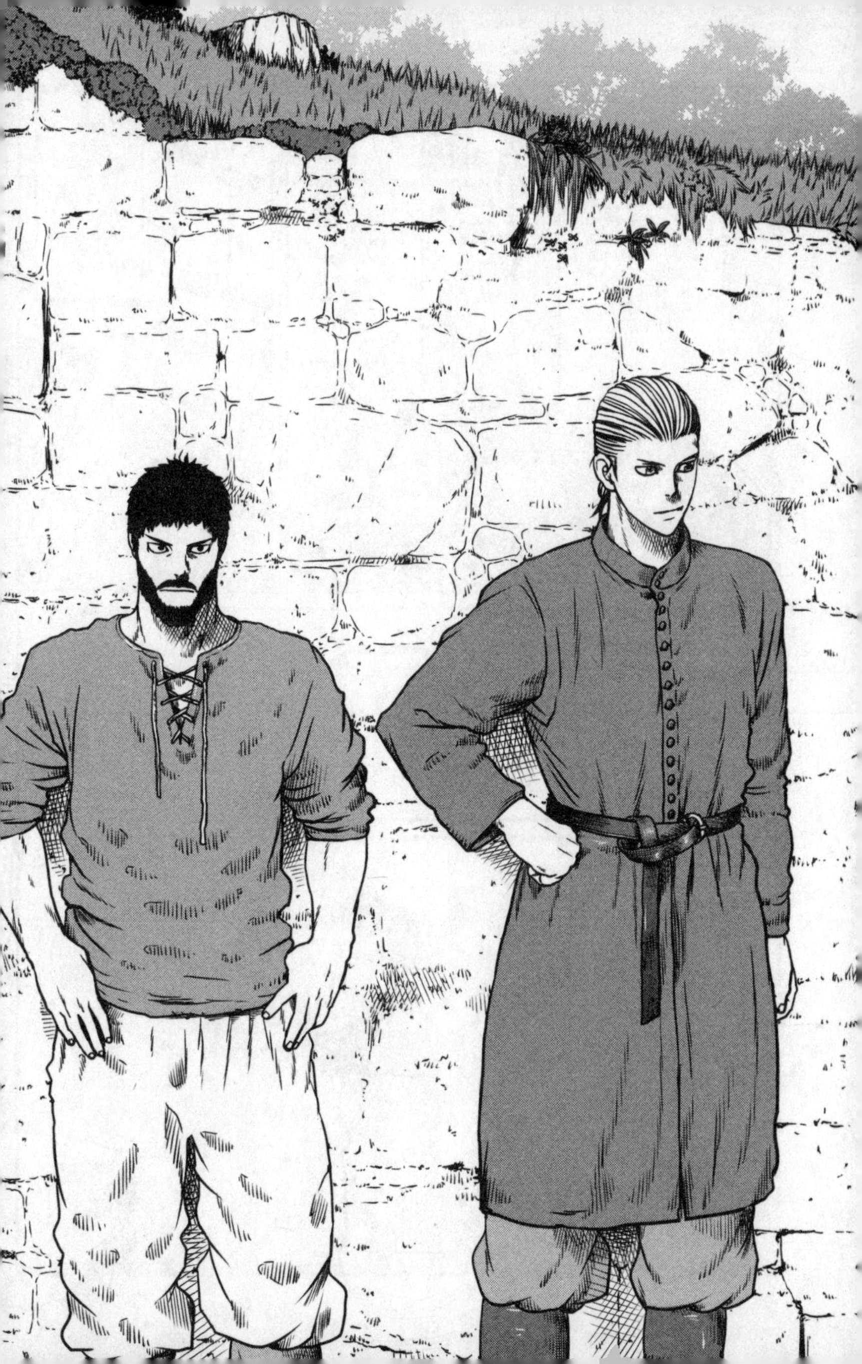

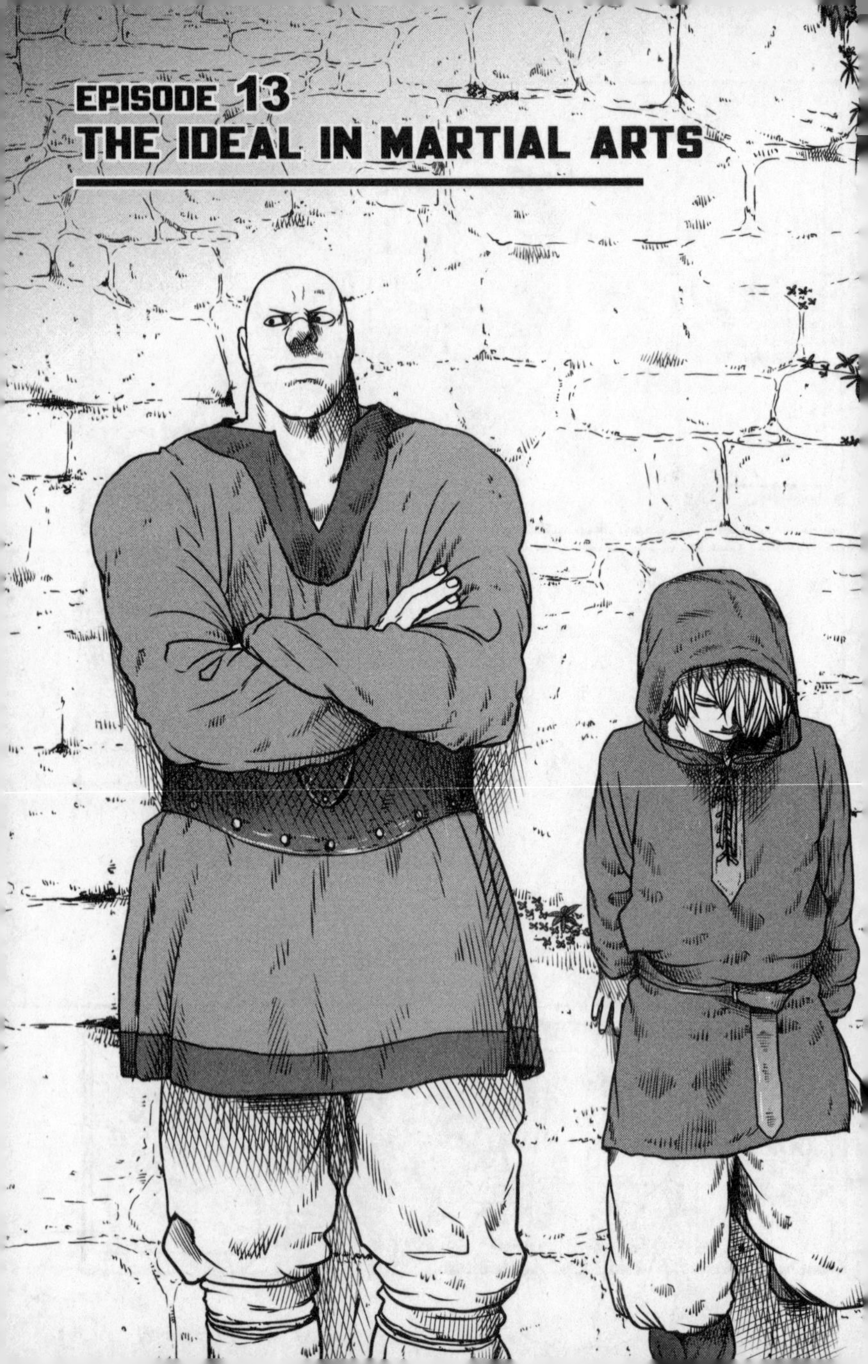
EPISODE 13
THE IDEAL IN MARTIAL ARTS

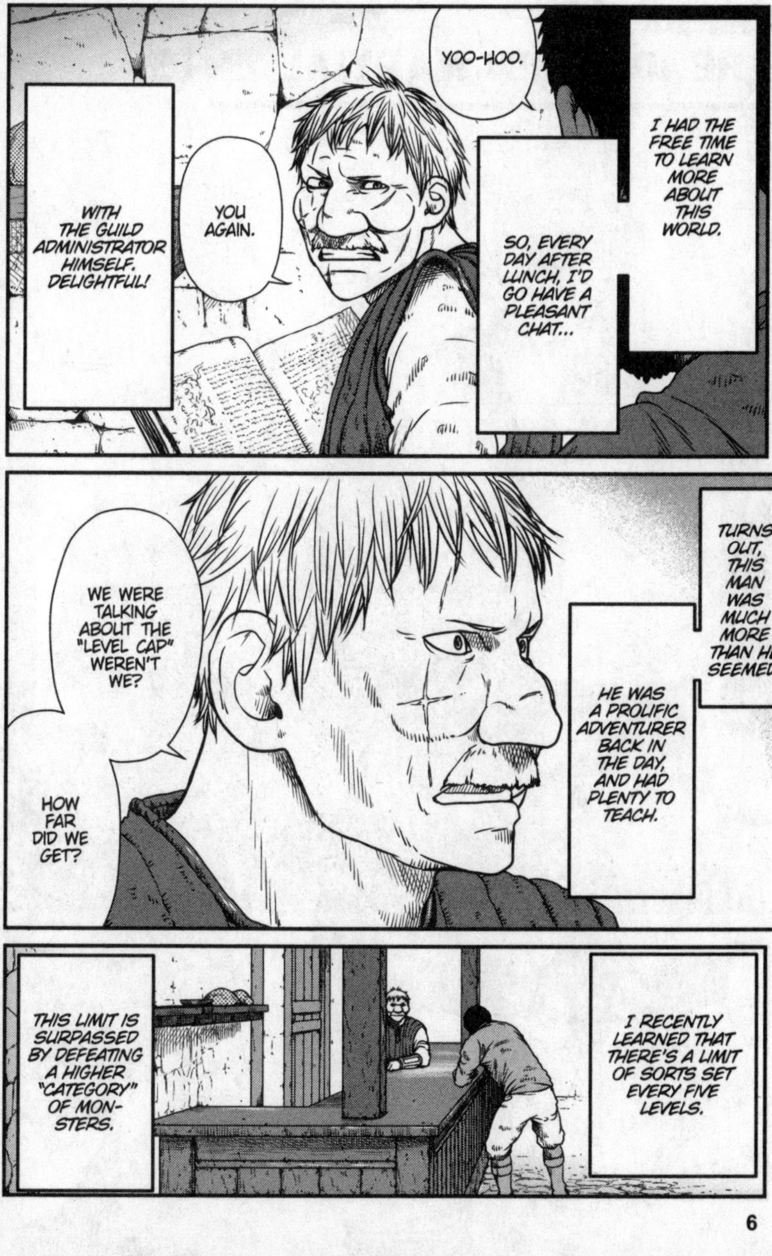
I HAD THE FREE TIME TO LEARN MORE ABOUT THIS WORLD.
SO, EVERY DAY AFTER LUNCH, I'D GO HAVE A PLEASANT CHAT...
YOO-HOO.
YOU AGAIN.
WITH THE GUILD ADMINISTRATOR HIMSELF. DELIGHTFUL!
TURNS OUT, THIS MAN WAS MUCH MORE THAN HE SEEMED.
HE WAS A PROLIFIC ADVENTURER BACK IN THE DAY, AND HAD PLENTY TO TEACH.
WE WERE TALKING ABOUT THE "LEVEL CAP" WEREN'T WE?
HOW FAR DID WE GET?
I RECENTLY LEARNED THAT THERE'S A LIMIT OF SORTS SET EVERY FIVE LEVELS.
THIS LIMIT IS SURPASSED BY DEFEATING A HIGHER "CATEGORY" OF MON-STERS.

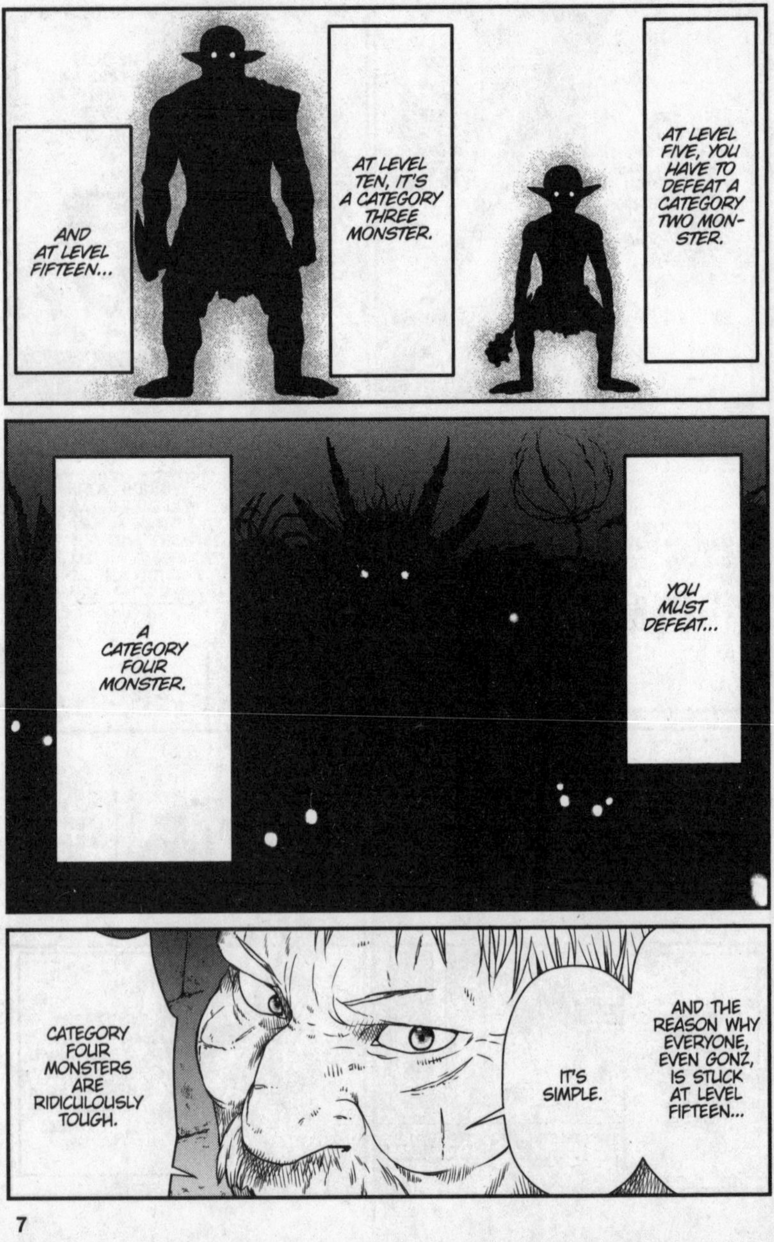
AT LEVEL FIVE, YOU HAVE TO DEFEAT A CATEGORY TWO MON-STER.
AT LEVEL TEN, IT'S A CATEGORY THREE MONSTER.
AND AT LEVEL FIFTEEN...
YOU MUST DEFEAT...
A CATEGORY FOUR MONSTER.
AND THE REASON WHY EVERYONE, EVEN GONZ, IS STUCK AT LEVEL FIFTEEN...
IT'S SIMPLE.
CATEGORY FOUR MONSTERS ARE RIDICULOUSLY TOUGH.

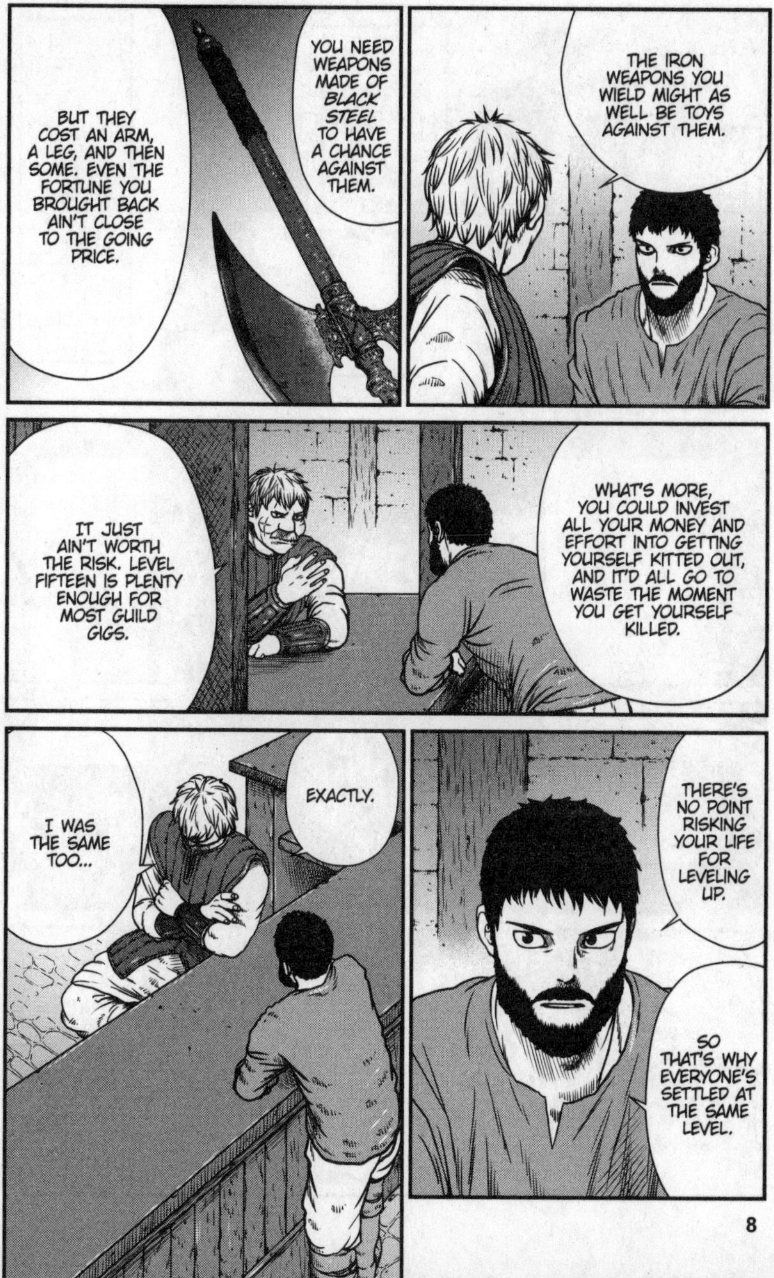
THE IRON WEAPONS YOU WIELD MIGHT AS WELL BE TOYS AGAINST THEM.
YOU NEED WEAPONS MADE OF *BLACK STEEL* TO HAVE A CHANCE AGAINST THEM.
BUT THEY COST AN ARM, A LEG, AND THEN SOME. EVEN THE FORTUNE YOU BROUGHT BACK AIN'T CLOSE TO THE GOING PRICE.
WHAT'S MORE, YOU COULD INVEST ALL YOUR MONEY AND EFFORT INTO GETTING YOURSELF KITTED OUT, AND IT'D ALL GO TO WASTE THE MOMENT YOU GET YOURSELF KILLED.
IT JUST AIN'T WORTH THE RISK. LEVEL FIFTEEN IS PLENTY ENOUGH FOR MOST GUILD GIGS.
THERE'S NO POINT RISKING YOUR LIFE FOR LEVELING UP.
SO THAT'S WHY EVERYONE'S SETTLED AT THE SAME LEVEL.
EXACTLY.
I WAS THE SAME TOO...

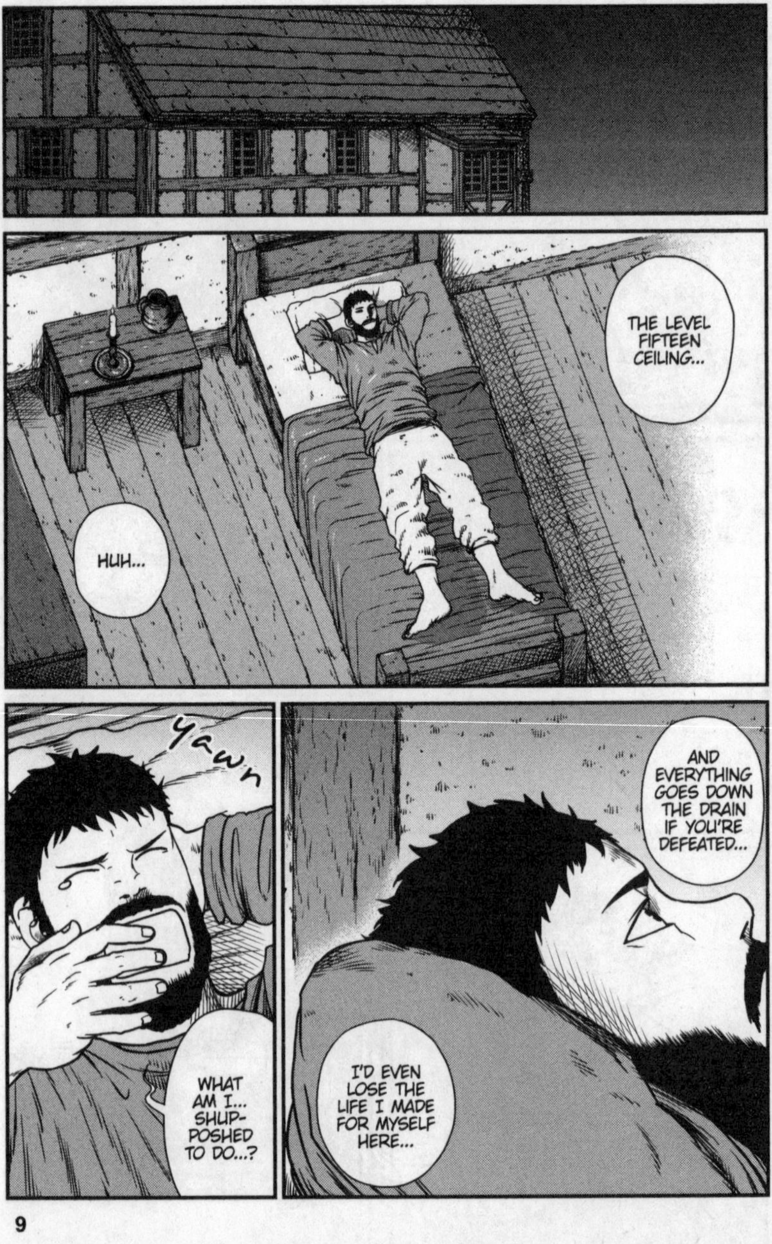
THE LEVEL FIFTEEN CEILING...
HUH...
AND EVERYTHING GOES DOWN THE DRAIN IF YOU'RE DEFEATED...
I'D EVEN LOSE THE LIFE I MADE FOR MYSELF HERE...
yawn
WHAT AM I... SHUP-POSHED TO DO...?

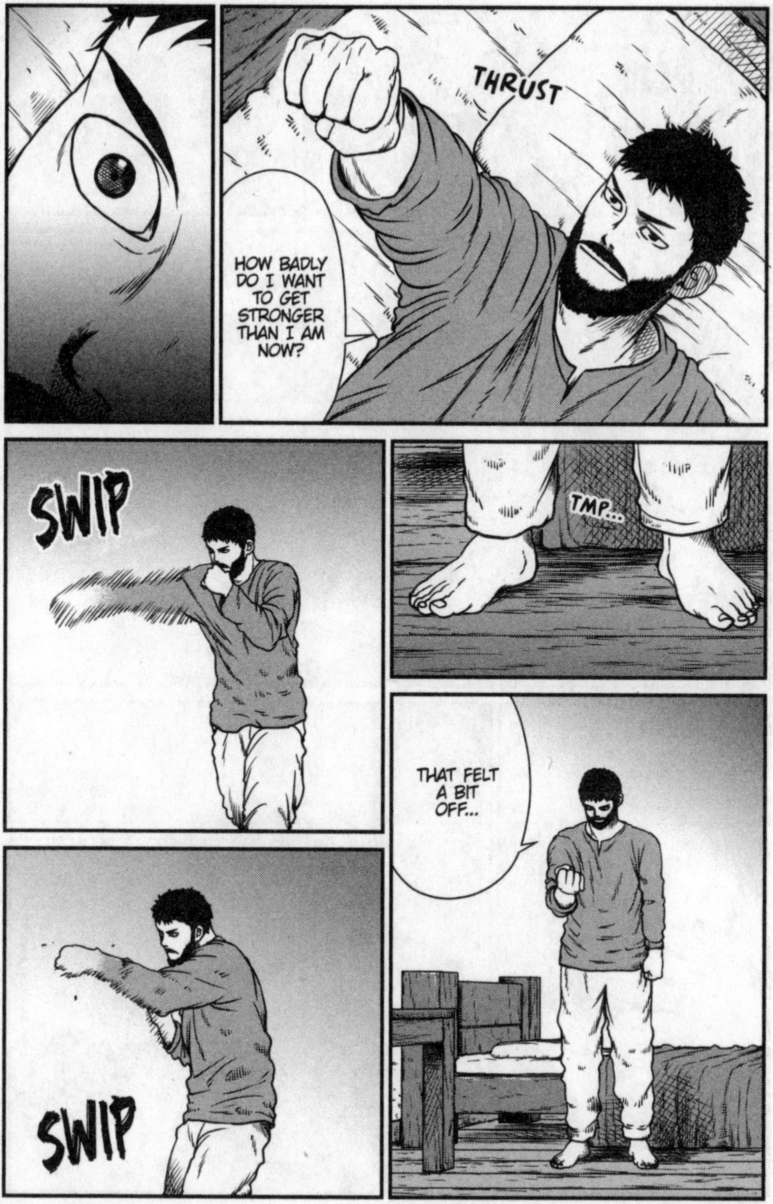
THRUST
HOW BADLY DO I WANT TO GET STRONGER THAN I AM NOW?
TMP...
SWIP
THAT FELT A BIT OFF...
SWIP

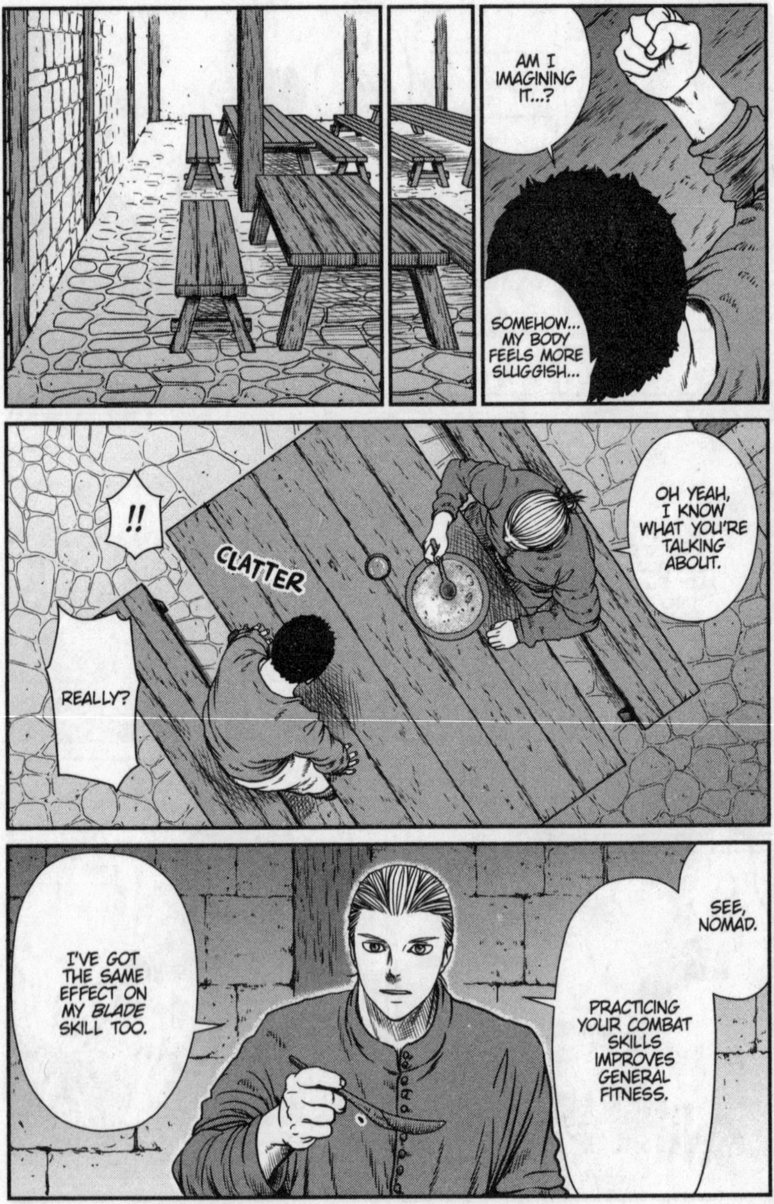
AM I IMAGINING IT...?
SOMEHOW... MY BODY FEELS MORE SLUGGISH...
OH YEAH, I KNOW WHAT YOU'RE TALKING ABOUT.
CLATTER
!!
REALLY?
SEE, NOMAD.
PRACTICING YOUR COMBAT SKILLS IMPROVES GENERAL FITNESS.
I'VE GOT THE SAME EFFECT ON MY *BLADE* SKILL TOO.

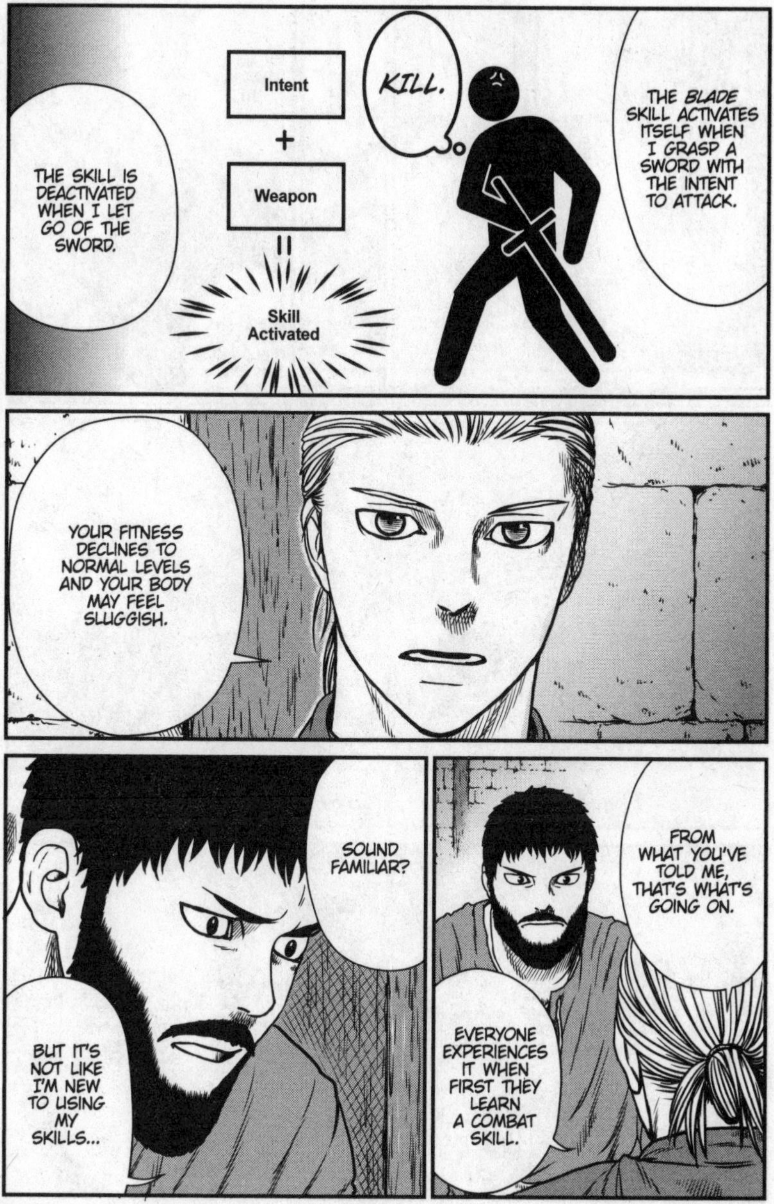

THE *BLADE* SKILL ACTIVATES ITSELF WHEN I GRASP A SWORD WITH THE INTENT TO ATTACK.
KILL.
Intent
+
Weapon
=
Skill Activated
THE SKILL IS DEACTIVATED WHEN I LET GO OF THE SWORD.
YOUR FITNESS DECLINES TO NORMAL LEVELS AND YOUR BODY MAY FEEL SLUGGISH.
FROM WHAT YOU'VE TOLD ME, THAT'S WHAT'S GOING ON.
EVERYONE EXPERIENCES IT WHEN FIRST THEY LEARN A COMBAT SKILL.
SOUND FAMILIAR?
BUT IT'S NOT LIKE I'M NEW TO USING MY SKILLS...

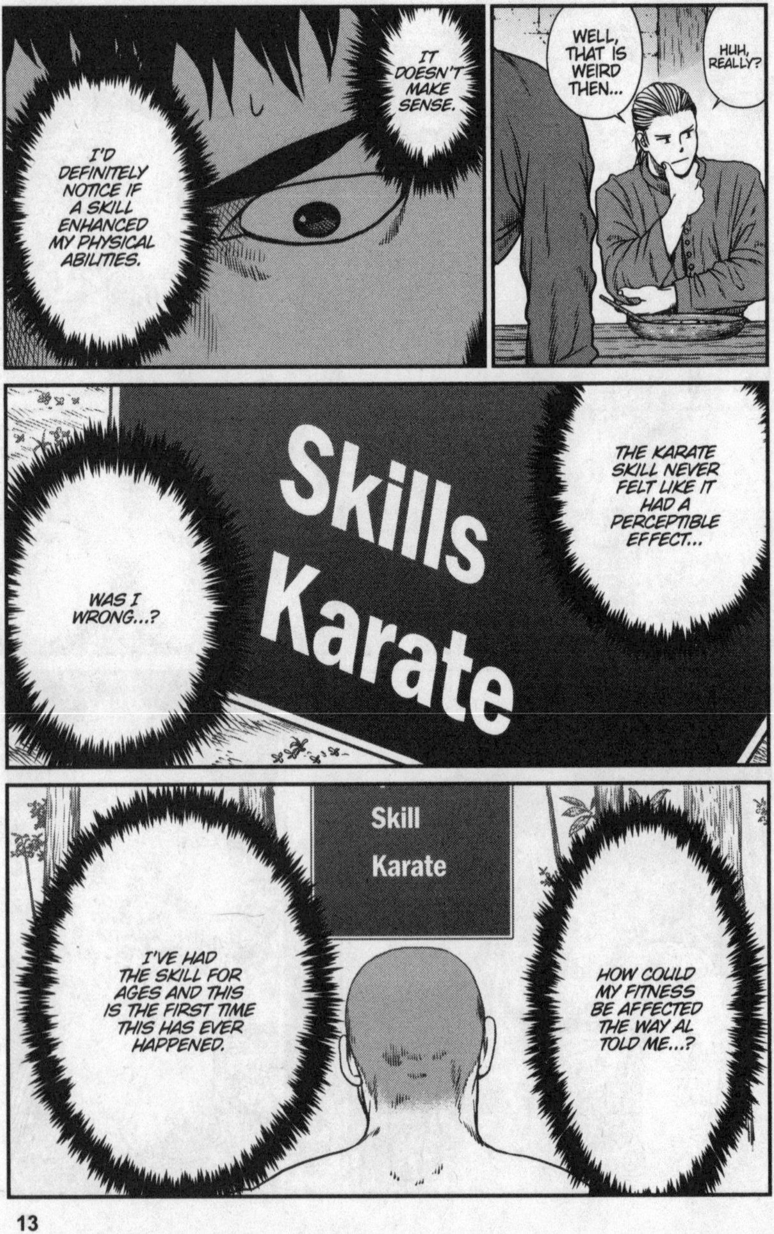
HUH, REALLY?
WELL, THAT IS WEIRD THEN...
IT DOESN'T MAKE SENSE.
I'D DEFINITELY NOTICE IF A SKILL ENHANCED MY PHYSICAL ABILITIES.
THE KARATE SKILL NEVER FELT LIKE IT HAD A PERCEPTIBLE EFFECT...
Skills
Karate
WAS I WRONG...?
Skill
Karate
HOW COULD MY FITNESS BE AFFECTED THE WAY AL TOLD ME...?
I'VE HAD THE SKILL FOR AGES AND THIS IS THE FIRST TIME THIS HAS EVER HAPPENED.

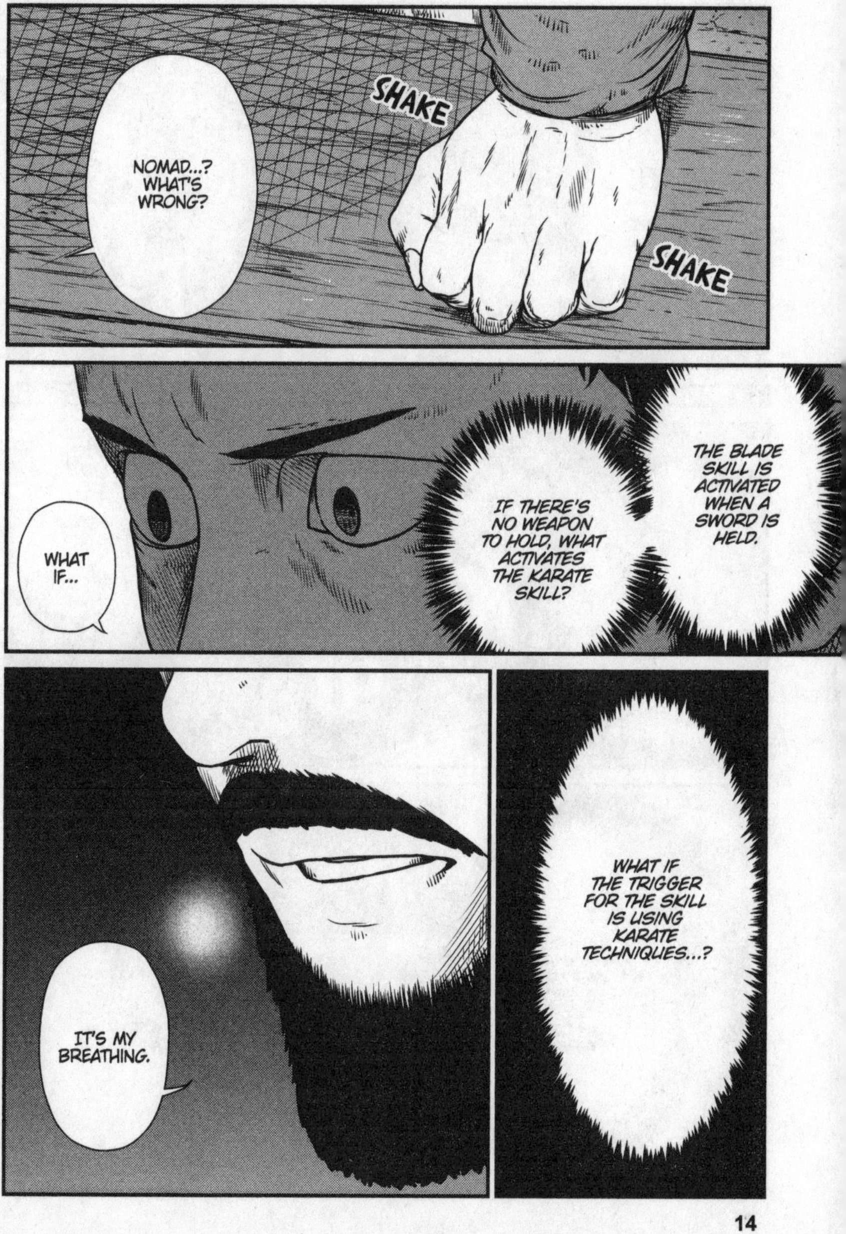
SHAKE
SHAKE
NOMAD...? WHAT'S WRONG?
THE BLADE SKILL IS ACTIVATED WHEN A SWORD IS HELD.
IF THERE'S NO WEAPON TO HOLD, WHAT ACTIVATES THE KARATE SKILL?
WHAT IF...
WHAT IF THE TRIGGER FOR THE SKILL IS USING KARATE TECHNIQUES...?
IT'S MY BREATHING.

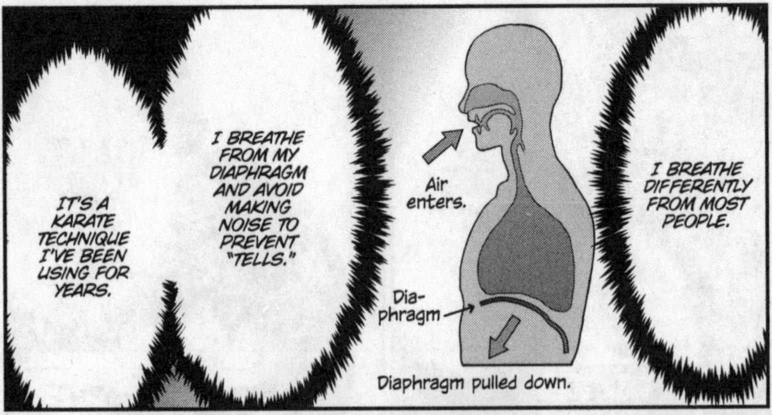
I BREATHE DIFFERENTLY FROM MOST PEOPLE.
Air enters.
Dia-phragm
Diaphragm pulled down.
I BREATHE FROM MY DIAPHRAGM AND AVOID MAKING NOISE TO PREVENT "TELLS."
IT'S A KARATE TECHNIQUE I'VE BEEN USING FOR YEARS.

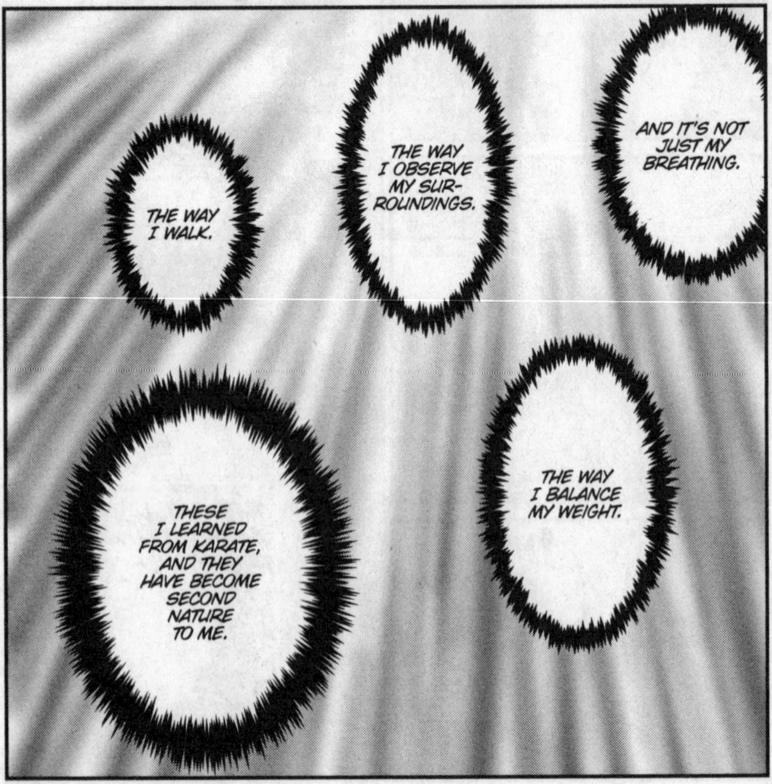
AND IT'S NOT JUST MY BREATHING.
THE WAY I OBSERVE MY SUR-ROUNDINGS.
THE WAY I WALK.
THE WAY I BALANCE MY WEIGHT.
THESE I LEARNED FROM KARATE, AND THEY HAVE BECOME SECOND NATURE TO ME.

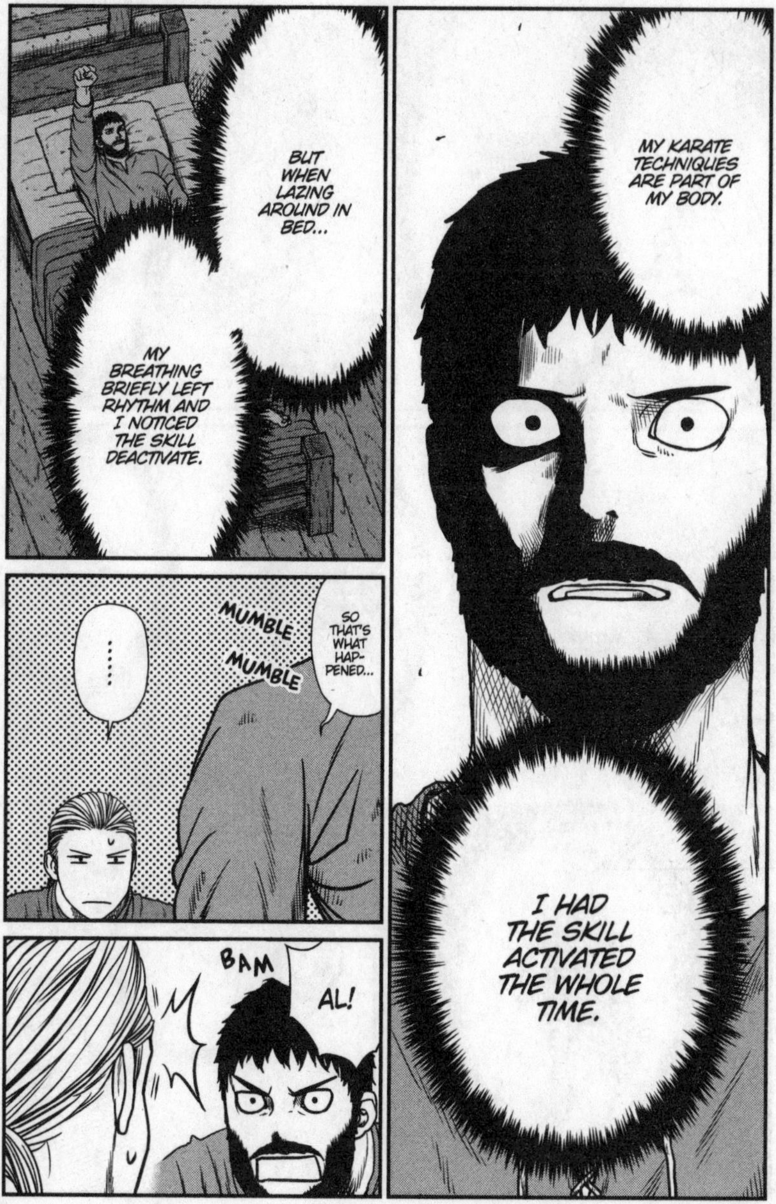
MY KARATE TECHNIQUES ARE PART OF MY BODY.
I HAD THE SKILL ACTIVATED THE WHOLE TIME.
BUT WHEN LAZING AROUND IN BED...
MY BREATHING BRIEFLY LEFT RHYTHM AND I NOTICED THE SKILL DEACTIVATE.
SO THAT'S WHAT HAP-PENED...
MUMBLE
MUMBLE
......
BAM
AL!

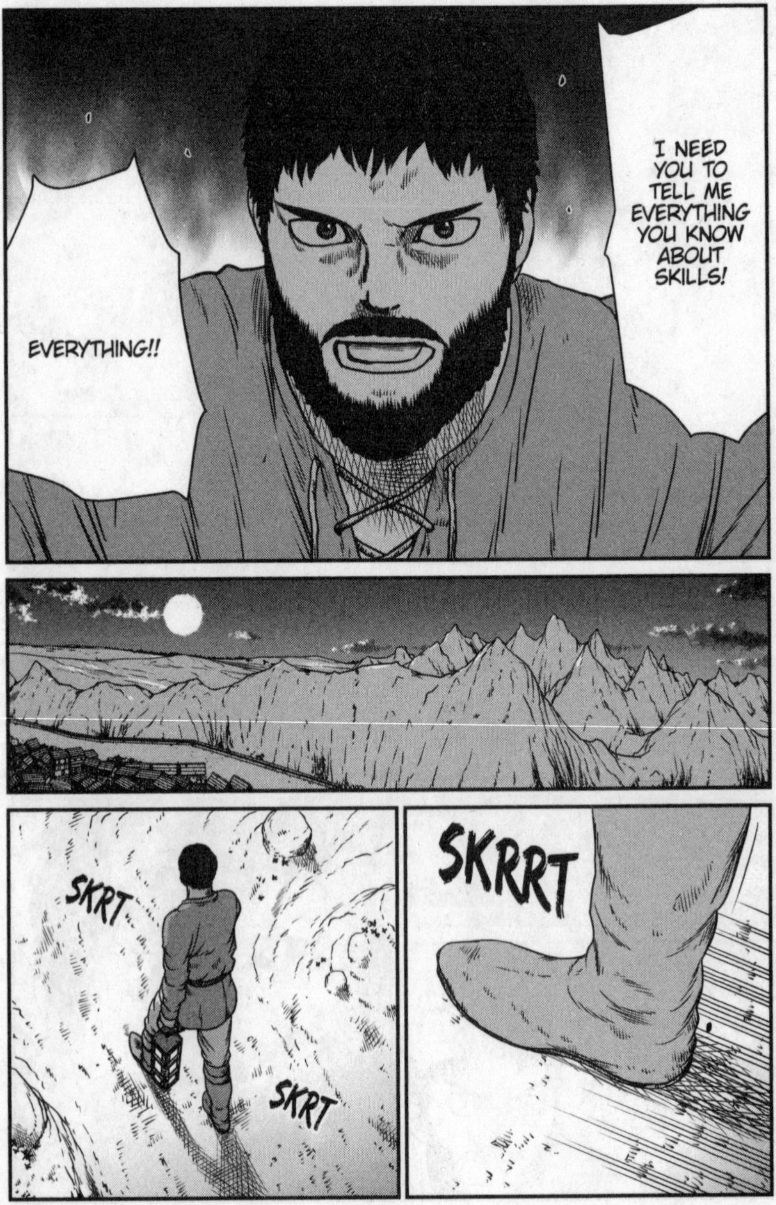
I NEED YOU TO TELL ME EVERYTHING YOU KNOW ABOUT SKILLS!
EVERYTHING!!
SKRRT
SKRT
SKRT

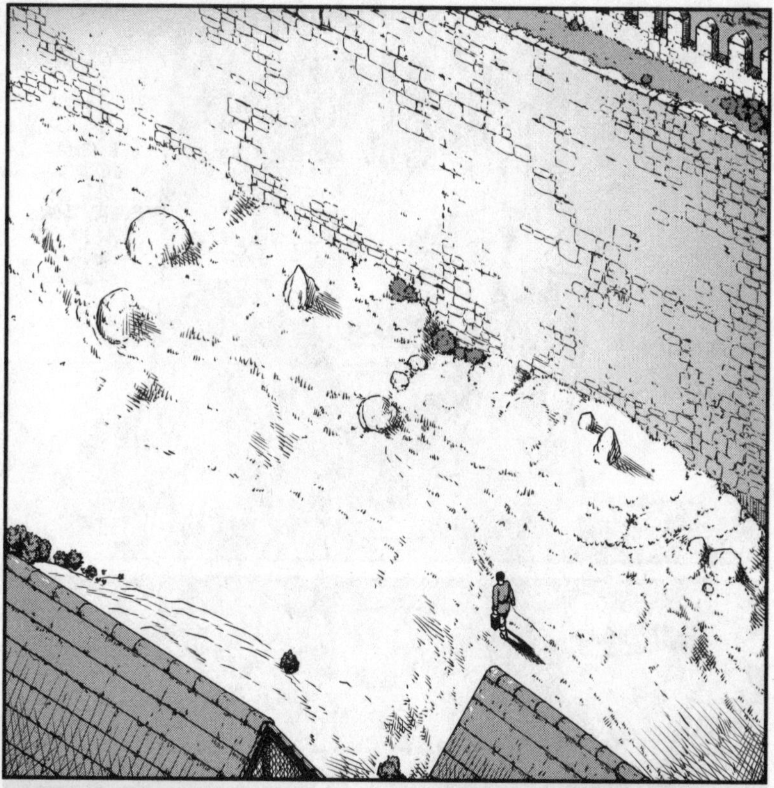

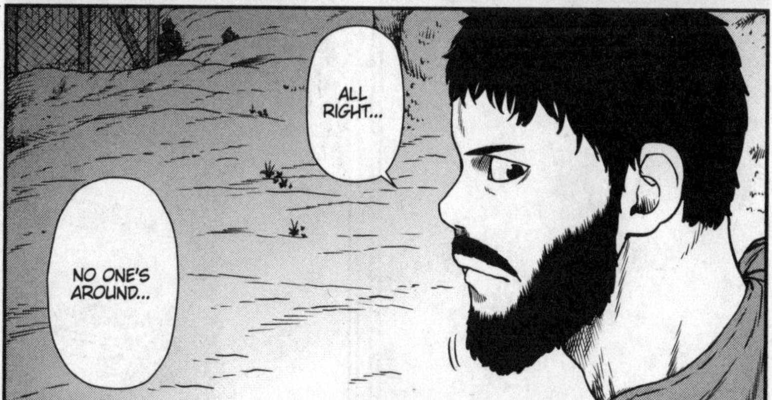
ALL RIGHT...
NO ONE'S AROUND...

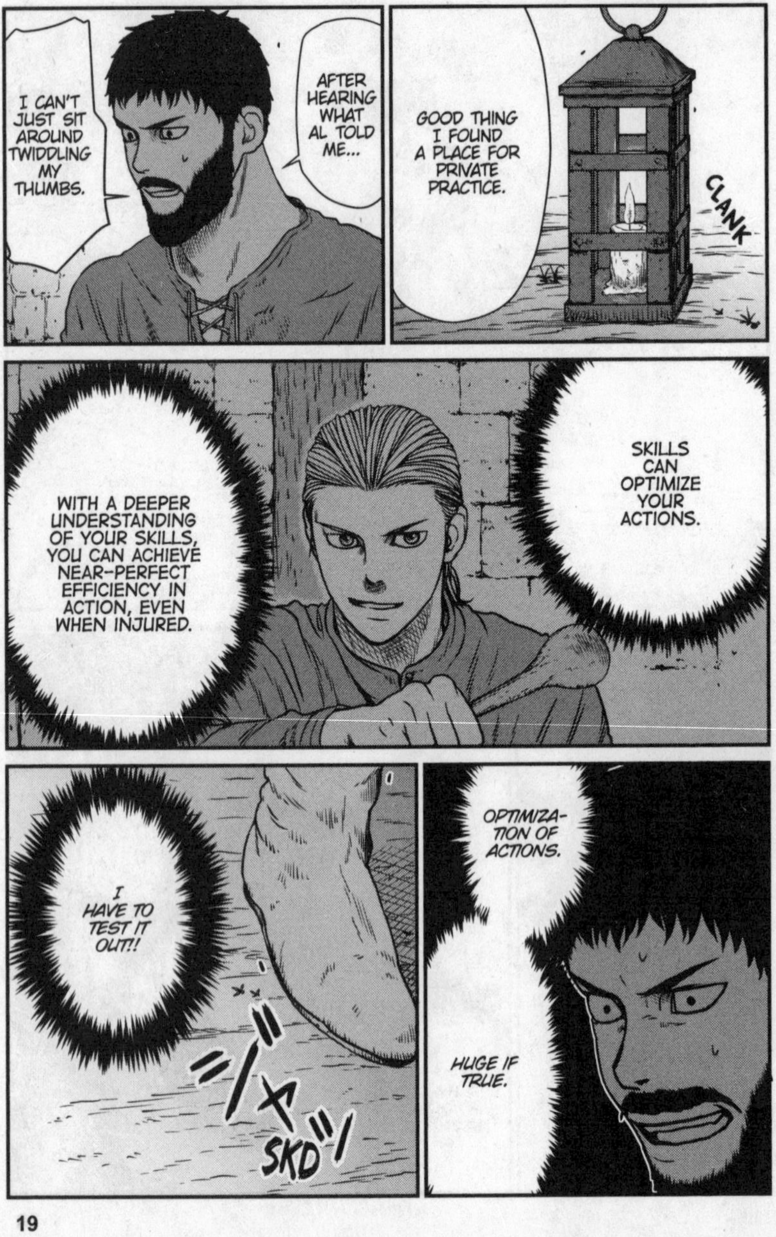
GOOD THING I FOUND A PLACE FOR PRIVATE PRACTICE.
CLANK
AFTER HEARING WHAT AL TOLD ME...
I CAN'T JUST SIT AROUND TWIDDLING MY THUMBS.
SKILLS CAN OPTIMIZE YOUR ACTIONS.
WITH A DEEPER UNDERSTANDING OF YOUR SKILLS, YOU CAN ACHIEVE NEAR-PERFECT EFFICIENCY IN ACTION, EVEN WHEN INJURED.
OPTIMIZA-TION OF ACTIONS.
HUGE IF TRUE.
I HAVE TO TEST IT OUT!!
SKD

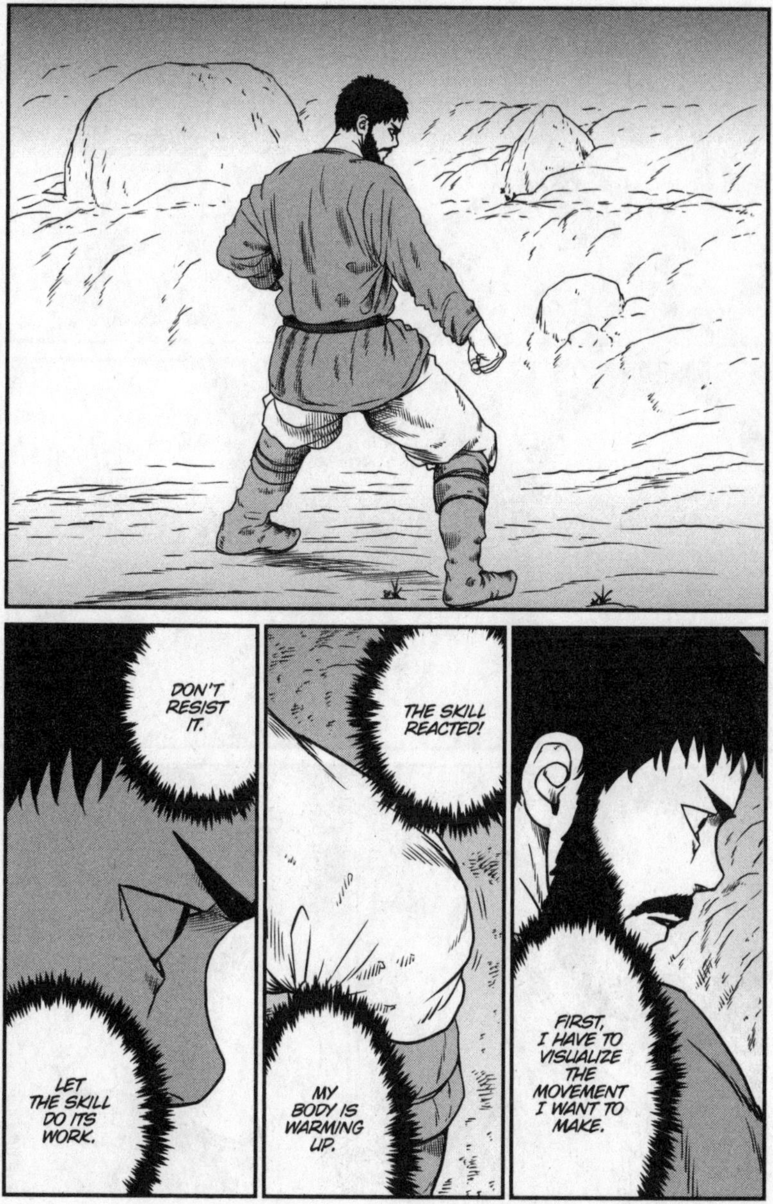
FIRST, I HAVE TO VISUALIZE THE MOVEMENT I WANT TO MAKE.
THE SKILL REACTED!
MY BODY IS WARMING UP.
DON'T RESIST IT.
LET THE SKILL DO ITS WORK.

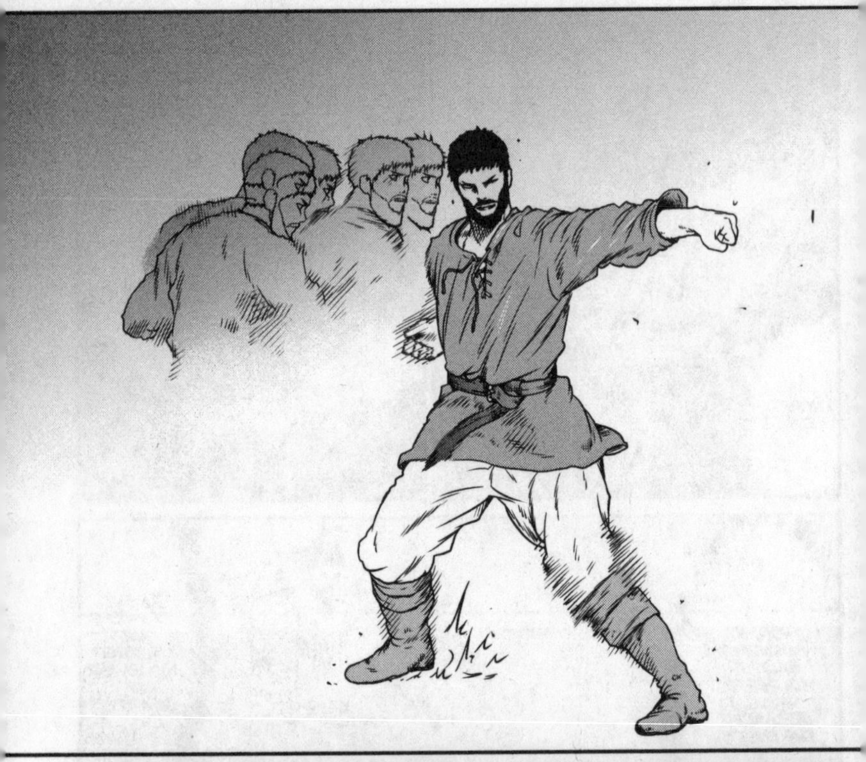

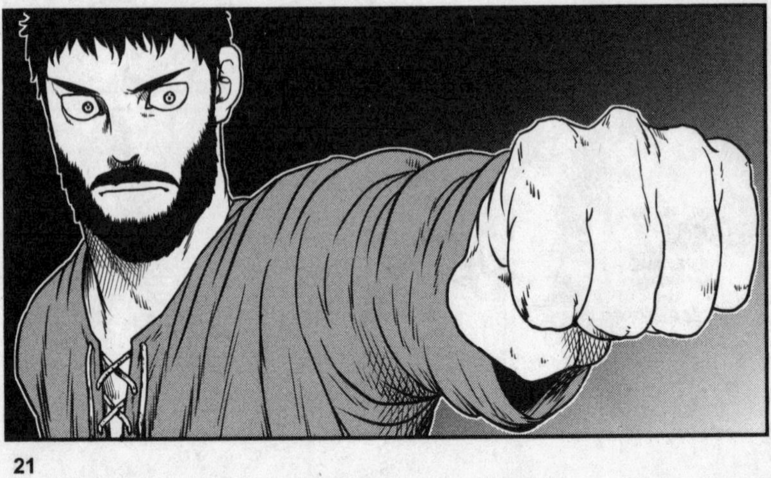

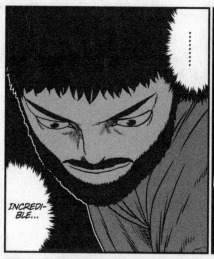

......

INCREDI-
BLE...

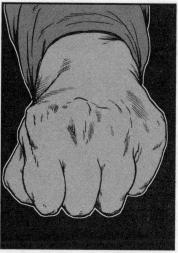

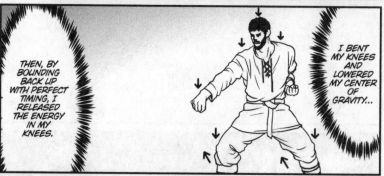

I BENT MY KNEES AND LOWERED MY CENTER OF GRAVITY...

THEN, BY BOUNDING BACK UP WITH PERFECT TIMING, I RELEASED THE ENERGY IN MY KNEES.

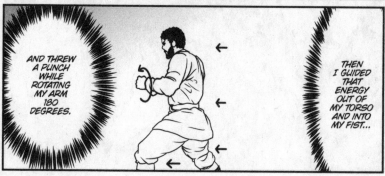

THEN I GUIDED THAT ENERGY OUT OF MY TORSO AND INTO MY FIST...

AND THREW A PUNCH WHILE ROTATING MY ARM 180 DEGREES.

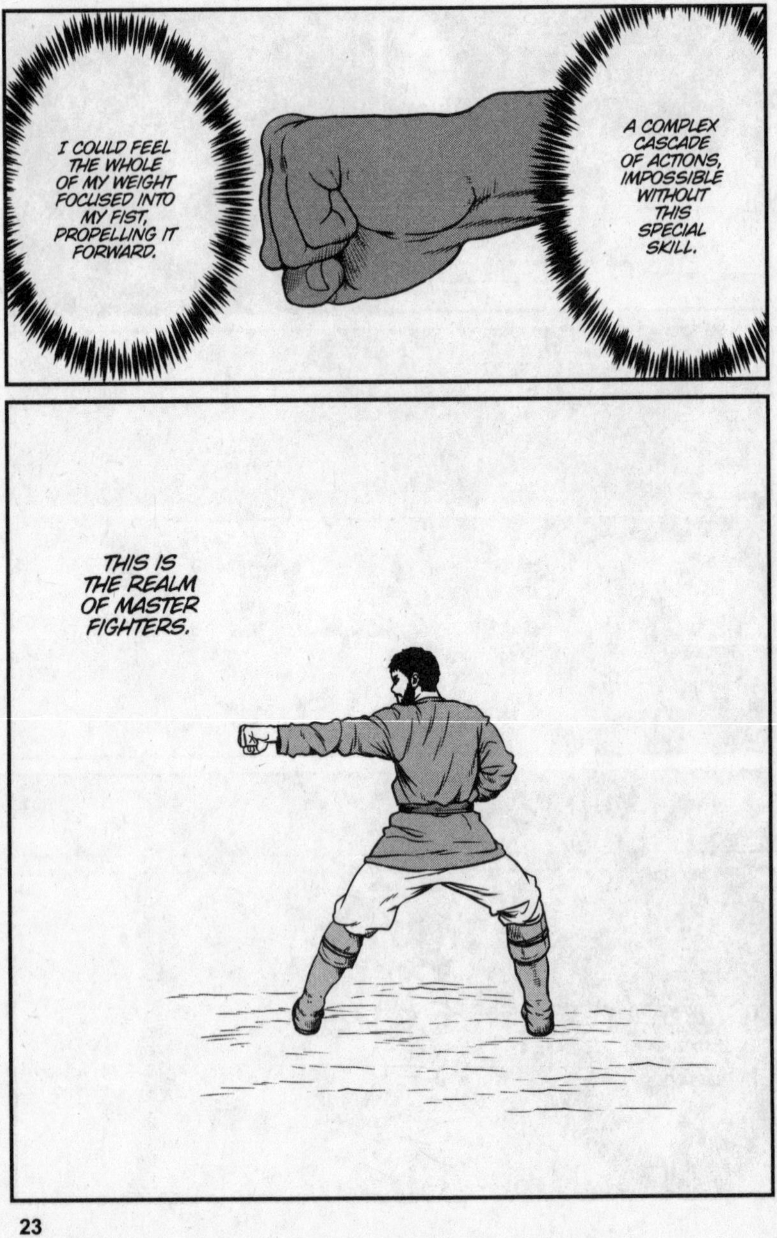
A COMPLEX CASCADE OF ACTIONS, IMPOSSIBLE WITHOUT THIS SPECIAL SKILL.
I COULD FEEL THE WHOLE OF MY WEIGHT FOCUSED INTO MY FIST, PROPELLING IT FORWARD.
THIS IS THE REALM OF MASTER FIGHTERS.

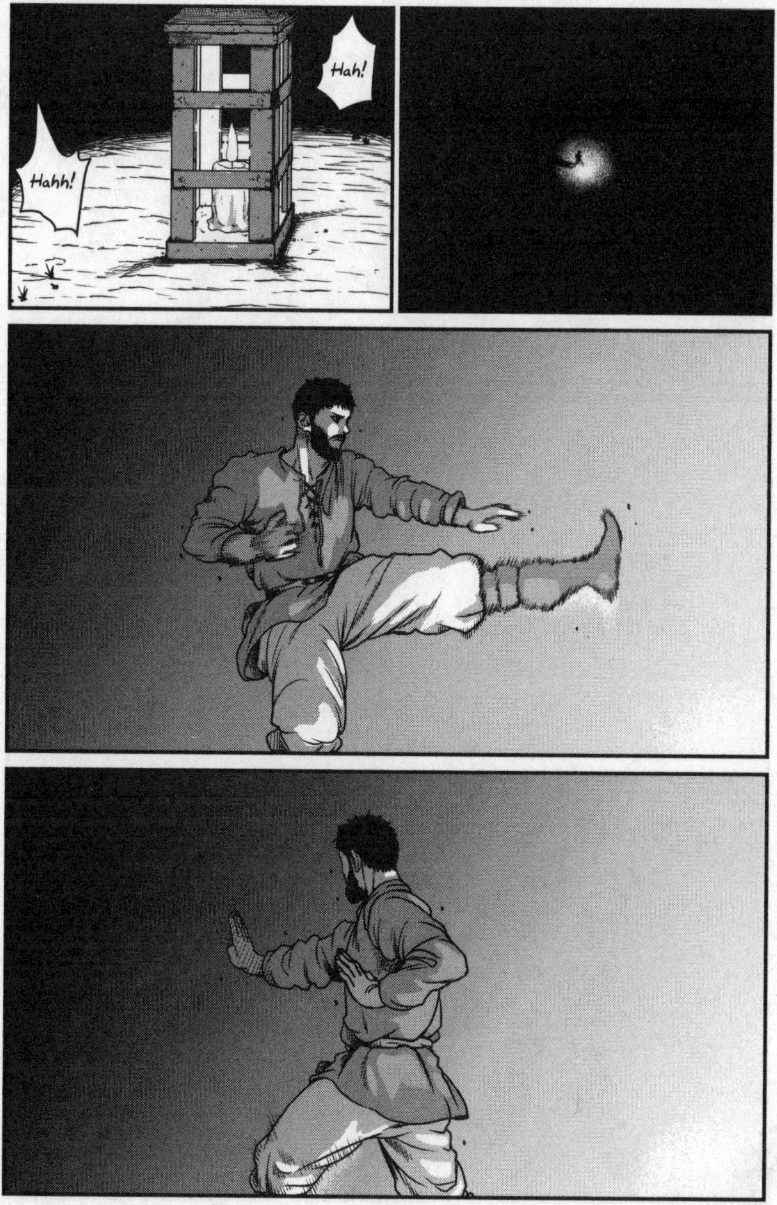
Hah!
Hahh!

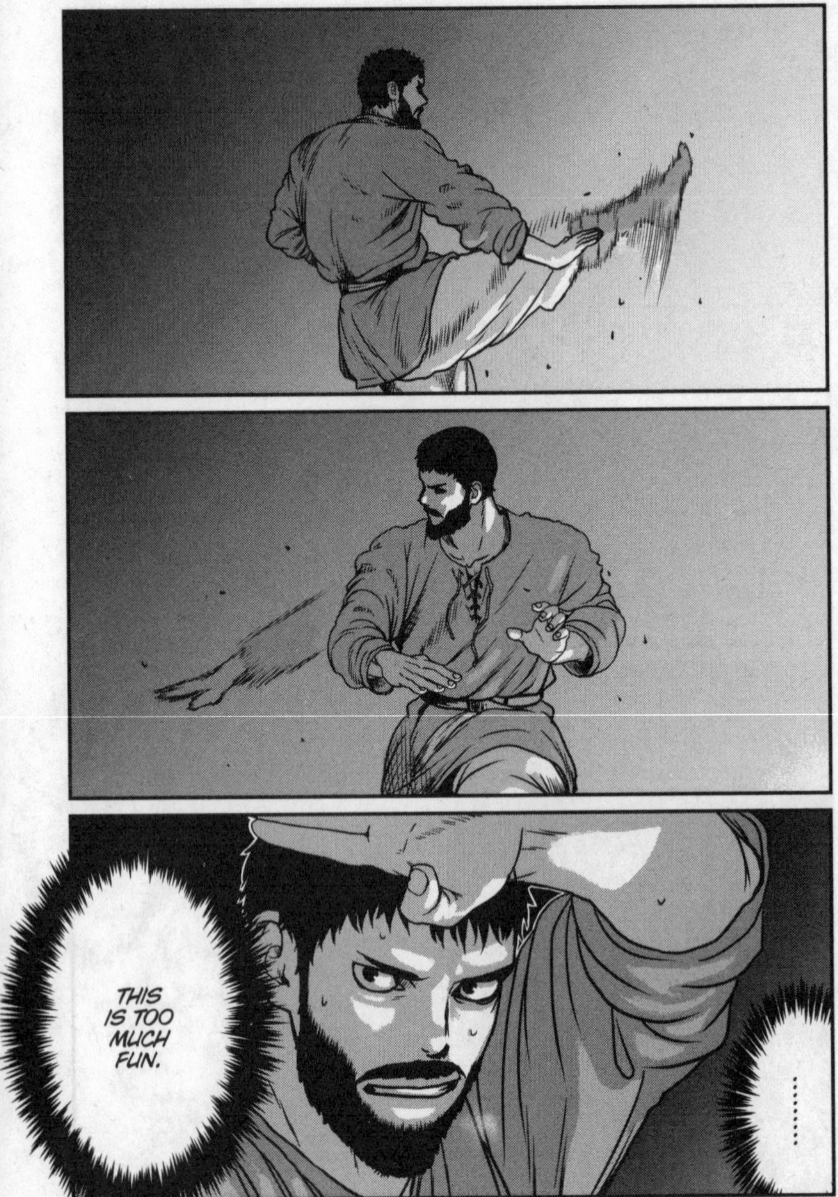
……
THIS IS TOO MUCH FUN.

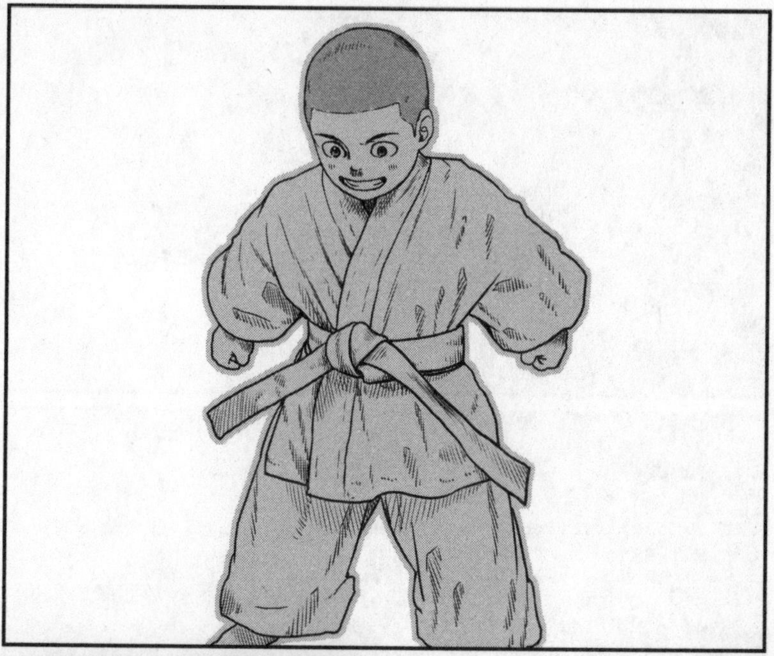

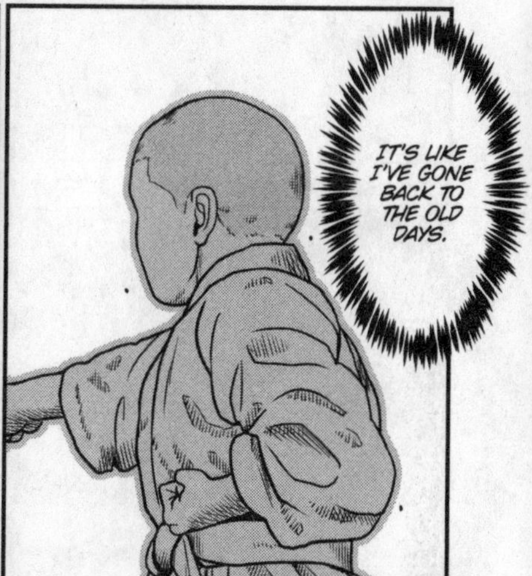
IT'S LIKE I'VE GONE BACK TO THE OLD DAYS.

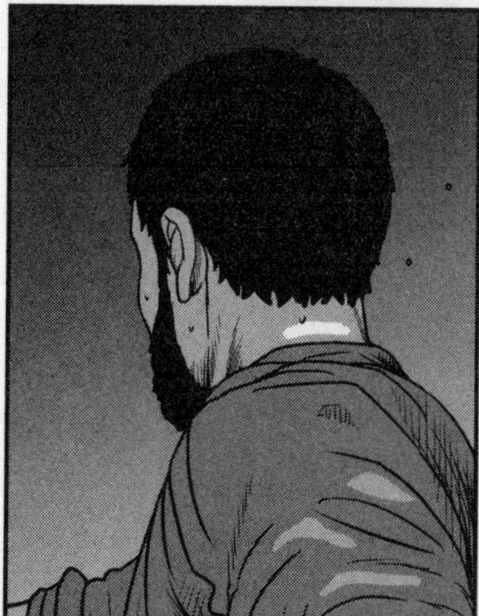

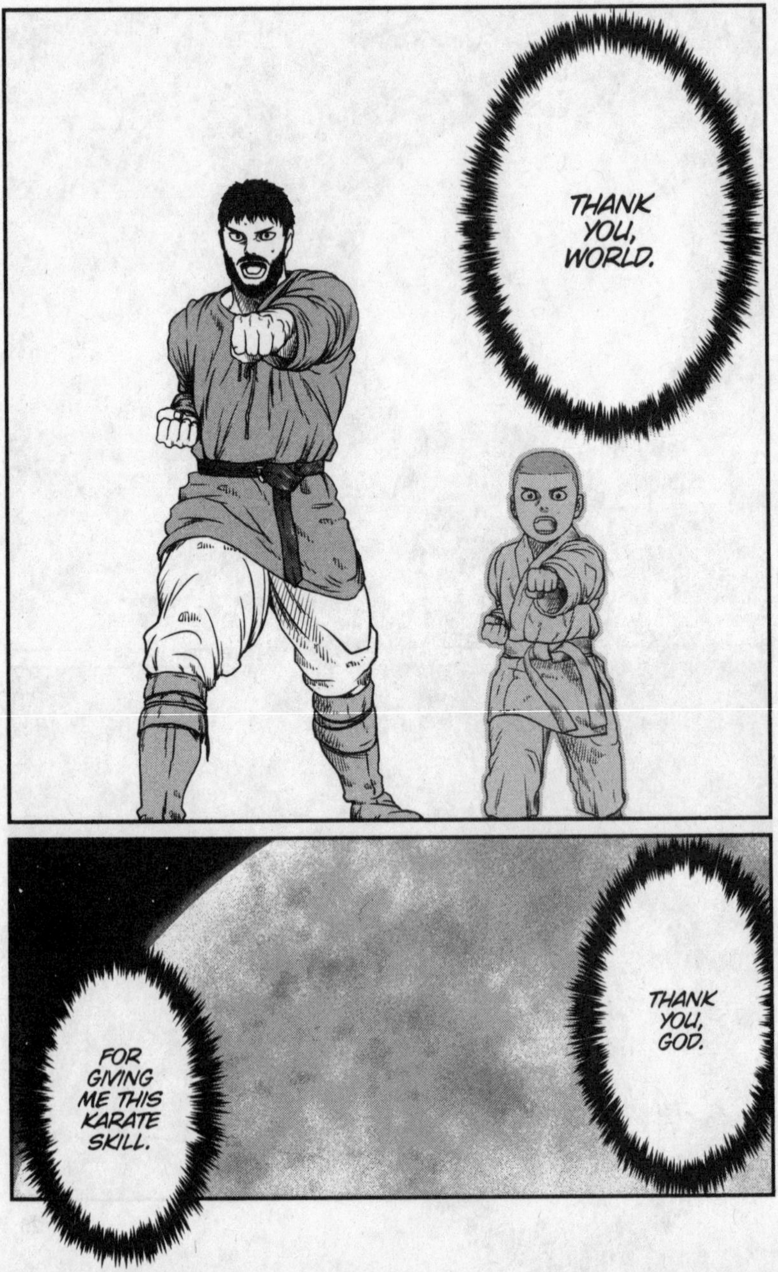
THANK YOU, WORLD.
THANK YOU, GOD.
FOR GIVING ME THIS KARATE SKILL.

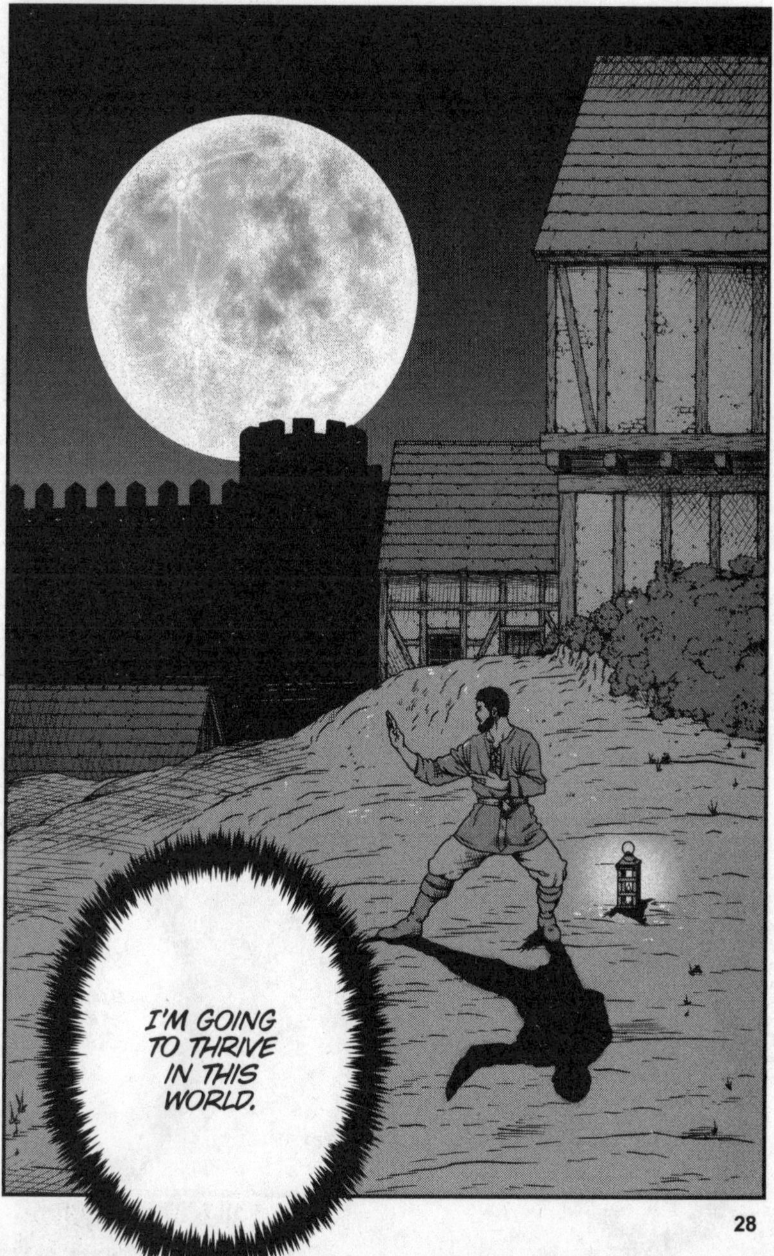
I'M GOING TO THRIVE IN THIS WORLD.

SPECIAL COLUMN BY
AUTHOR, YAZIN

KARATE SURVIVOR IN ANOTHER WORLD

INTERMISSION
SAVAGE RULES 13

THE REALM OF THE ENLIGHTENED

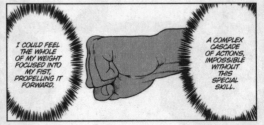

Various shams over the ages have given masters of martial arts an air of mystique and thus they are often confused for something extraordinary. However, masters of martial arts are just as ubiquitous as masters in any craft.

Mastery is not limited to martial arts. Masters exist at the top of every field. Experienced craftsmen can feel a gap of a fraction of a millimeter simply by touch. An experienced soba-noodle chef can consistently produce high-quality noodles by adjusting the amount of water they add in response to the humidity they feel in the air. The most accomplished of professional athletes are obviously masters of their disciplines. You can find experts and masters anywhere you look.

A COMPLEX CASCADE OF ACTIONS, IMPOSSIBLE WITHOUT THIS SPECIAL SKILL.
I COULD FEEL THE WHOLE OF MY WEIGHT FOCUSED INTO MY FIST, PROPELLING IT FORWARD.

My mentor was a middle-aged man of modest frame. He was about 160 cm tall and weighed only 50 kg. He did not believe in specific training exercises and only had minimal calluses on his knuckles. The casual observer would never guess that he did karate. He was an ordinary civil servant, and appeared as such.

Despite the impression that he gave, he dealt a brutal front kick. The impact would penetrate the thick strike pads we used, triggering a tortuous wave of pain that would enter and twist up my guts. It felt as though the kick was delivered straight to my body. A well-placed kick could have easily incapacitated me, and this was from a man 20 kg lighter than me. Indeed, his kick was almost like a "special move" from a manga. However, he did nothing special to achieve this. He was merely taught the kick by his own master. He adapted it to suit his own physique and drilled the kick until the move was ingrained in his own body. He earned this "special ability" by simply repeating this motion over and over again.

Make no mistake, this is an incredible accomplishment. You must first have a knack for the craft, and you must be able to correctly apply yourself to the task. Only then will you be able to reach this special realm: the world of masters that Nomad was able to catch a glimpse into. This is a world that exists only for the most talented and hardworking of people. There is nothing inherently special in play. Only practice and effort. Yet it is a realm that is inaccessible to ordinary people.

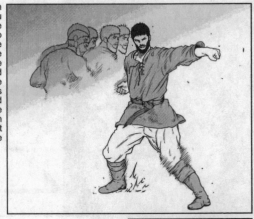

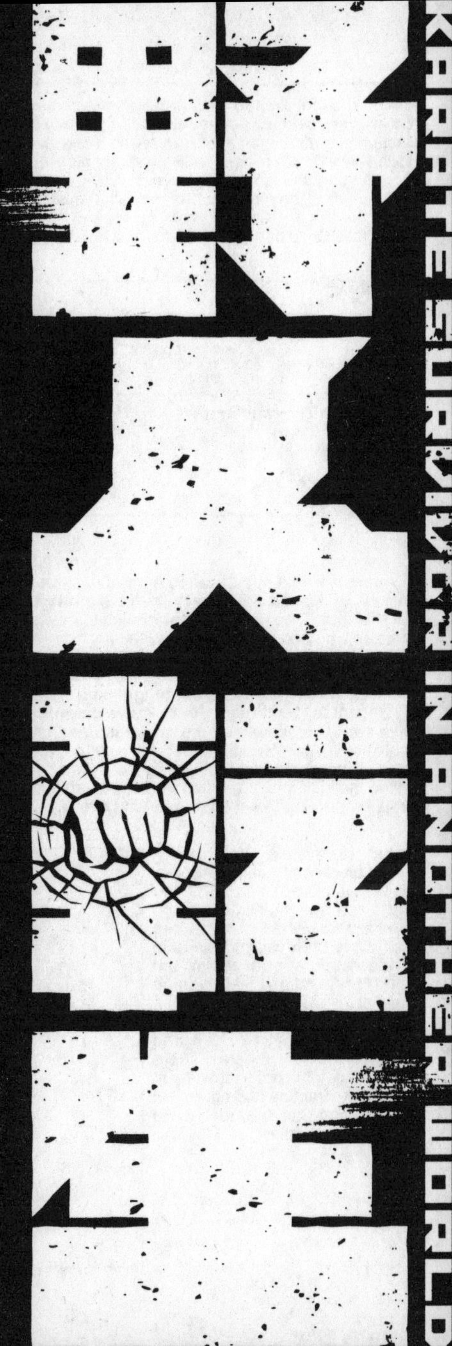
KARATE SURVIVOR IN ANOTHER WORLD

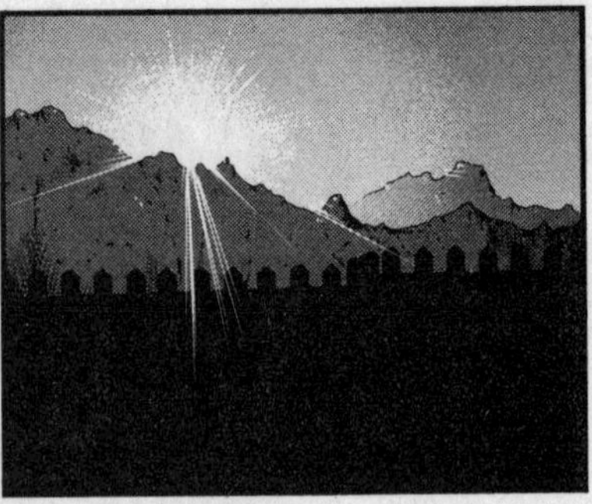

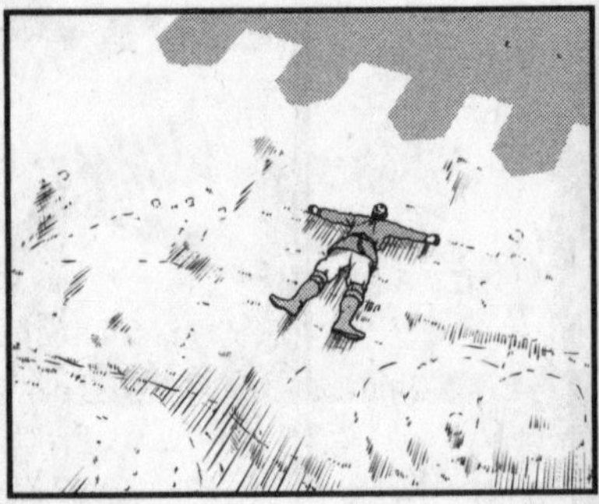

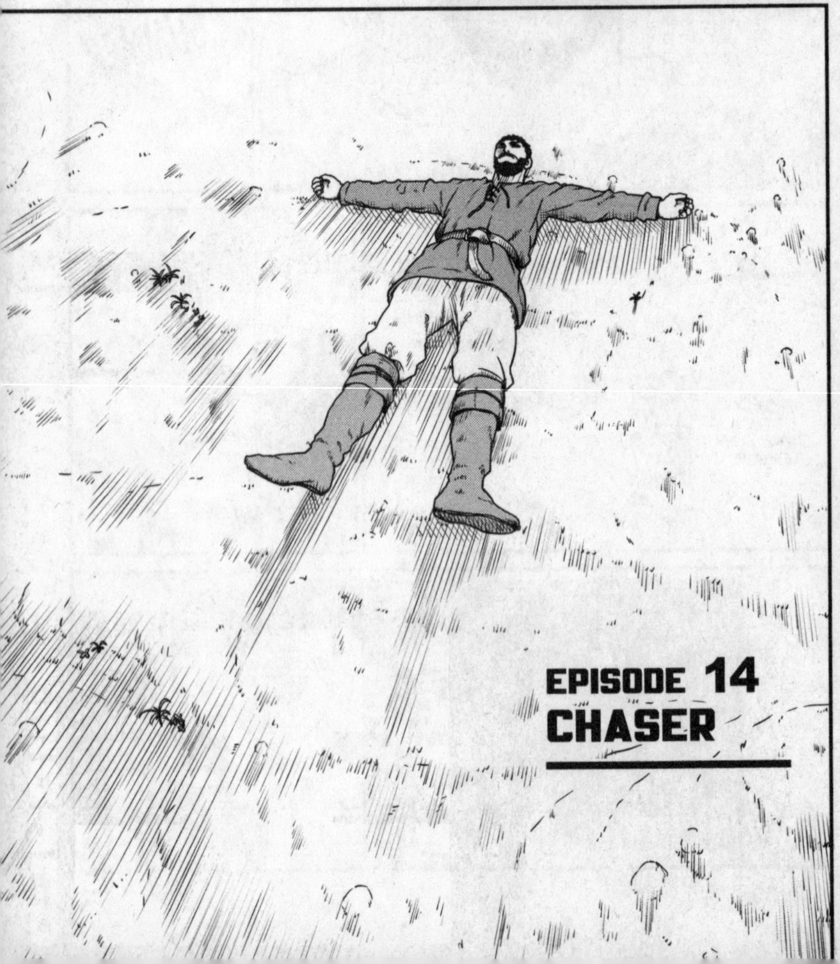
EPISODE 14
CHASER

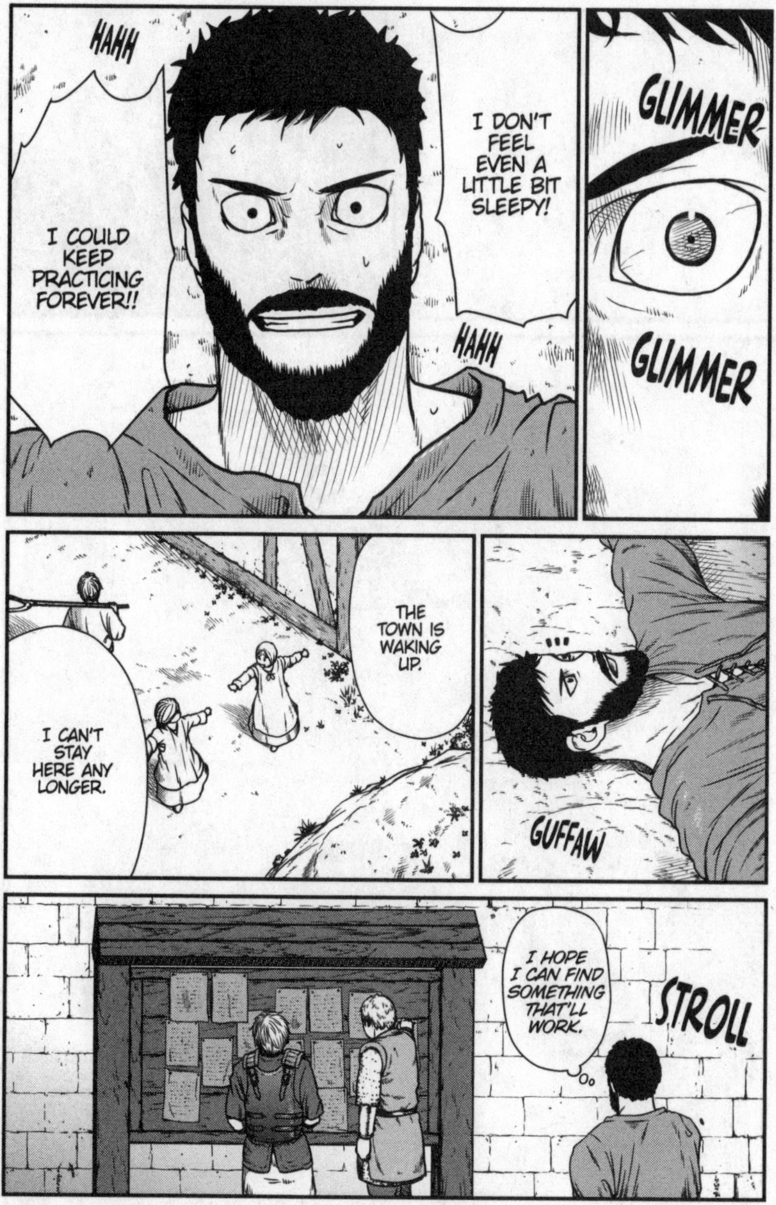
GLIMMER
GLIMMER
I DON'T FEEL EVEN A LITTLE BIT SLEEPY!
HAHH
I COULD KEEP PRACTICING FOREVER!!
HAHH
...
GUFFAW
THE TOWN IS WAKING UP.
I CAN'T STAY HERE ANY LONGER.
STROLL
I HOPE I CAN FIND SOMETHING THAT'LL WORK.

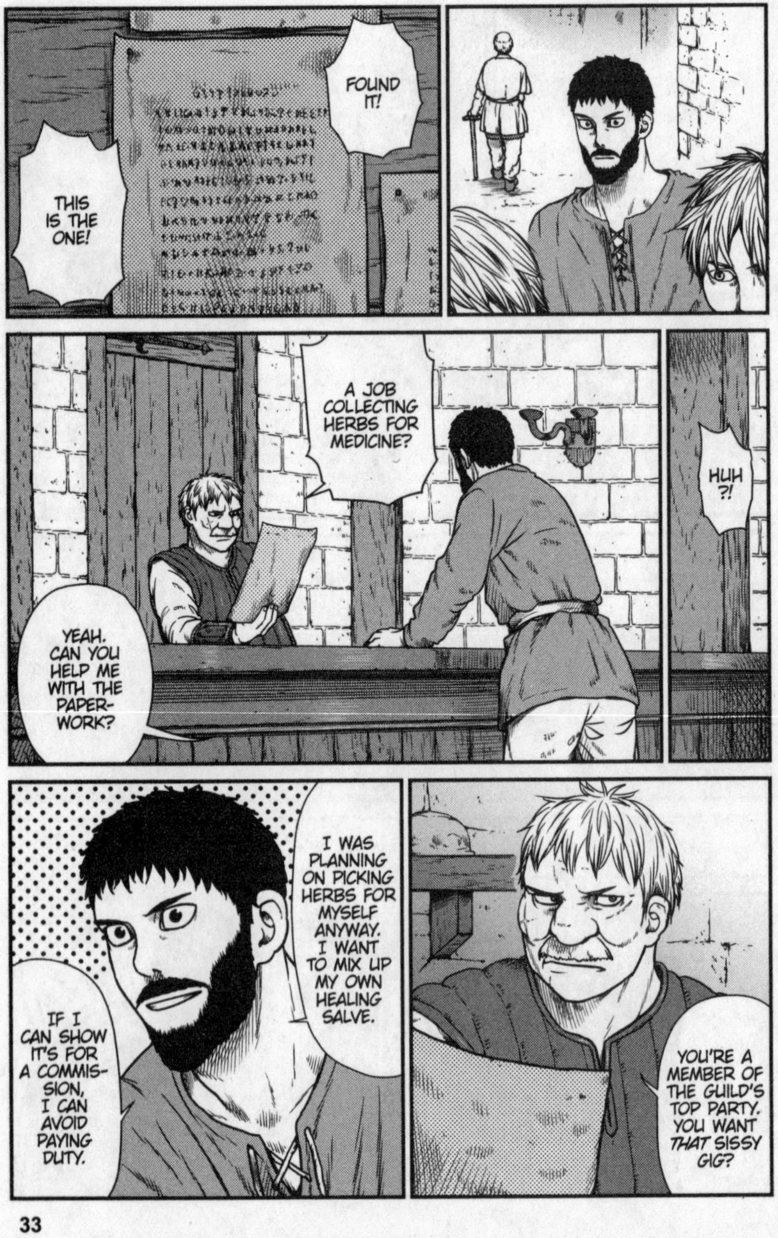
FOUND IT!
THIS IS THE ONE!
HUH ?!
A JOB COLLECTING HERBS FOR MEDICINE?
YEAH. CAN YOU HELP ME WITH THE PAPER-WORK?
YOU'RE A MEMBER OF THE GUILD'S TOP PARTY. YOU WANT *THAT* SISSY GIG?
I WAS PLANNING ON PICKING HERBS FOR MYSELF ANYWAY. I WANT TO MIX UP MY OWN HEALING SALVE.
IF I CAN SHOW IT'S FOR A COMMISSION, I CAN AVOID PAYING DUTY.

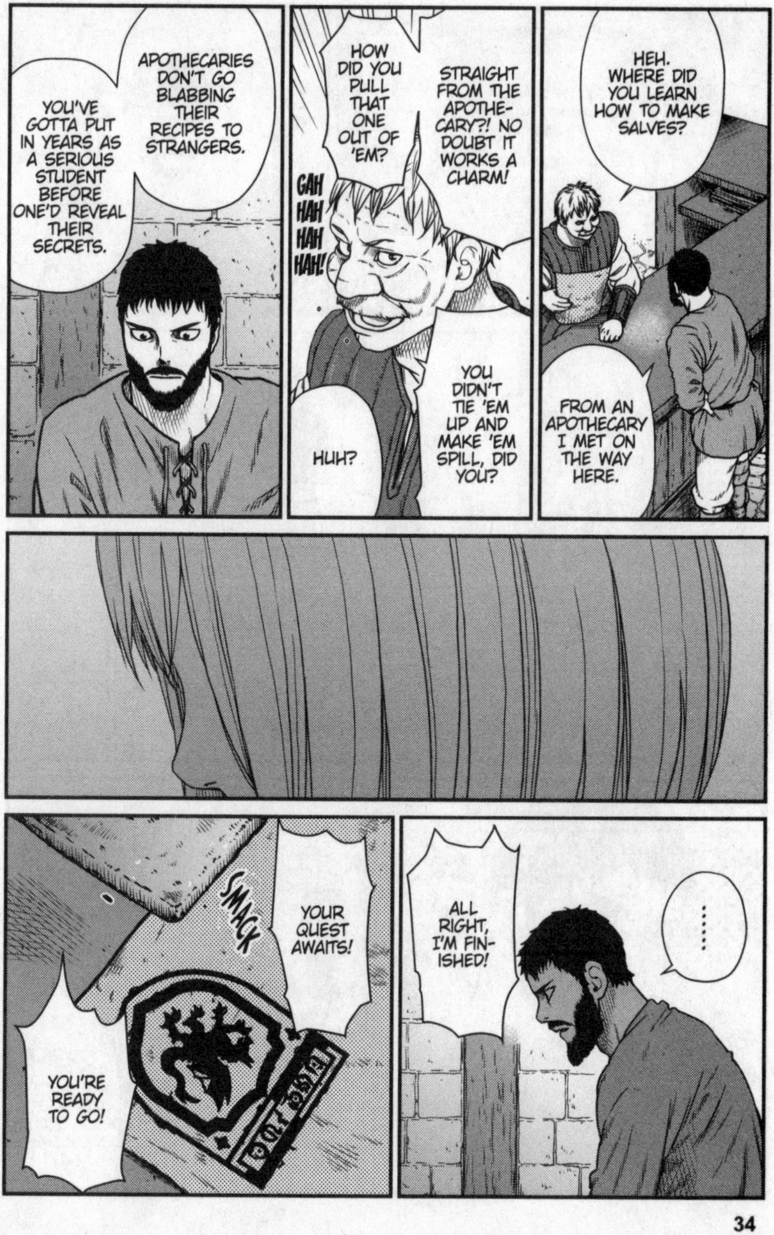
HEH. WHERE DID YOU LEARN HOW TO MAKE SALVES?
FROM AN APOTHECARY I MET ON THE WAY HERE.
STRAIGHT FROM THE APOTHE-CARY?! NO DOUBT IT WORKS A CHARM!
HOW DID YOU PULL THAT ONE OUT OF 'EM?
GAH HAH HAH HAH!
YOU DIDN'T TIE 'EM UP AND MAKE 'EM SPILL, DID YOU?
HUH?
APOTHECARIES DON'T GO BLABBING THEIR RECIPES TO STRANGERS.
YOU'VE GOTTA PUT IN YEARS AS A SERIOUS STUDENT BEFORE ONE'D REVEAL THEIR SECRETS.
......
ALL RIGHT, I'M FIN-ISHED!
YOUR QUEST AWAITS!
SMACK
YOU'RE READY TO GO!

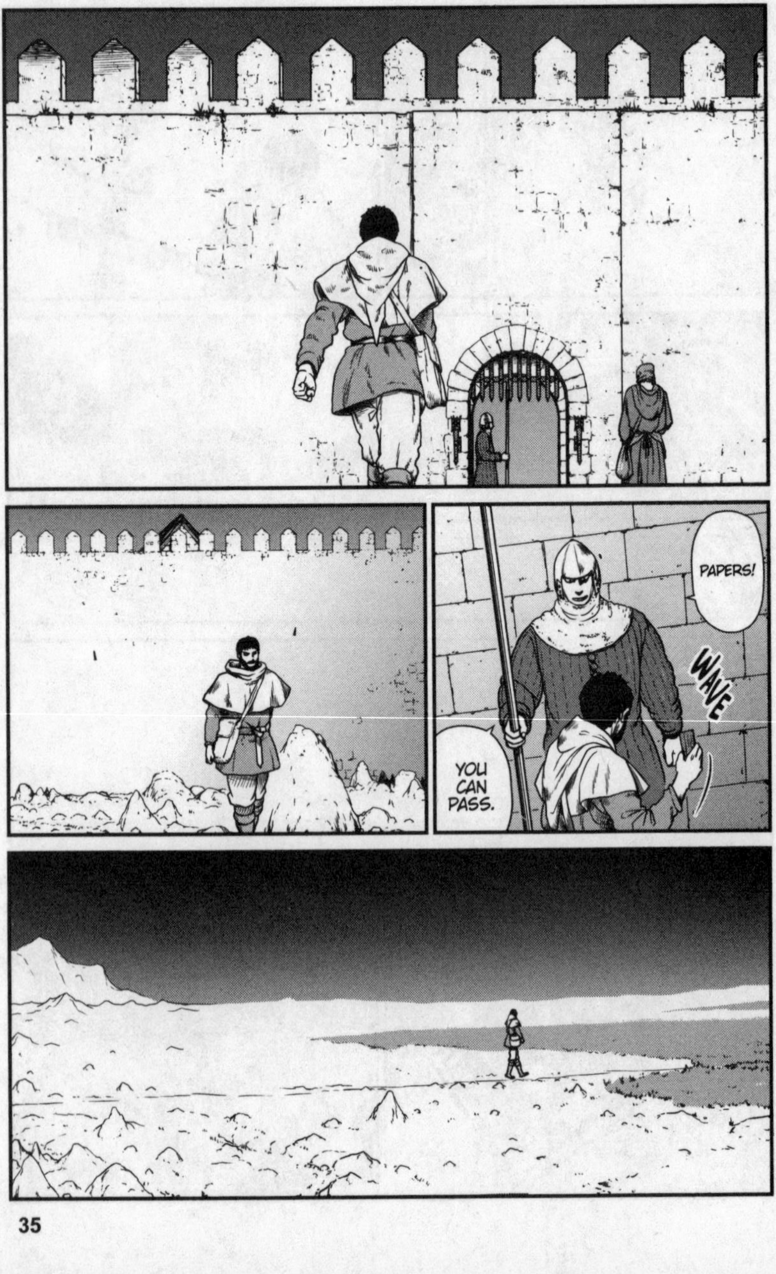
PAPERS!
WAVE
YOU CAN PASS.

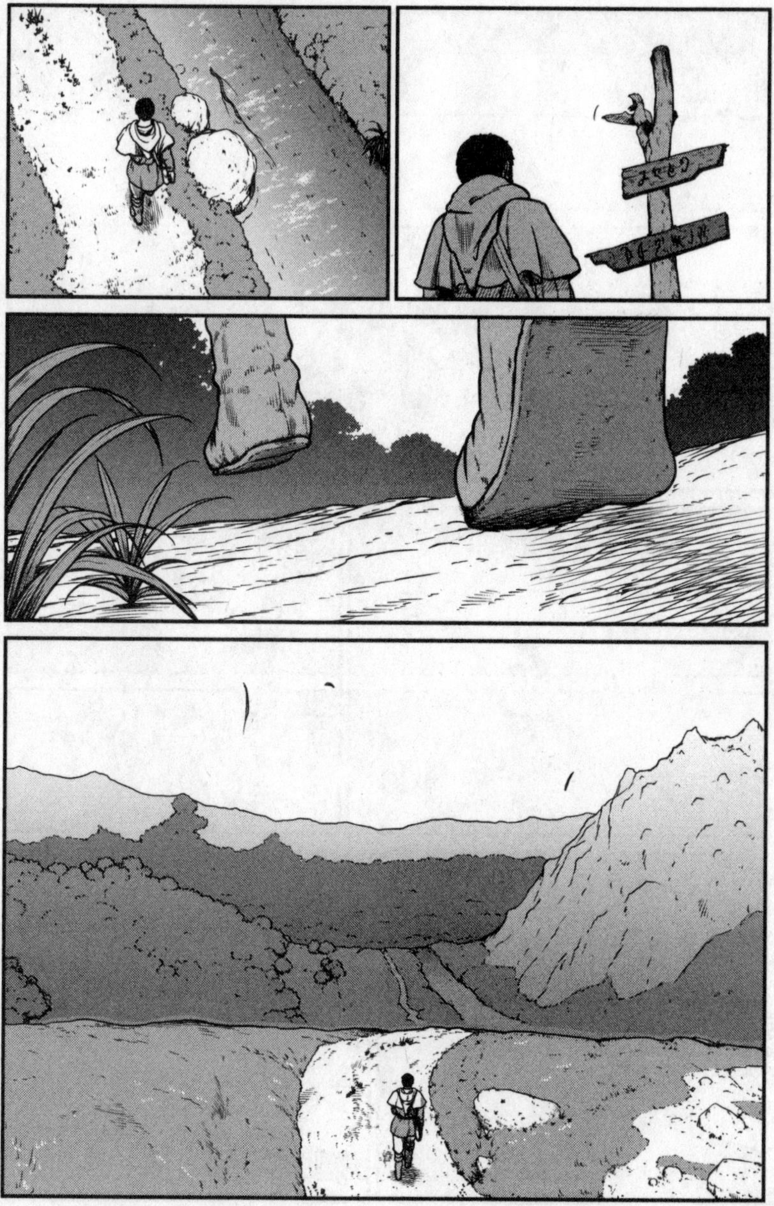

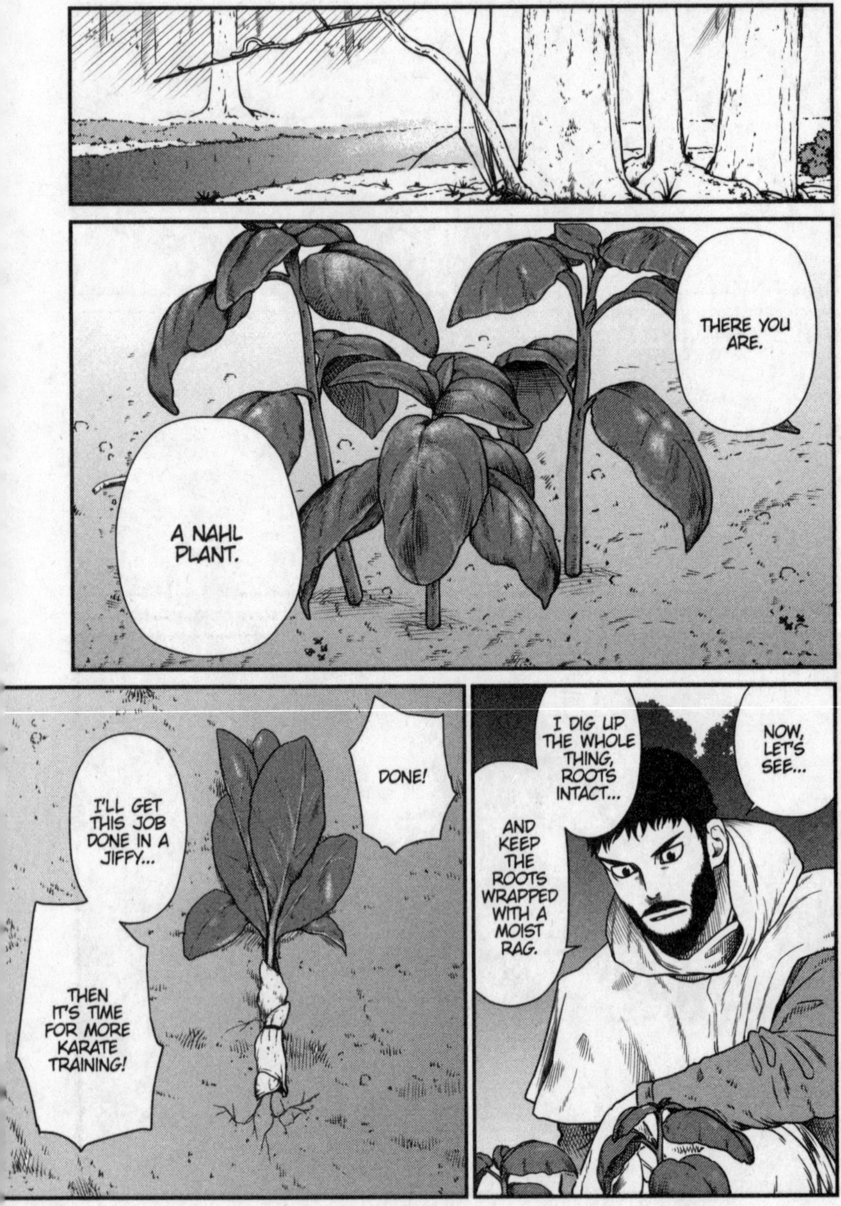
THERE YOU ARE.
A NAHL PLANT.
NOW, LET'S SEE...
I DIG UP THE WHOLE THING, ROOTS INTACT...
AND KEEP THE ROOTS WRAPPED WITH A MOIST RAG.
DONE!
I'LL GET THIS JOB DONE IN A JIFFY...
THEN IT'S TIME FOR MORE KARATE TRAINING!

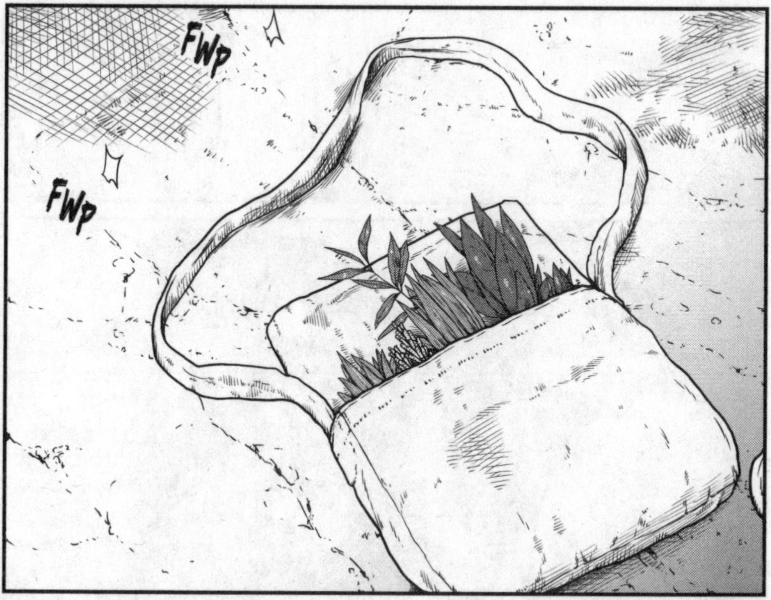
FWp
FWp

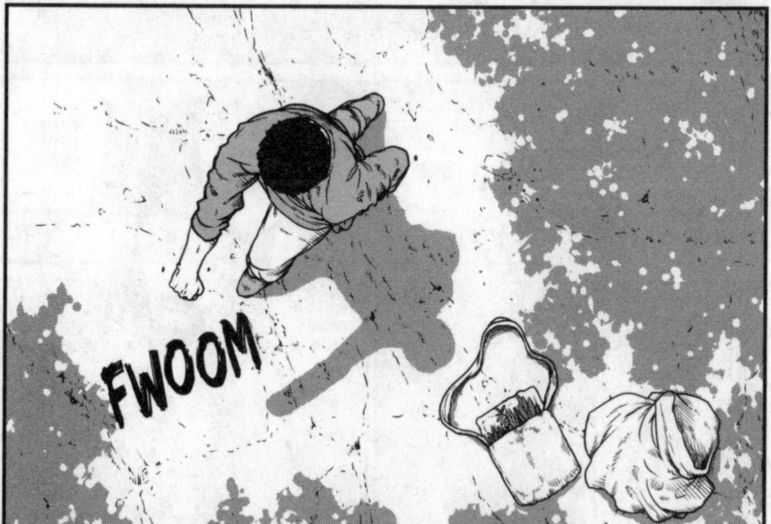
FWOOM

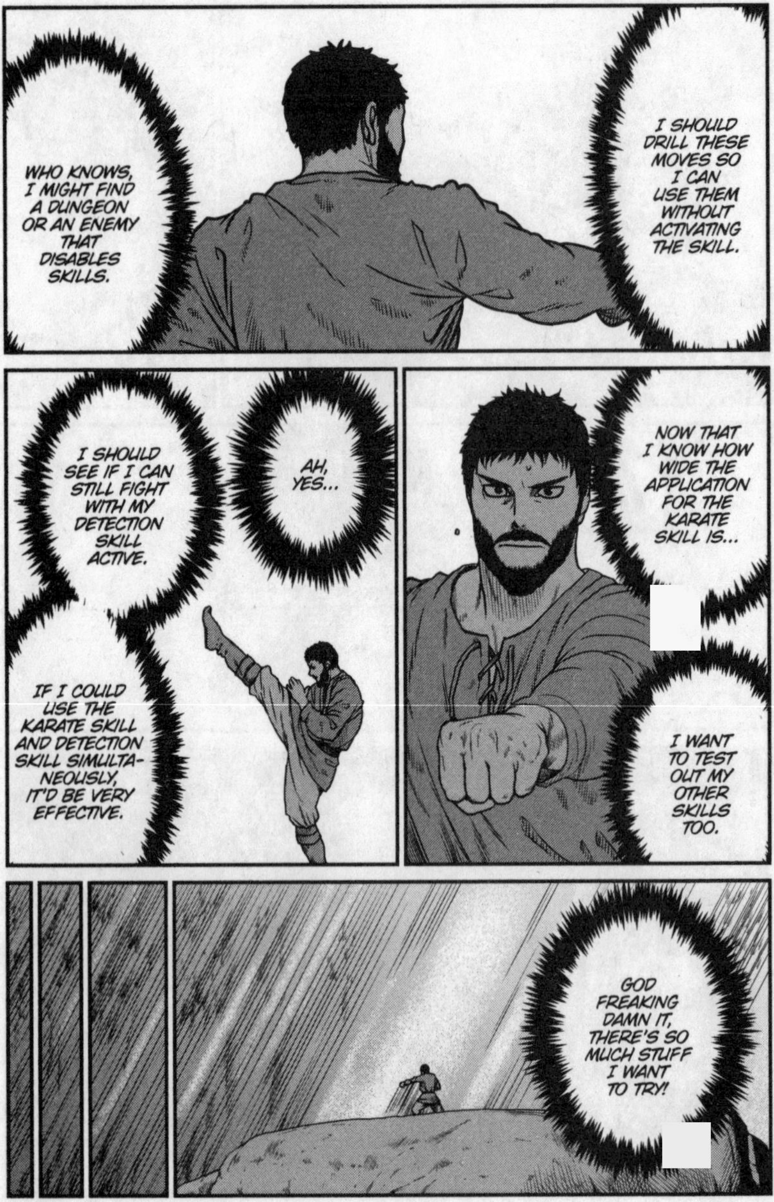
I SHOULD DRILL THESE MOVES SO I CAN USE THEM WITHOUT ACTIVATING THE SKILL.
WHO KNOWS, I MIGHT FIND A DUNGEON OR AN ENEMY THAT DISABLES SKILLS.
NOW THAT I KNOW HOW WIDE THE APPLICATION FOR THE KARATE SKILL IS...
I WANT TO TEST OUT MY OTHER SKILLS TOO.
AH, YES...
I SHOULD SEE IF I CAN STILL FIGHT WITH MY DETECTION SKILL ACTIVE.
IF I COULD USE THE KARATE SKILL AND DETECTION SKILL SIMULTA-NEOUSLY, IT'D BE VERY EFFECTIVE.
GOD FREAKING DAMN IT, THERE'S SO MUCH STUFF I WANT TO TRY!

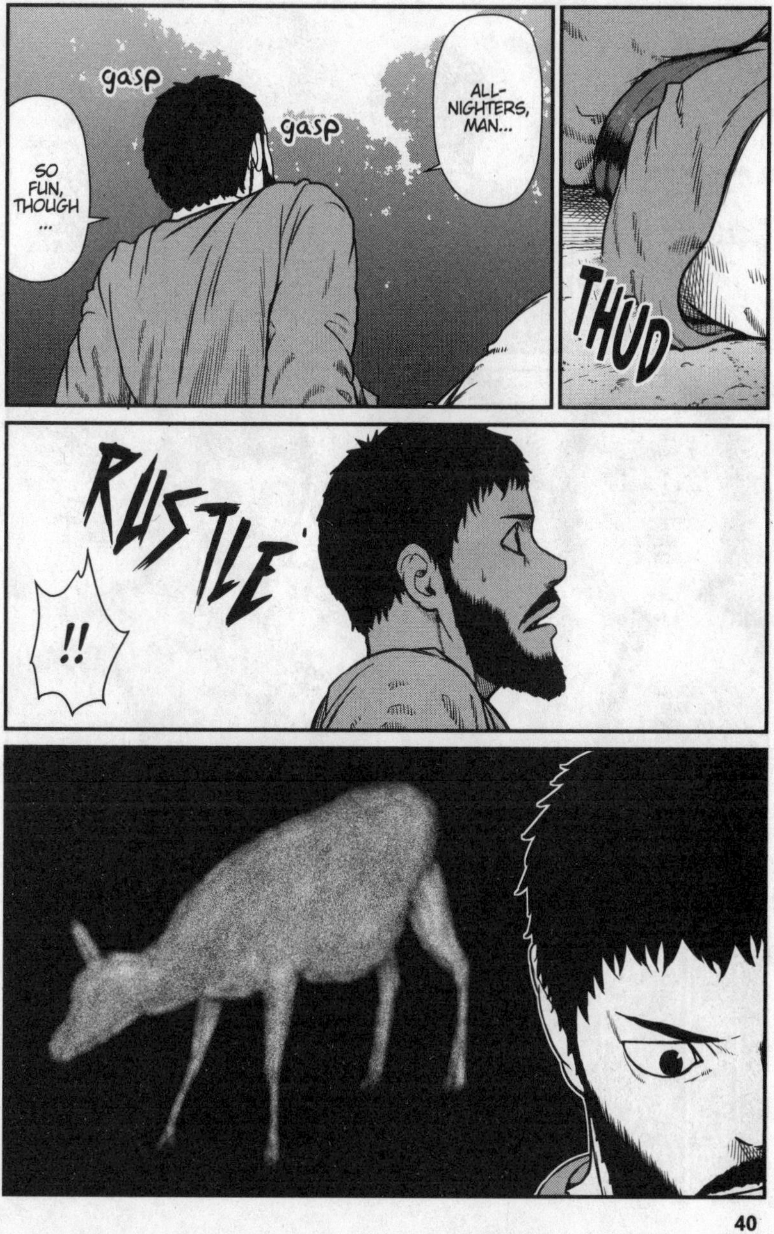
THUD
ALL-NIGHTERS, MAN...
gasp
gasp
SO FUN, THOUGH...
RUSTLE
!!

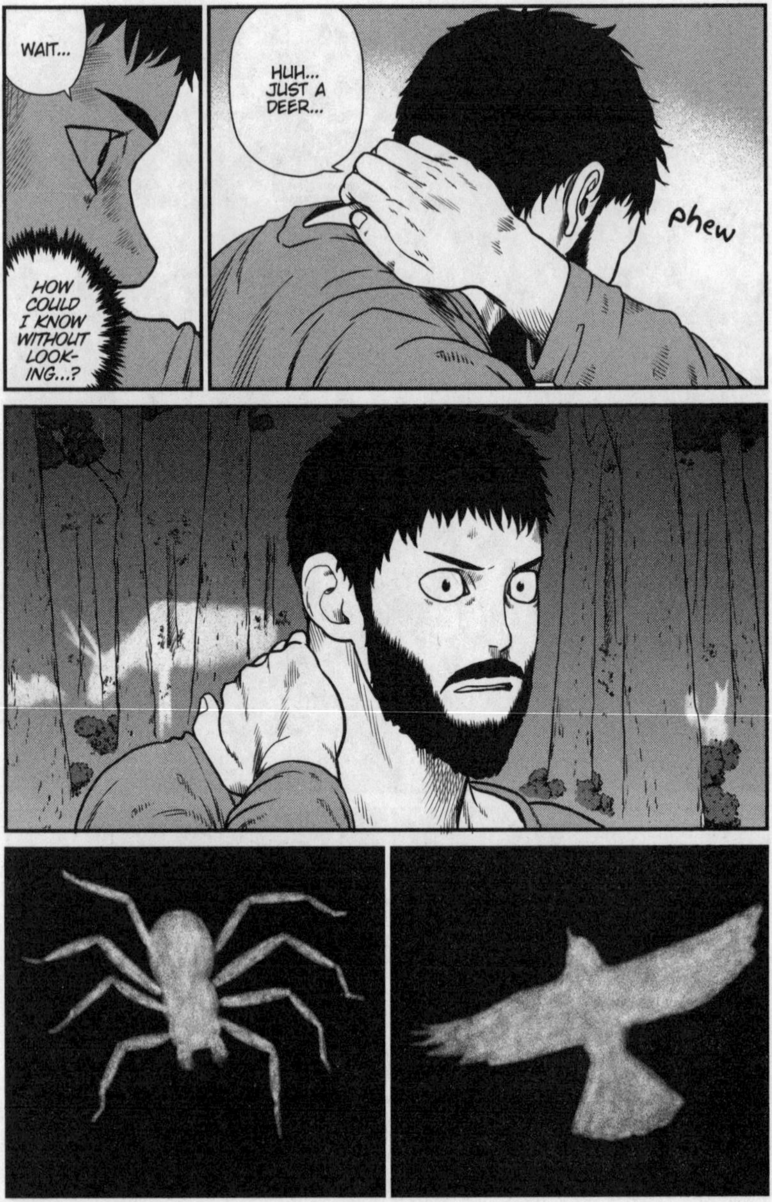
HUH... JUST A DEER...
phew
WAIT...
HOW COULD I KNOW WITHOUT LOOK-ING...?

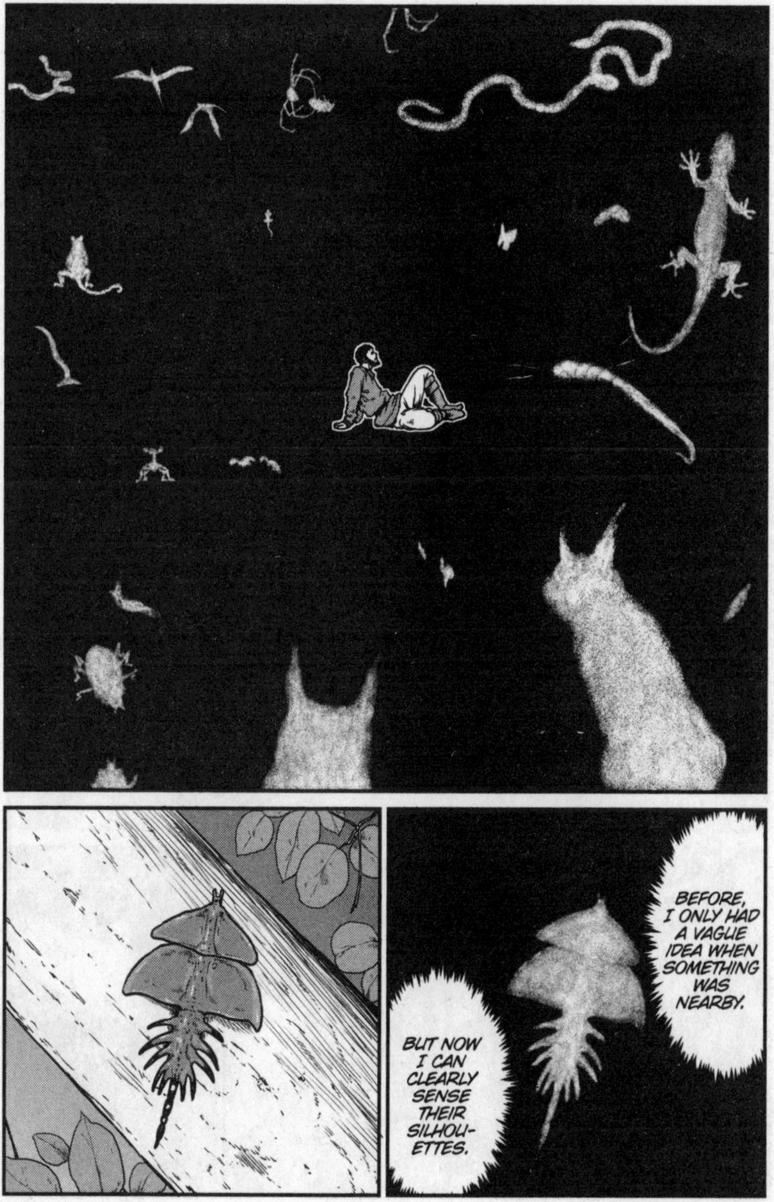
BEFORE, I ONLY HAD A VAGUE IDEA WHEN SOMETHING WAS NEARBY.
BUT NOW I CAN CLEARLY SENSE THEIR SILHOU-ETTES.

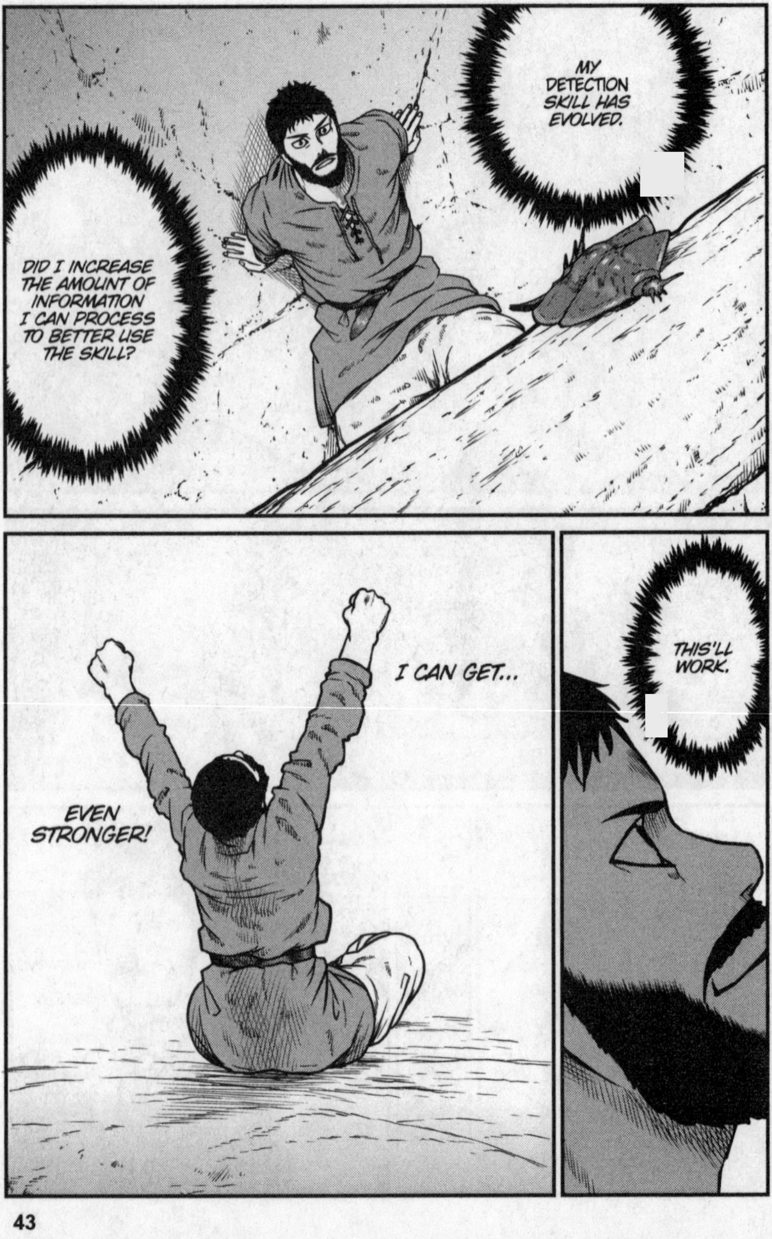
MY DETECTION SKILL HAS EVOLVED.
DID I INCREASE THE AMOUNT OF INFORMATION I CAN PROCESS TO BETTER USE THE SKILL?
THIS'LL WORK.
I CAN GET...
EVEN STRONGER!

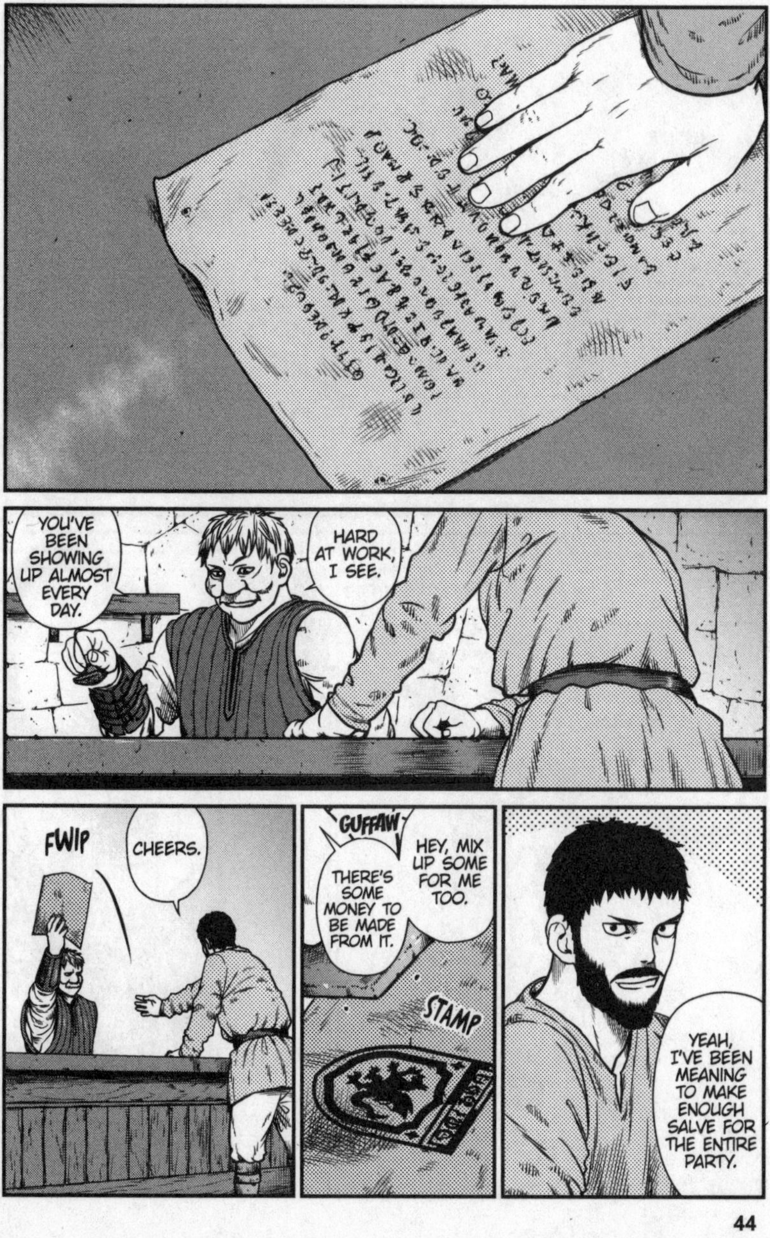
HARD AT WORK, I SEE.
YOU'VE BEEN SHOWING UP ALMOST EVERY DAY.
YEAH, I'VE BEEN MEANING TO MAKE ENOUGH SALVE FOR THE ENTIRE PARTY.
GUFFAW
HEY, MIX UP SOME FOR ME TOO.
THERE'S SOME MONEY TO BE MADE FROM IT.
STAMP
CHEERS.
FWIP

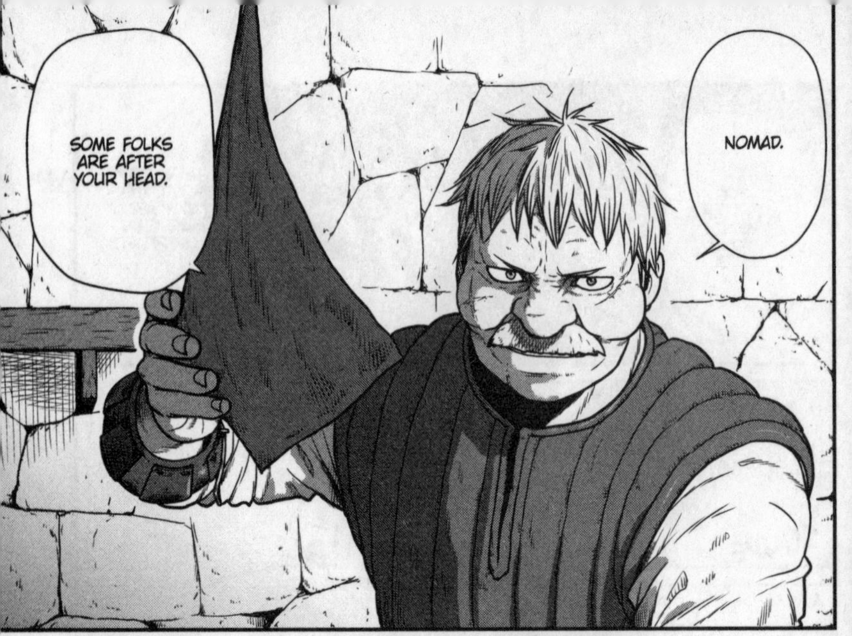
NOMAD.
SOME FOLKS ARE AFTER YOUR HEAD.

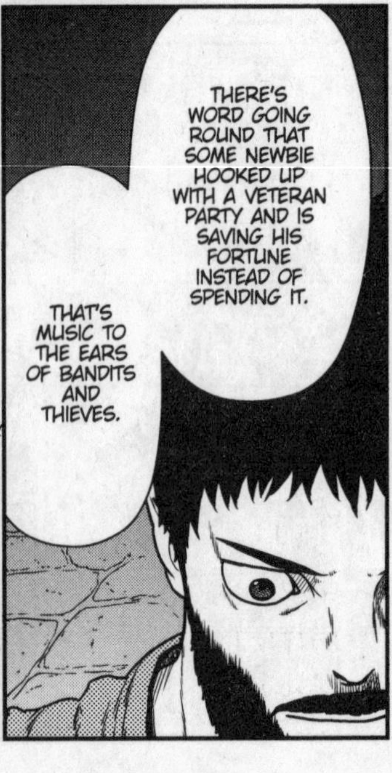
THERE'S WORD GOING ROUND THAT SOME NEWBIE HOOKED UP WITH A VETERAN PARTY AND IS SAVING HIS FORTUNE INSTEAD OF SPENDING IT.
THAT'S MUSIC TO THE EARS OF BANDITS AND THIEVES.

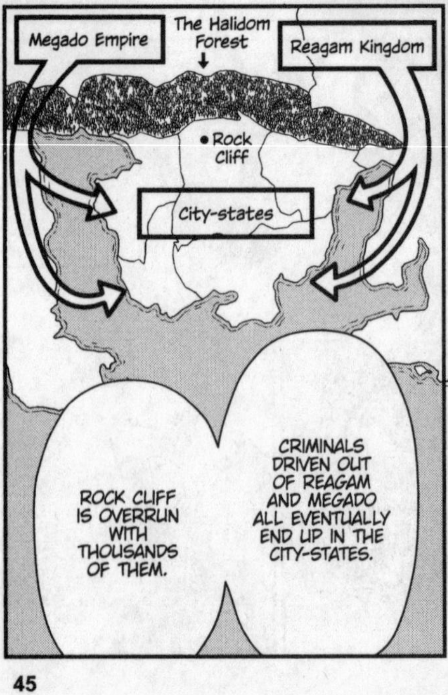
Reagam Kingdom
The Halidom Forest
Megado Empire
Rock Cliff
City-states
CRIMINALS DRIVEN OUT OF REAGAM AND MEGADO ALL EVENTUALLY END UP IN THE CITY-STATES.
ROCK CLIFF IS OVERRUN WITH THOUSANDS OF THEM.

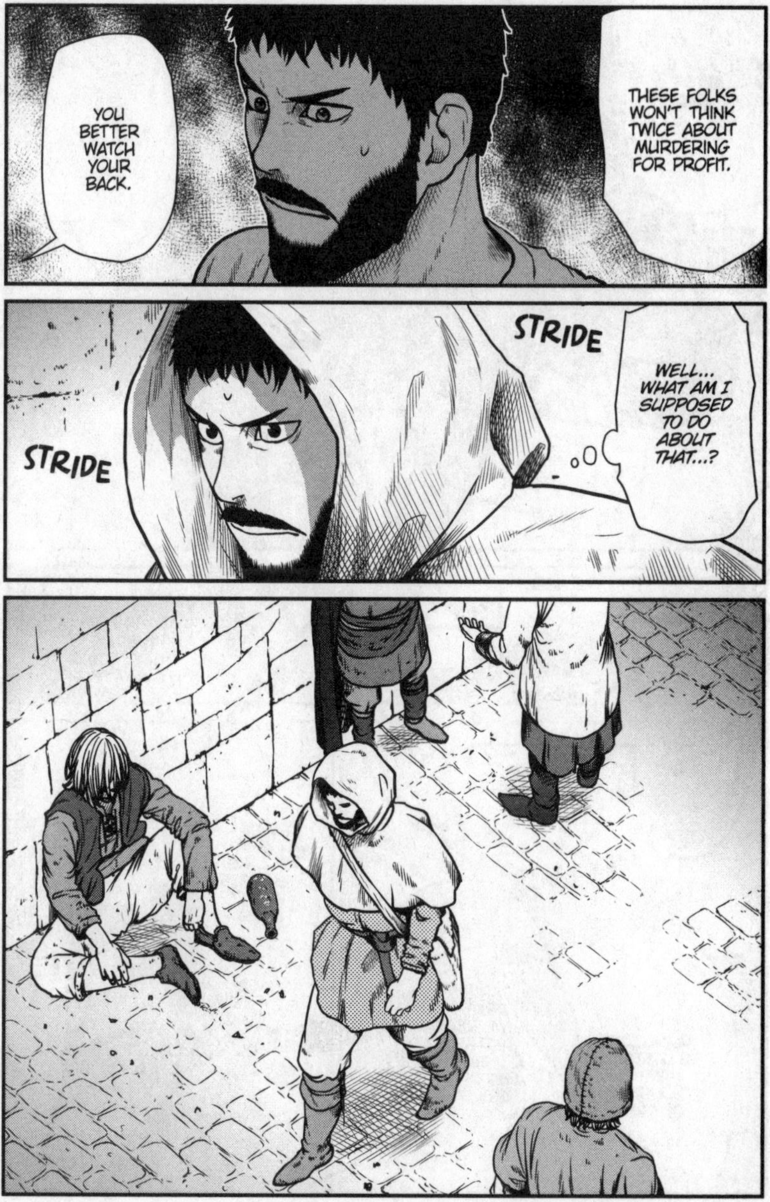
THESE FOLKS WON'T THINK TWICE ABOUT MURDERING FOR PROFIT.
YOU BETTER WATCH YOUR BACK.
WELL... WHAT AM I SUPPOSED TO DO ABOUT THAT...?
STRIDE
STRIDE

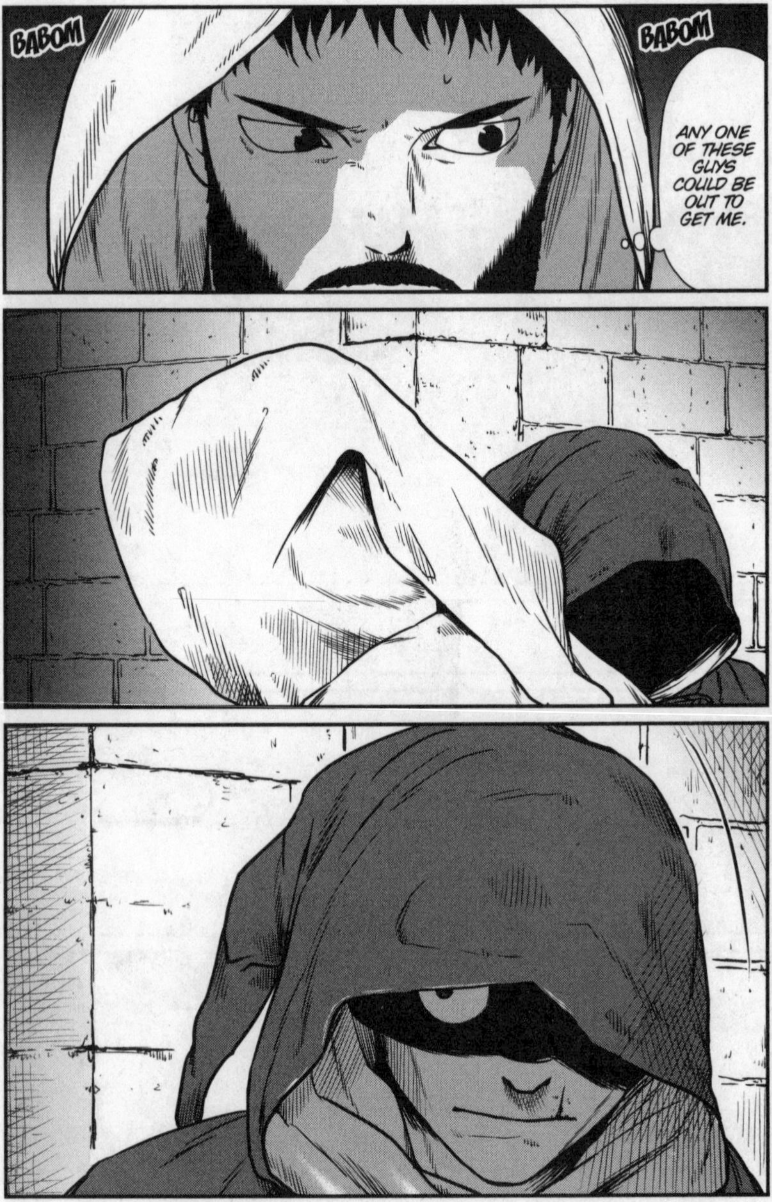
BABOM
ANY ONE OF THESE GUYS COULD BE OUT TO GET ME.
BABOM

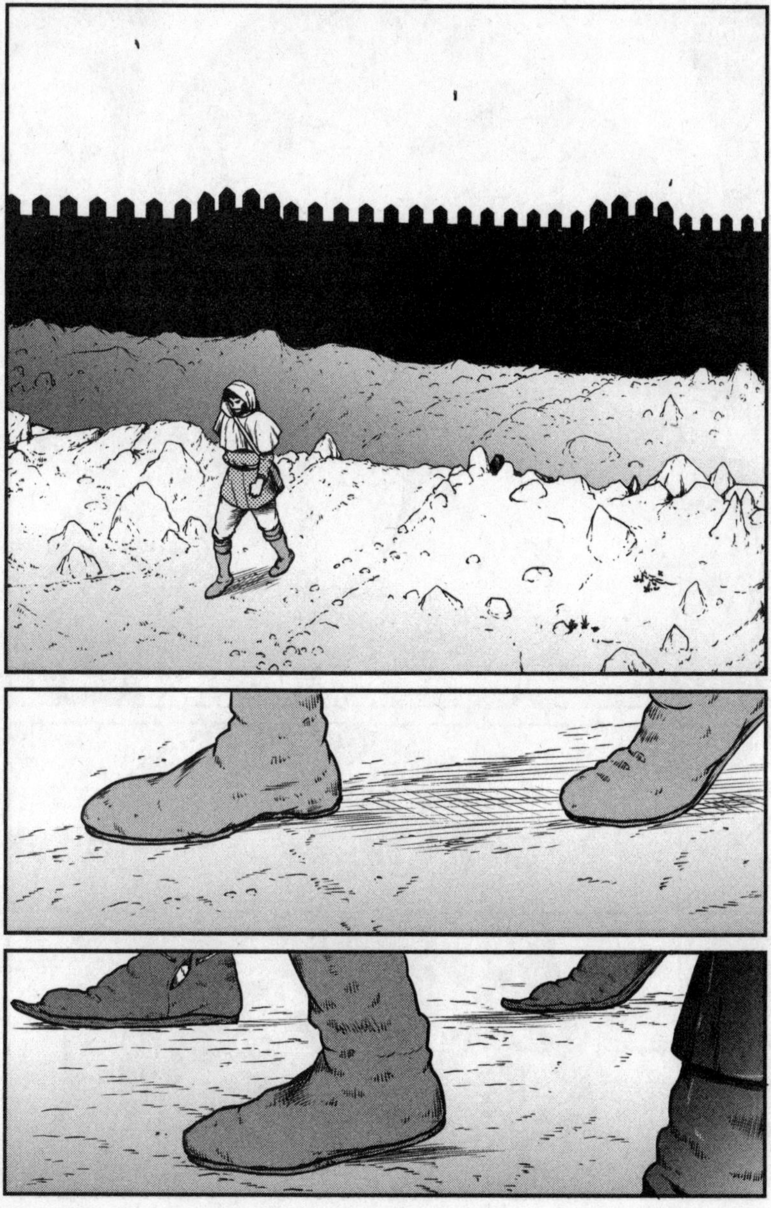

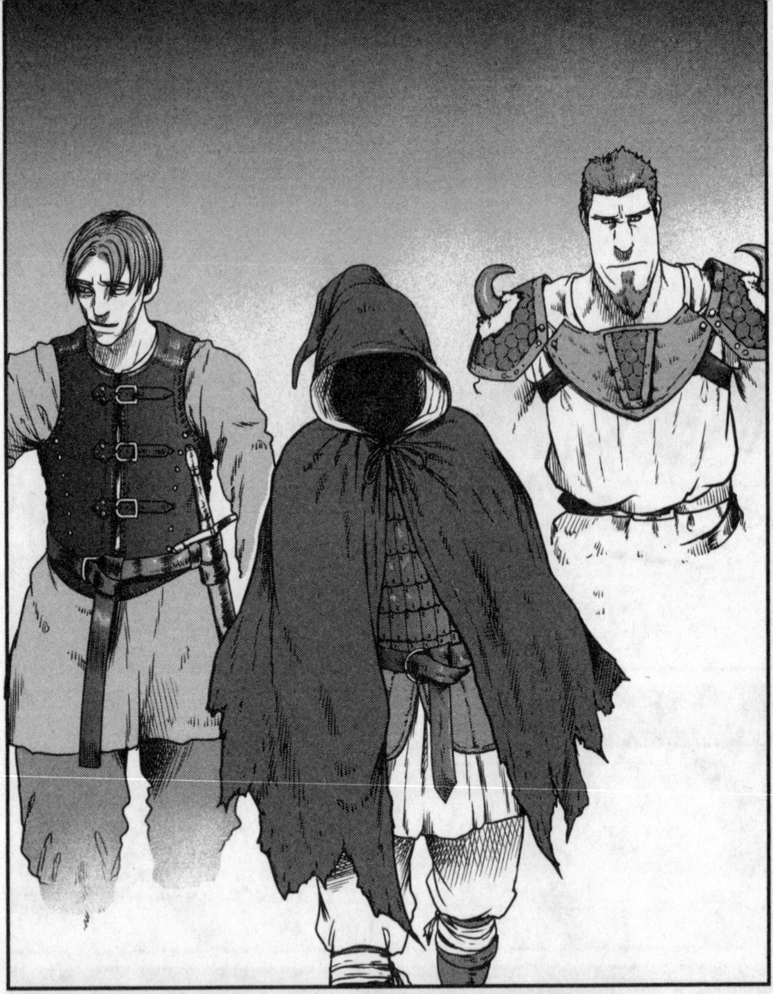
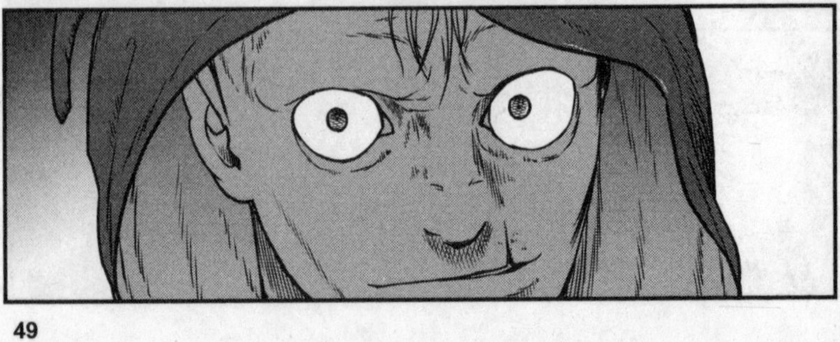

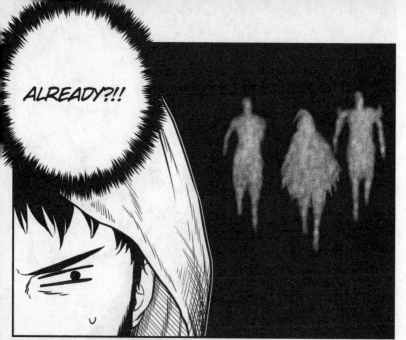

ALREADY?!!

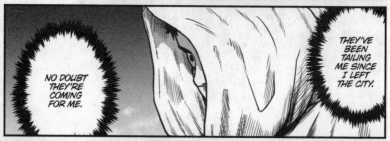

THEY'VE BEEN TAILING ME SINCE I LEFT THE CITY.

NO DOUBT THEY'RE COMING FOR ME.

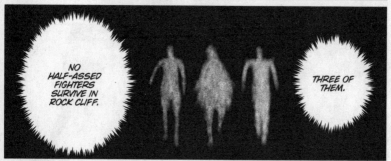

NO HALF-ASSED FIGHTERS SURVIVE IN ROCK CLIFF.

THREE OF THEM.

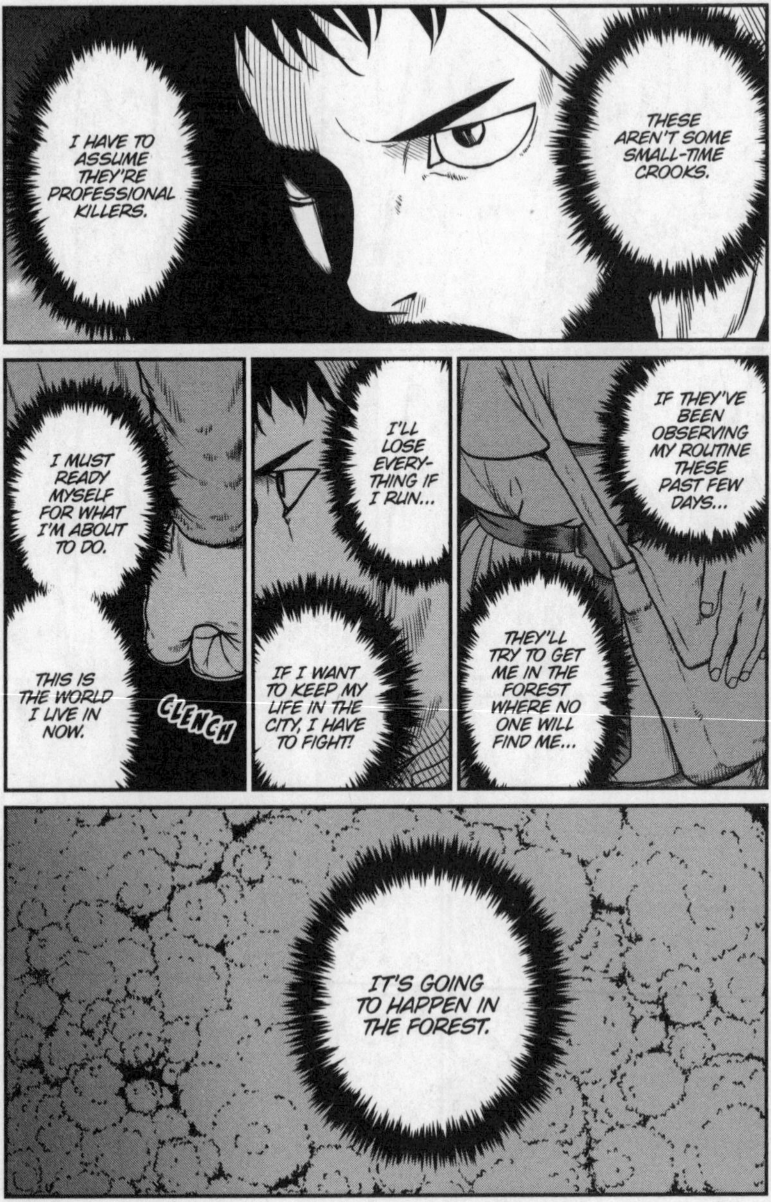
THESE AREN'T SOME SMALL-TIME CROOKS.
I HAVE TO ASSUME THEY'RE PROFESSIONAL KILLERS.
IF THEY'VE BEEN OBSERVING MY ROUTINE THESE PAST FEW DAYS...
THEY'LL TRY TO GET ME IN THE FOREST WHERE NO ONE WILL FIND ME...
I'LL LOSE EVERY-THING IF I RUN...
IF I WANT TO KEEP MY LIFE IN THE CITY, I HAVE TO FIGHT!
I MUST READY MYSELF FOR WHAT I'M ABOUT TO DO.
CLENCH
THIS IS THE WORLD I LIVE IN NOW.
IT'S GOING TO HAPPEN IN THE FOREST.

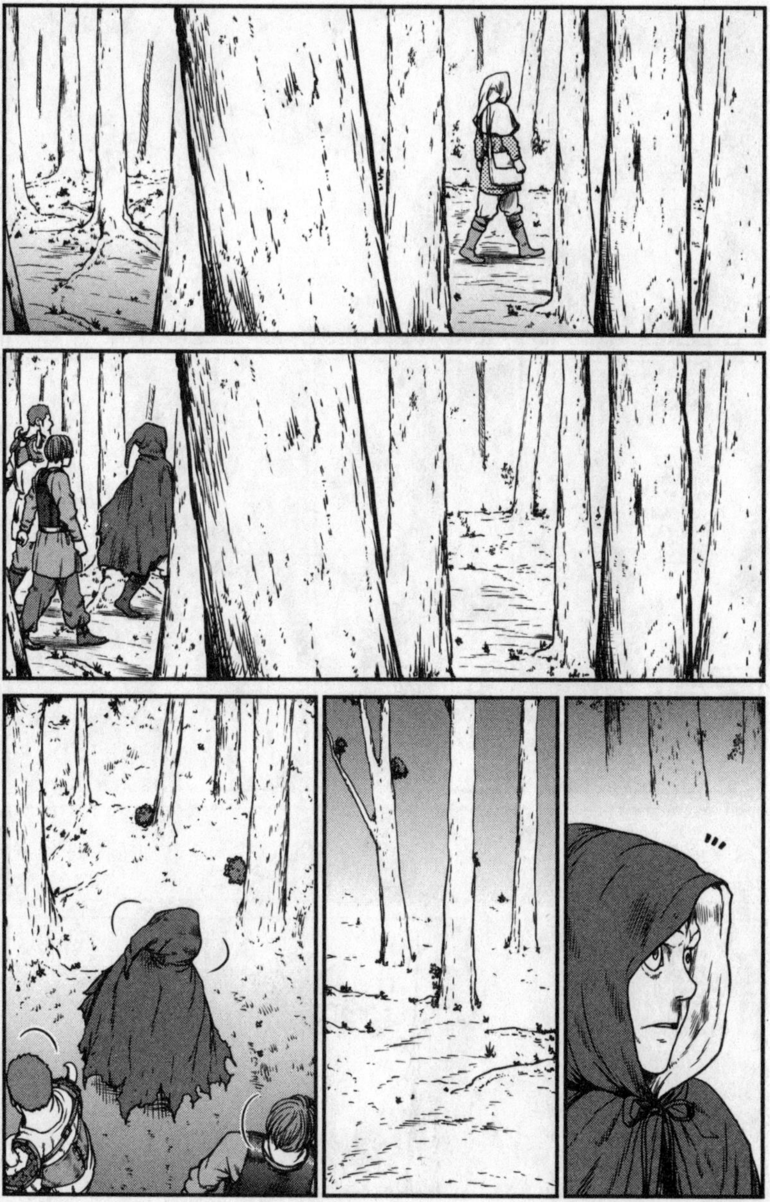
...

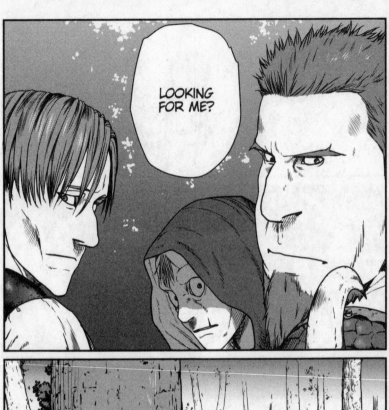

LOOKING FOR ME?

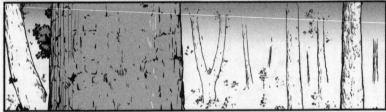

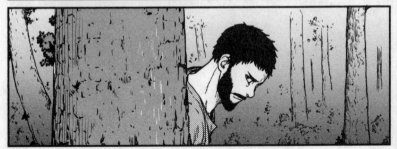

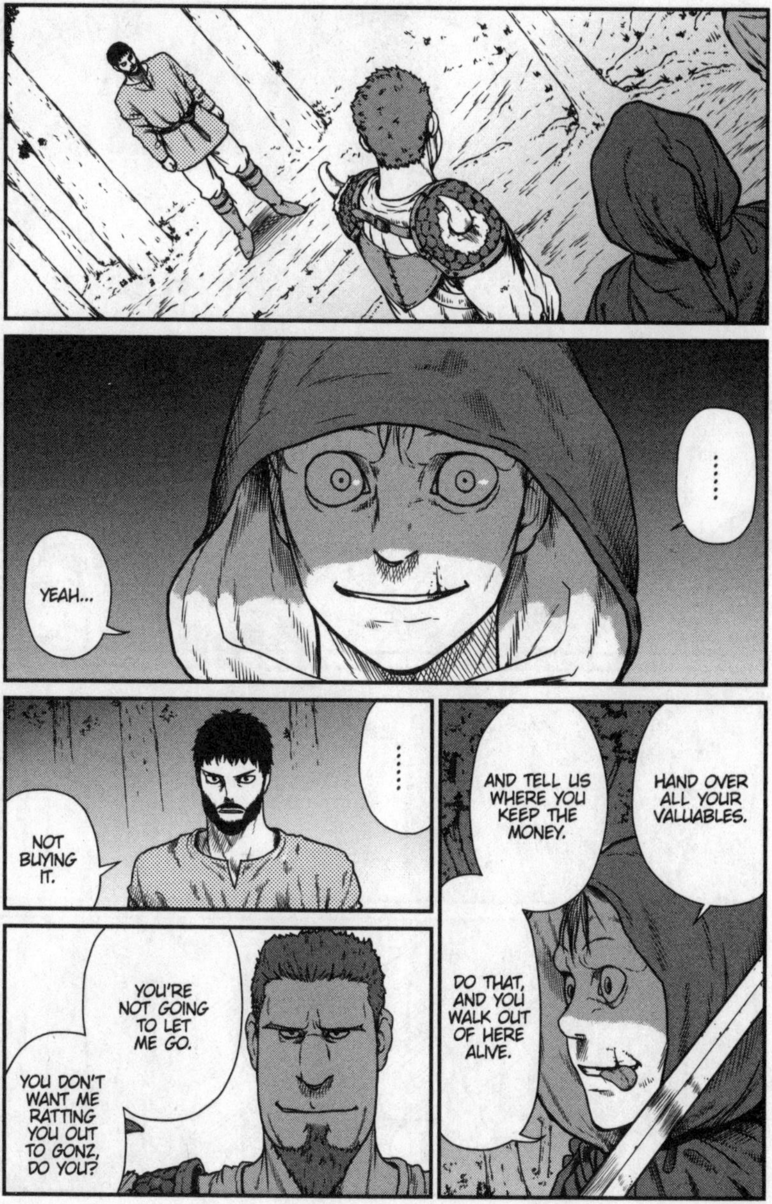
......
YEAH...
HAND OVER ALL YOUR VALUABLES.
AND TELL US WHERE YOU KEEP THE MONEY.
DO THAT, AND YOU WALK OUT OF HERE ALIVE.
......
NOT BUYING IT.
YOU'RE NOT GOING TO LET ME GO.
YOU DON'T WANT ME RATTING YOU OUT TO GONZ, DO YOU?

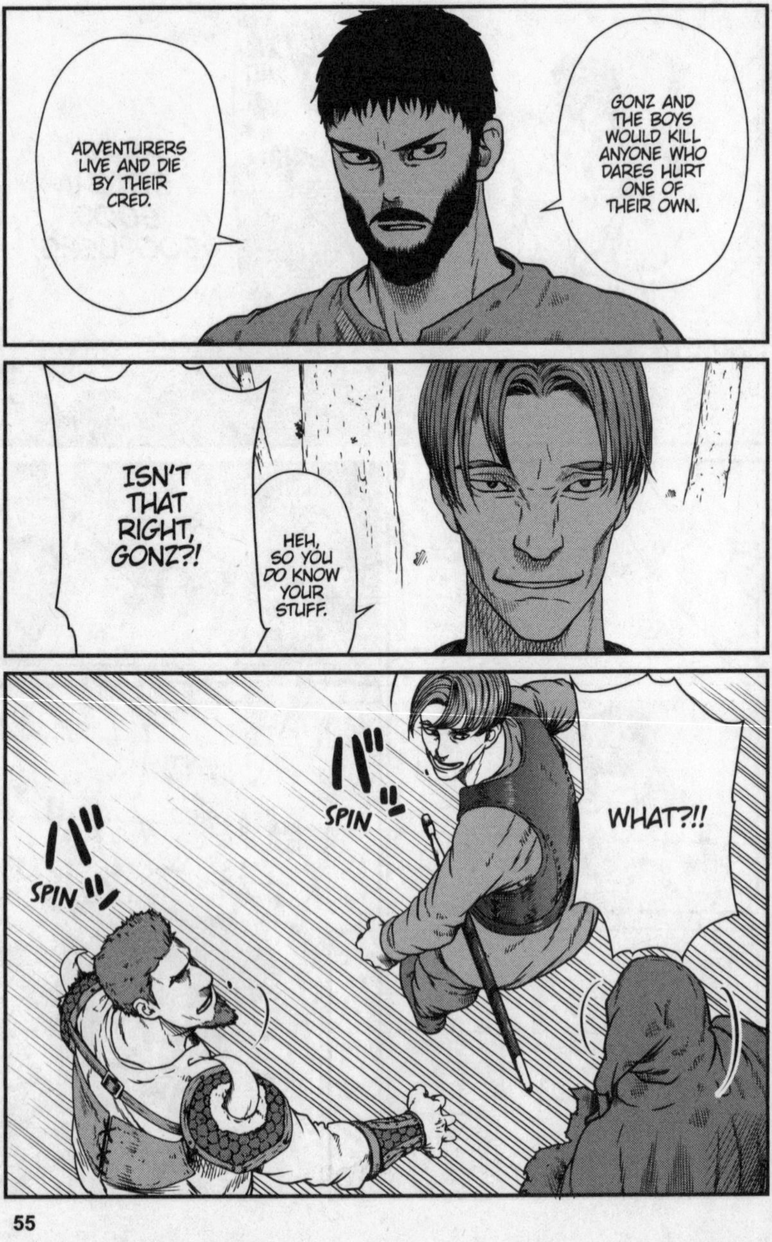
GONZ AND THE BOYS WOULD KILL ANYONE WHO DARES HURT ONE OF THEIR OWN.
ADVENTURERS LIVE AND DIE BY THEIR CRED.
HEH, SO YOU DO KNOW YOUR STUFF.
ISN'T THAT RIGHT, GONZ?!
WHAT?!!
バッ
SPIN
バッ
SPIN

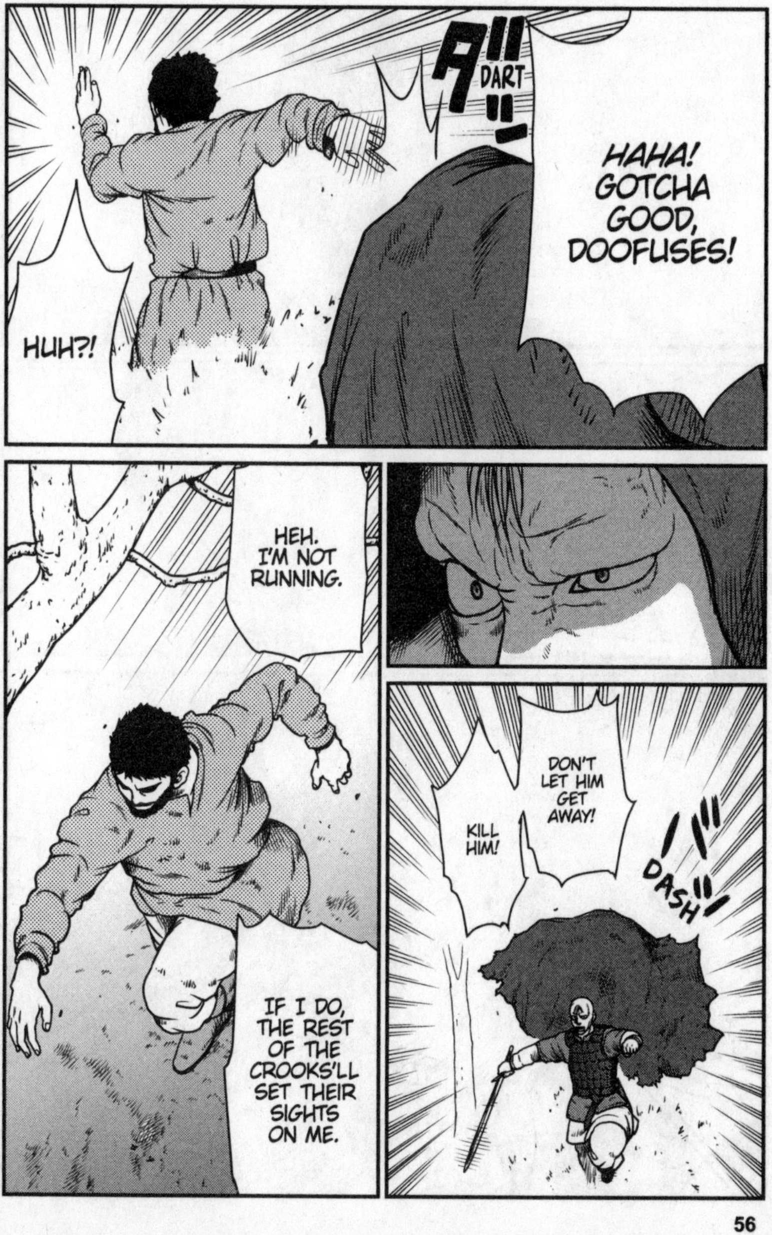
DART
HAHA! GOTCHA GOOD, DOOFUSES!
HUH?!
DASH
DON'T LET HIM GET AWAY!
KILL HIM!
HEH. I'M NOT RUNNING.
IF I DO, THE REST OF THE CROOKS'LL SET THEIR SIGHTS ON ME.

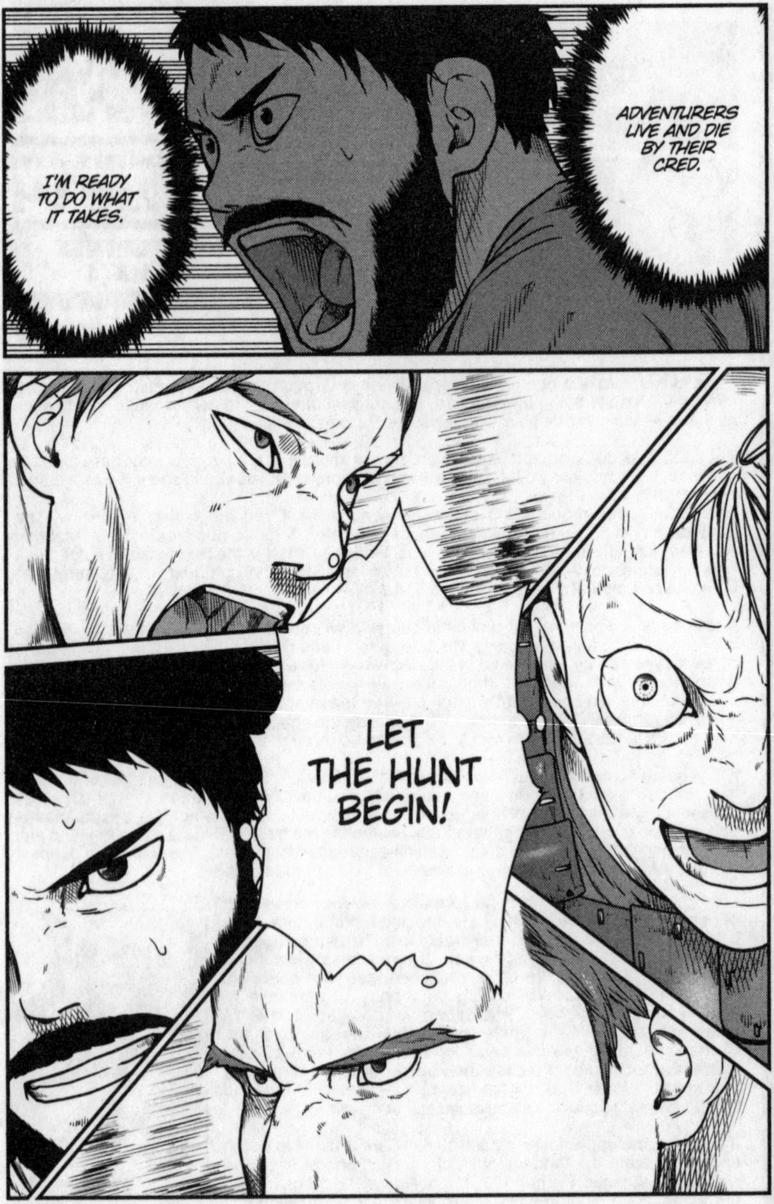
ADVENTURERS LIVE AND DIE BY THEIR CRED.
I'M READY TO DO WHAT IT TAKES.
LET THE HUNT BEGIN!

SPECIAL COLUMN BY AUTHOR, YAZIN

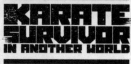

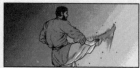

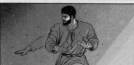

KARATE SURVIVOR IN ANOTHER WORLD

INTERMISSION SAVAGE RULES 14

THE PURPOSE OF KATA

Karate events were included in the 2020 Tokyo Olympics. Since the announcement, kata has started to feature frequently on TV and gained increased public recognition. Kata, the Japanese word for "form," is a mode of training that involves repeating a specific pattern of moves. However, kata can have different purposes and goals between its use in sport and its use in combat training. Nomad can be seen practicing his kata in the story as well. Let us explore this in more detail.

Competitive kata is a contest of expressiveness through the performance of a standard move set. Despite being a martial art, it is somewhat similar to performance sports such as figure skating, in that points are awarded for artistic expression.

But what role does artistic expression play in martial arts? As you may have already guessed, it is completely different to the sort of expression you would see in figure skating.

Competitive kata requires the athlete to perform as if you are facing an enemy. The purpose is to express to the judges a sense of tension, ferocity, and create the illusion that you were actually in combat during the performance. That is the "expression" judged in a kata performance. Just as figure skaters deliver a story through their routine, karatekas fabricate one side of a fight through their kata.

Accuracy is a highly valued quality in competitive kata. Accurate kata must be learned in order to teach future students the correct form and motions. Yet as times change, the same moves can be interpreted in different ways. For example, you might perform a foot sweep to trip your opponent, then poke your fingers into their eyes. In our current, less violent society, we could hardly teach children these applications. Instead, we adjust the content appropriately for the context. But despite the change in interpretation, competitive kata allows these specific moves to be preserved through the ages.

Katas serve as examples of basic moves for beginners. This is true regardless of where it is performed, even the world stage as prominent as the Olympic Games. Competitive kata is essentially a contest involving the world's most practiced fundamentals. (By no means do I mean to disparage competitive kata. Perfecting the basic moves is a challenge in and of itself, and you could easily spend a lifetime trying to master kata. I have only the deepest respect for how dedicated these athletes are to the fundamentals.)

AH, YES...
I SHOULD SEE IF I CAN STILL FIGHT WITH MY DETECTION SKILL ACTIVE.
IF I COULD USE THE KARATE SKILL AND DETECTION SKILL SIMULTANEOUSLY, IT'D BE VERY EFFECTIVE.

Kata for competition aims to preserve perfect form, but opponents rarely move as they are imagined to in a kata. Kata is only a record of basic patterns meant to be expanded upon. If your opponent deviates from the kata, then you must also adapt. You plan for several different approaches that your opponent might take. You practice moving your body in response to your simulated opponent. This allows you to react on the fly when you encounter a similar move from a real opponent. By deconstructing the basics of kata, you can learn several alternative forms and increase the number of types of attacks you are able to deal with. This is kata for combat, and it is in direct contrast to sports kata, which aims to preserve.

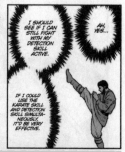

If you have the opportunity, please take the opportunity to watch kata. These are the fundamentals of karate, performed by the world's top athletes. Perhaps you might admire the grace of their perfected motions, or imagine alternative practical moves for different situations. Kata offers plenty for spectators to enjoy.

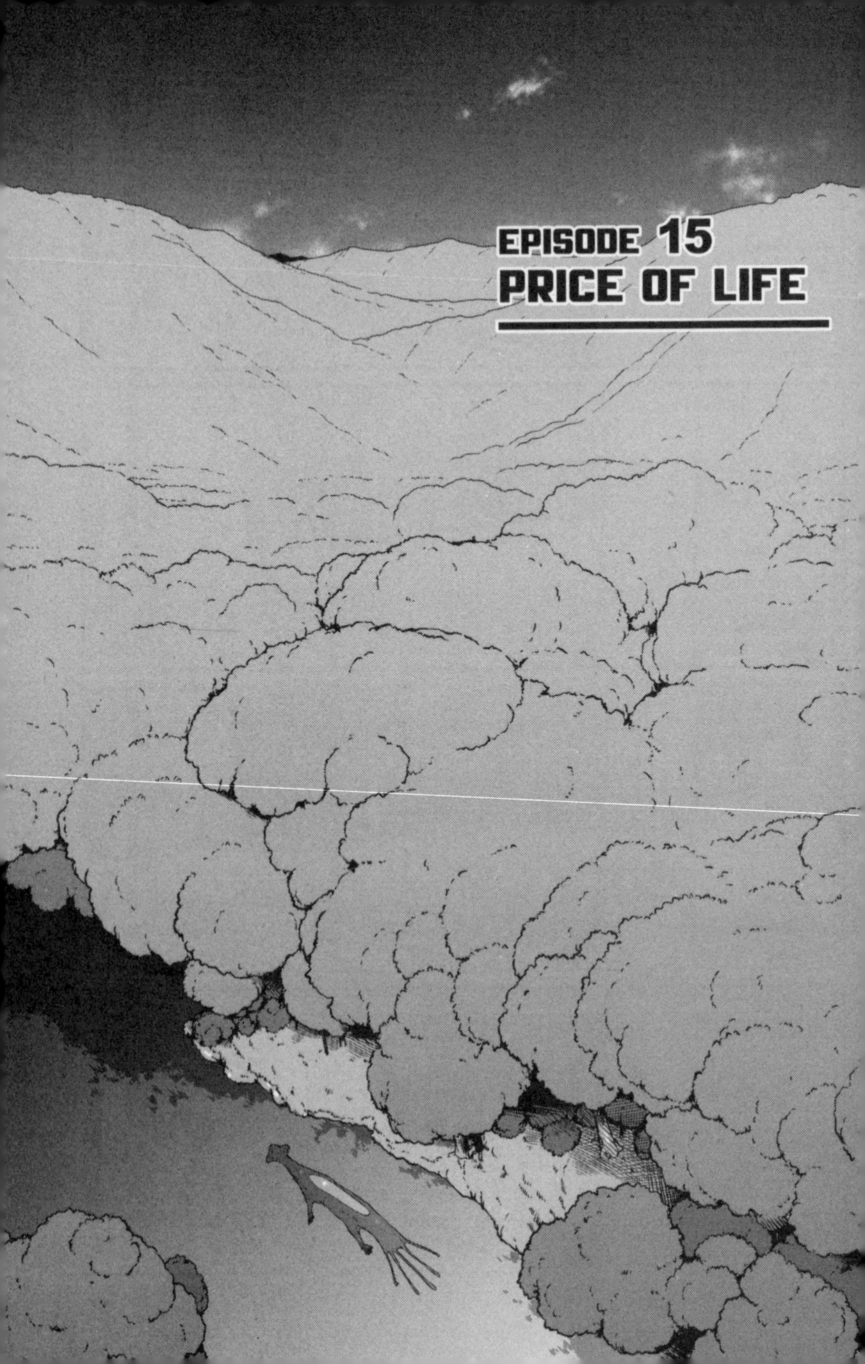
EPISODE 15
PRICE OF LIFE

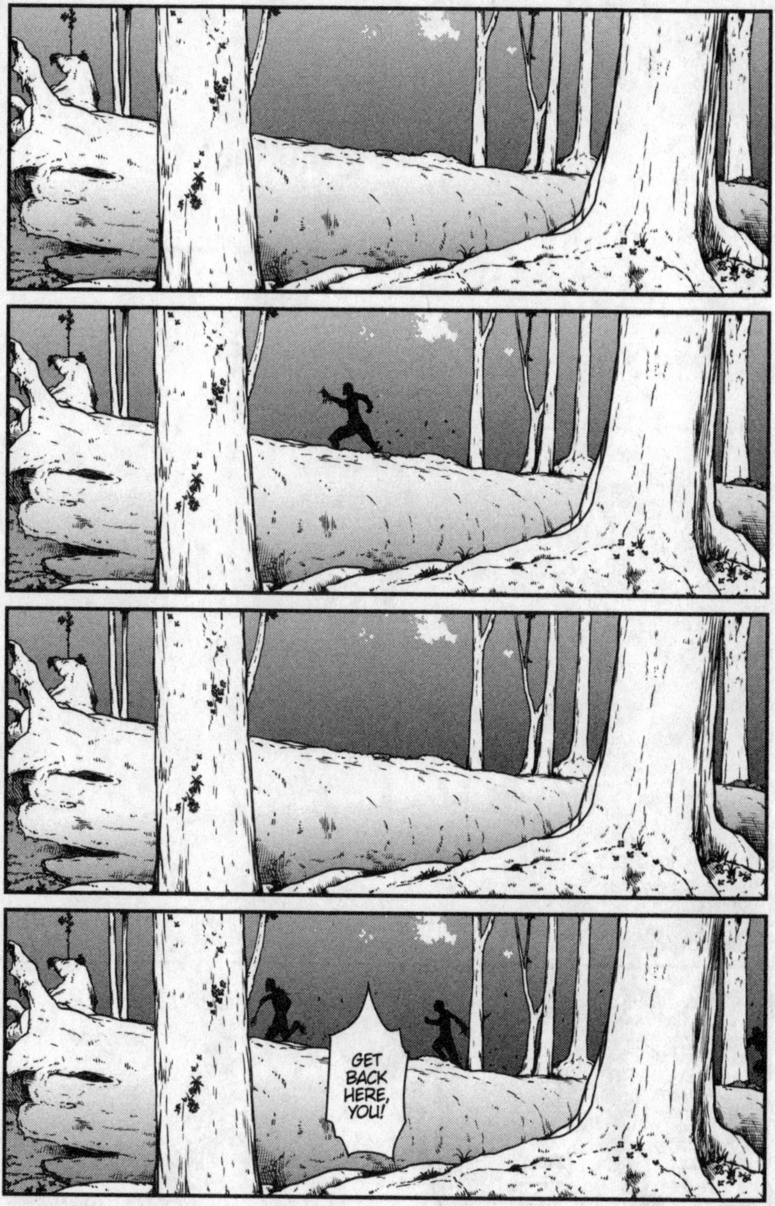
GET BACK HERE, YOU!

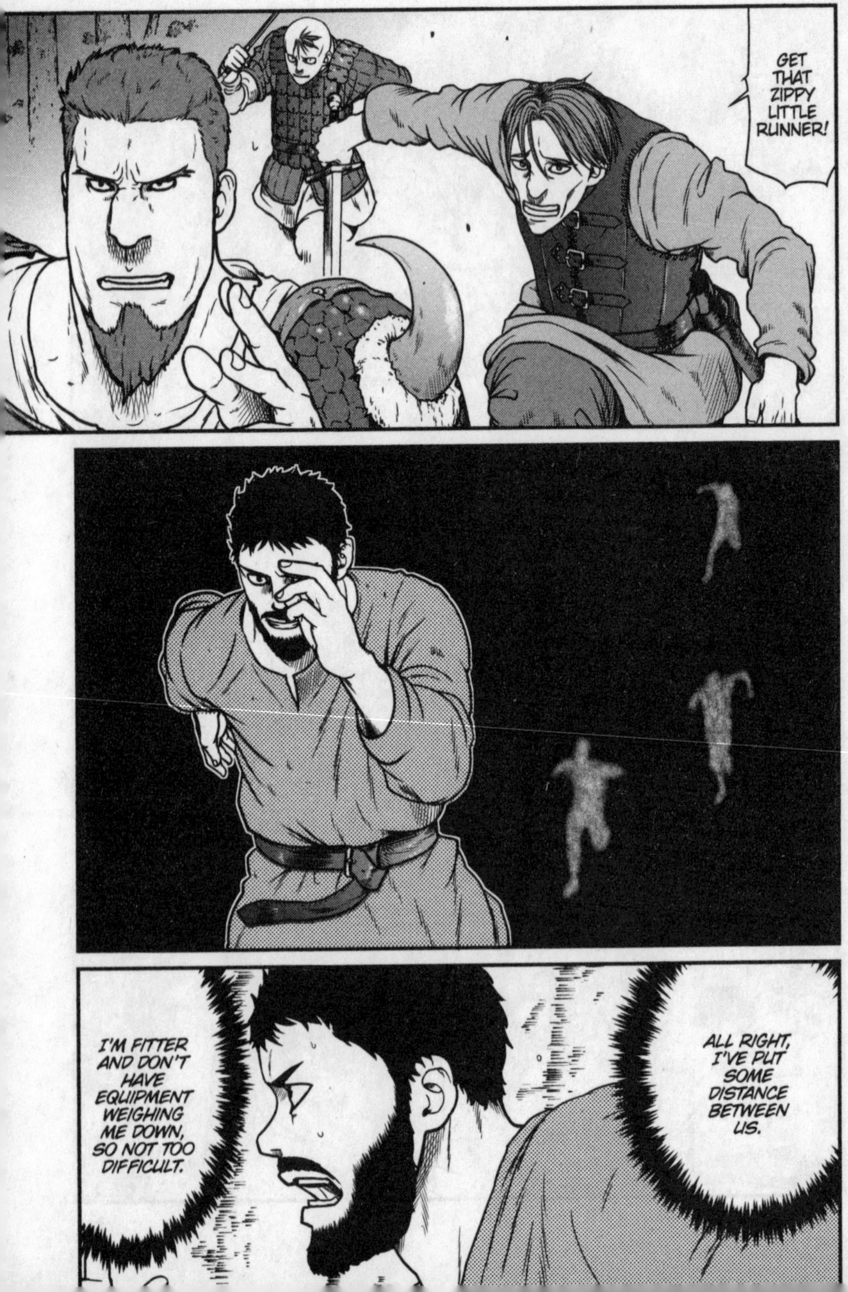
GET THAT ZIPPY LITTLE RUNNER!
ALL RIGHT, I'VE PUT SOME DISTANCE BETWEEN US.
I'M FITTER AND DON'T HAVE EQUIPMENT WEIGHING ME DOWN, SO NOT TOO DIFFICULT.

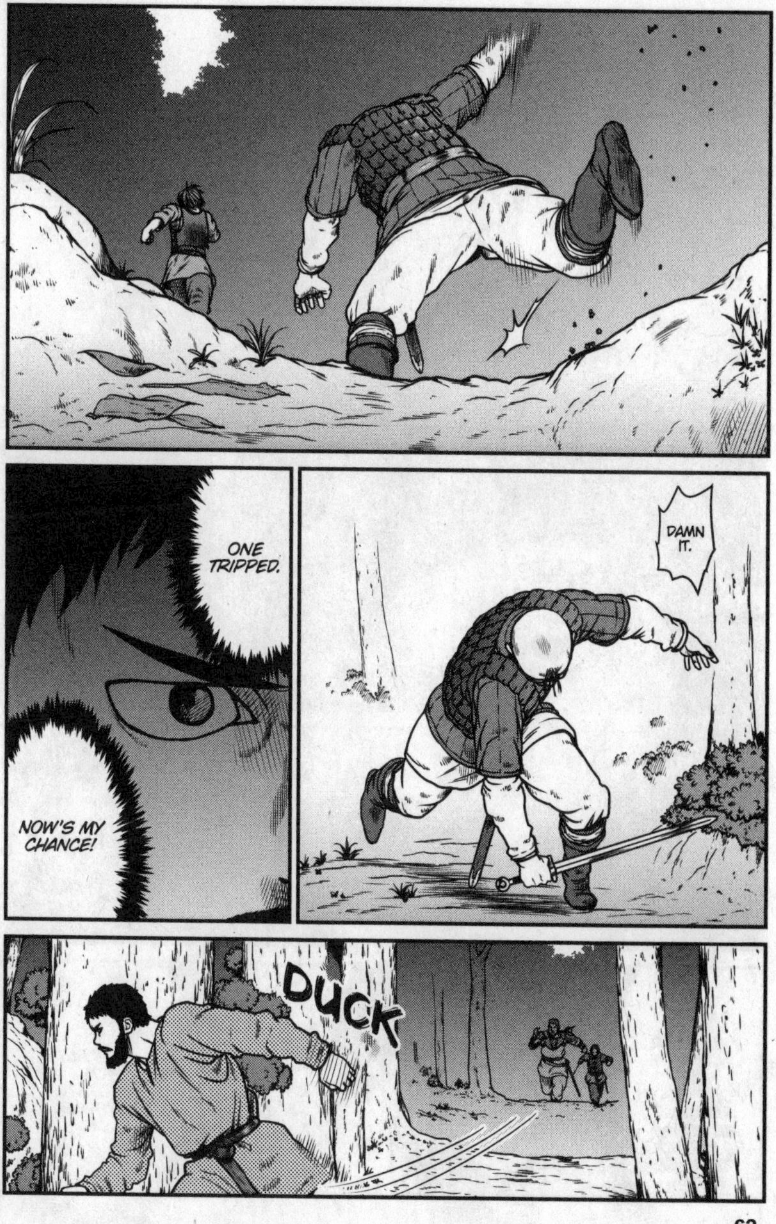
DAMN IT.
ONE TRIPPED.
NOW'S MY CHANCE!
DUCK

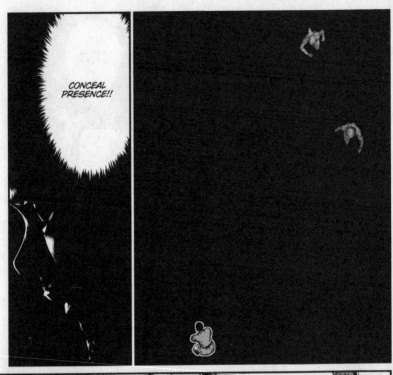

CONCEAL PRESENCE!!

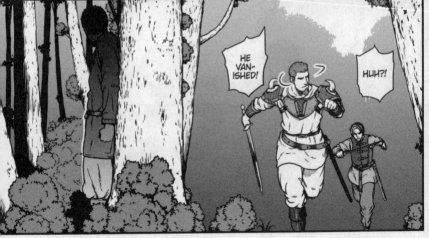

HE VAN- ISHED!

HUH?!

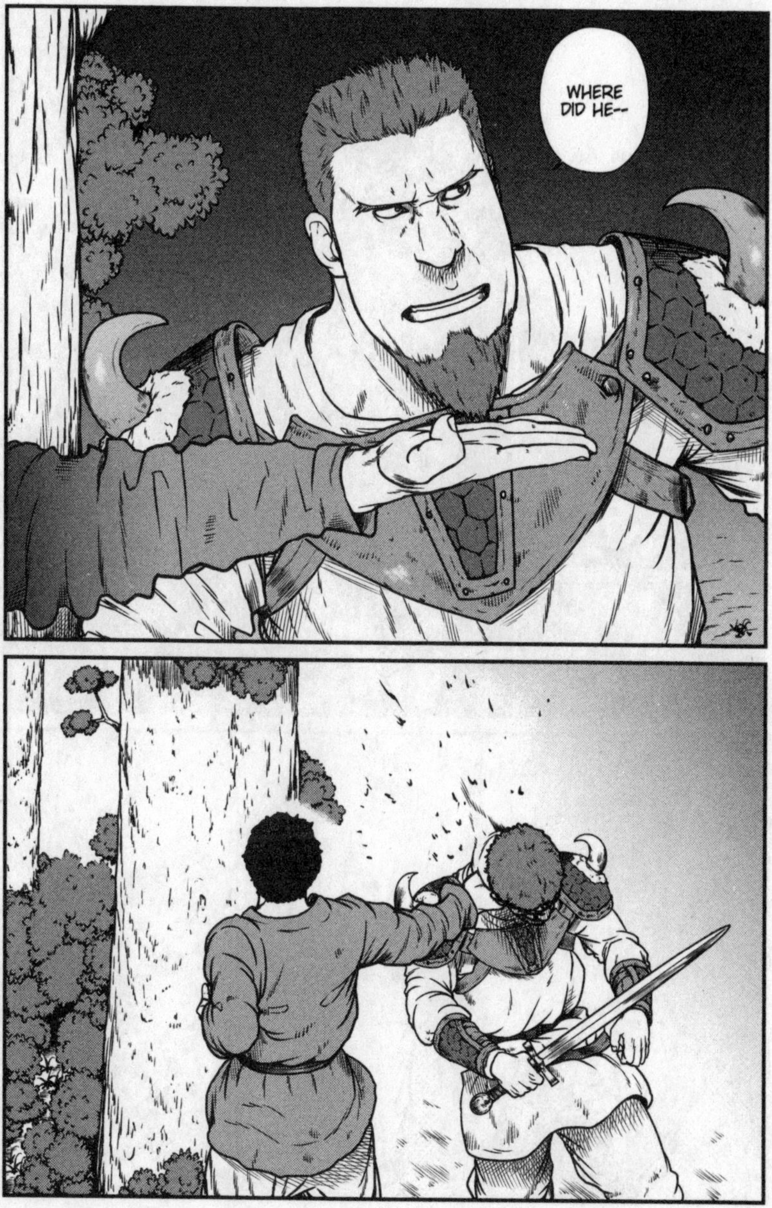
WHERE DID HE--

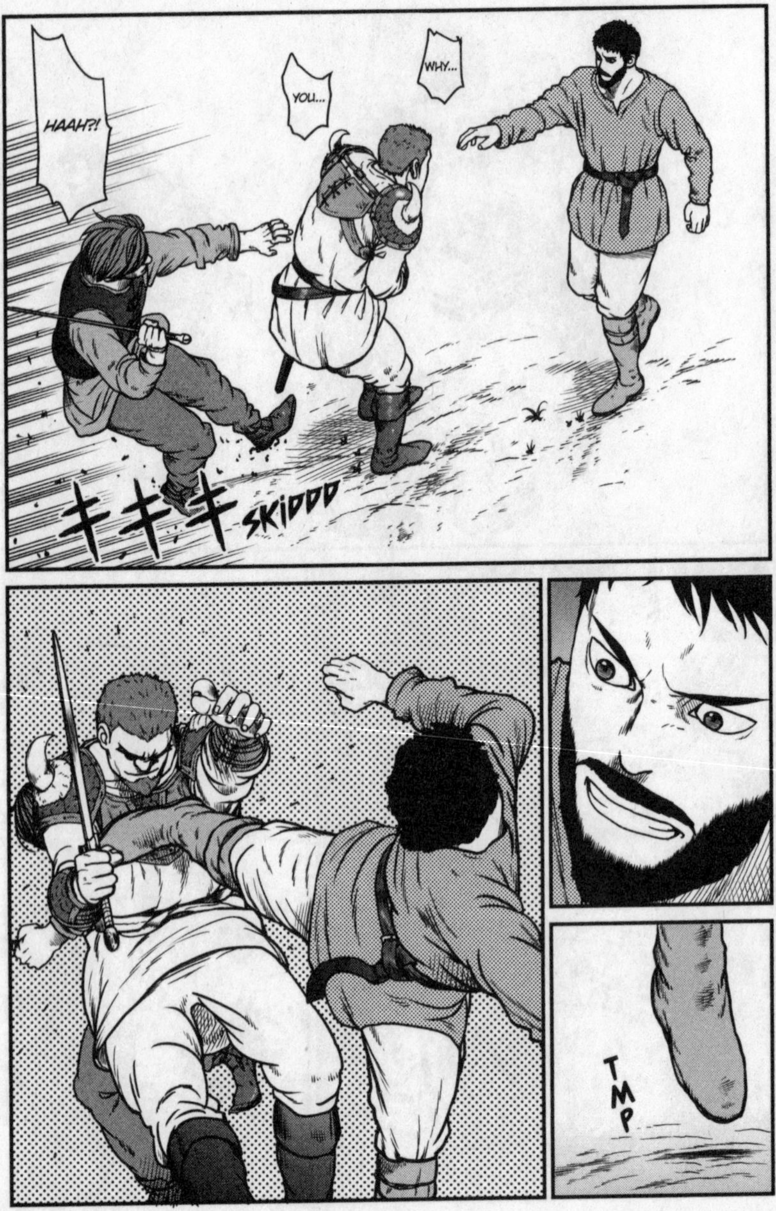
WHY...
YOU...
HAAH?!
キキキ
SKIDDD
TMP

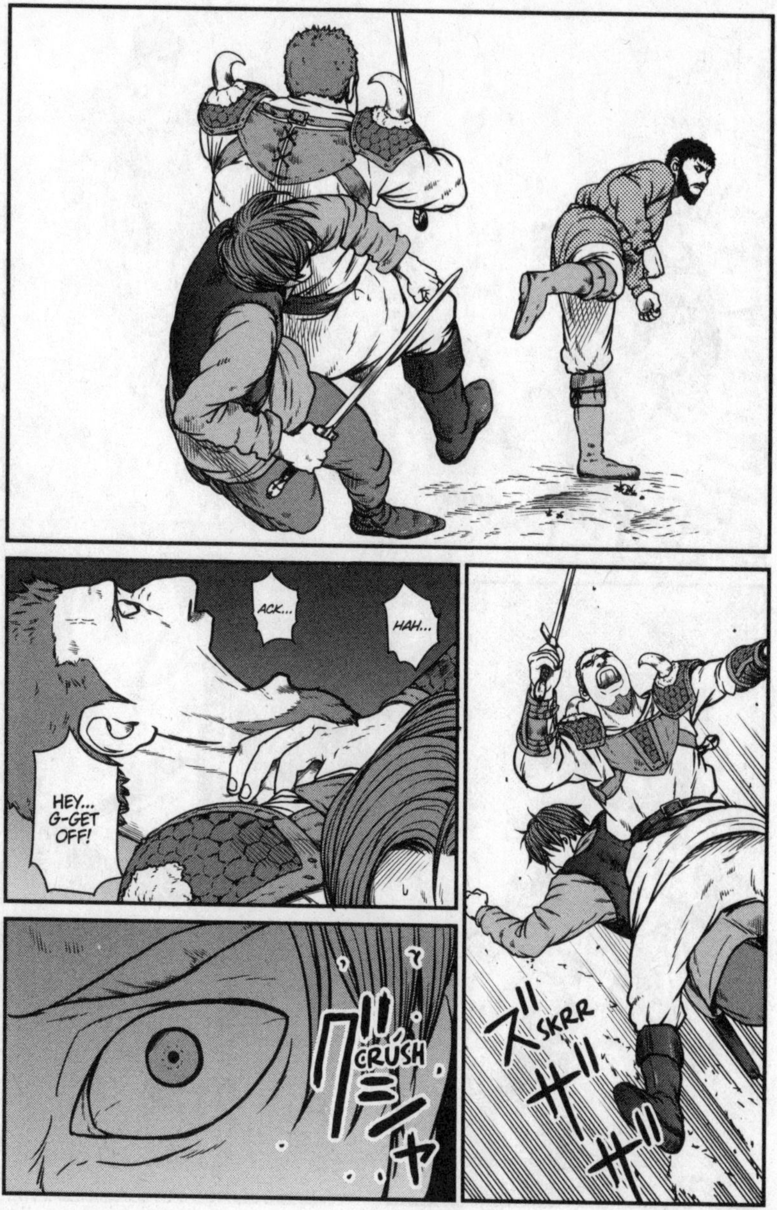
ズザザ
SKRR
HAH...
ACK...
HEY...
G-GET
OFF!
グシャ
CRUSH

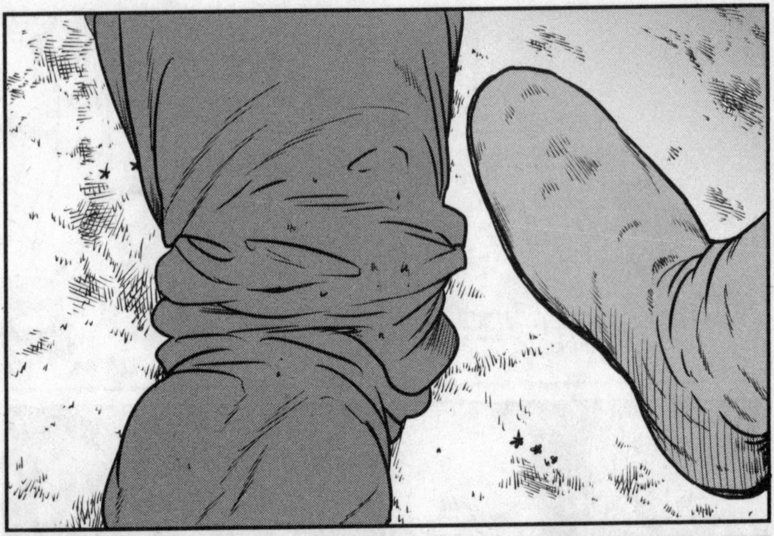

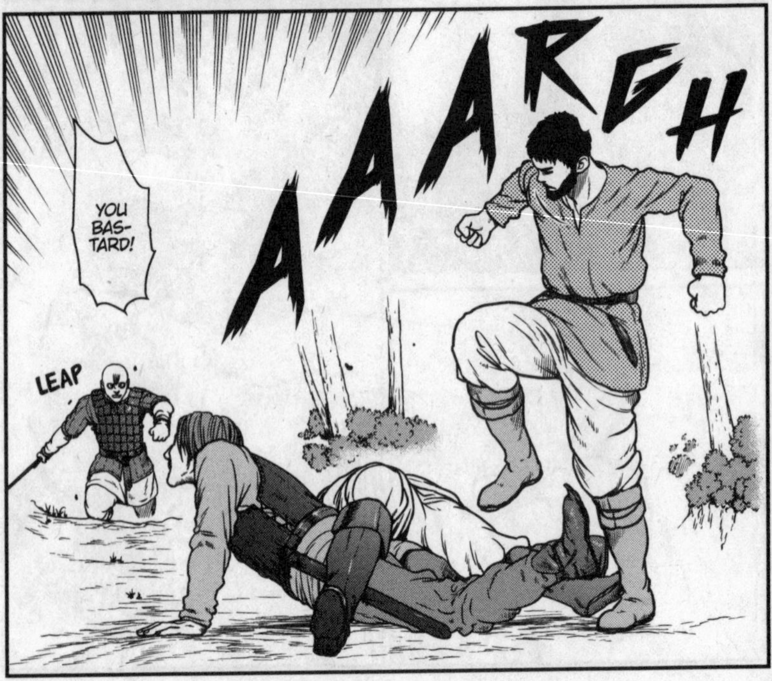
AAARGH
YOU BASTARD!
LEAP

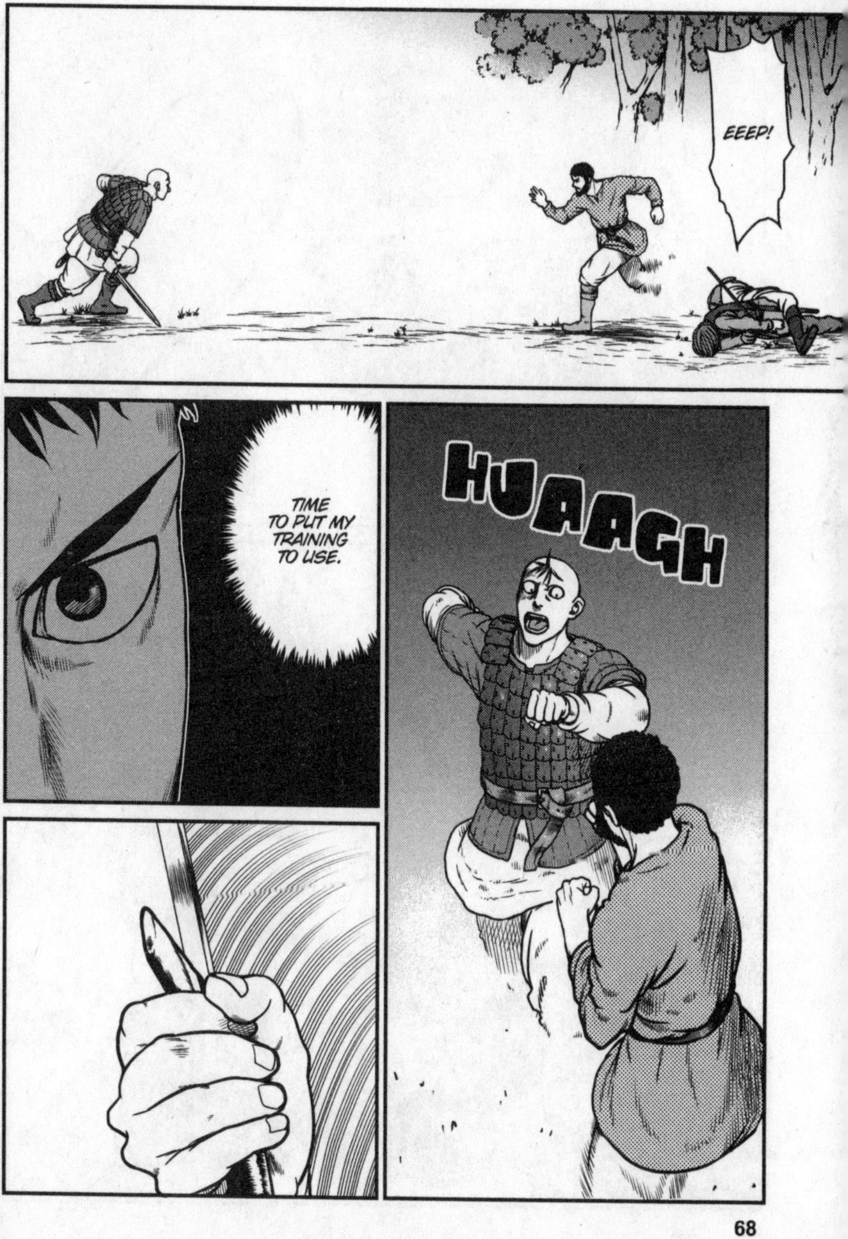
EEEP!
HUAAAGH
TIME TO PUT MY TRAINING TO USE.

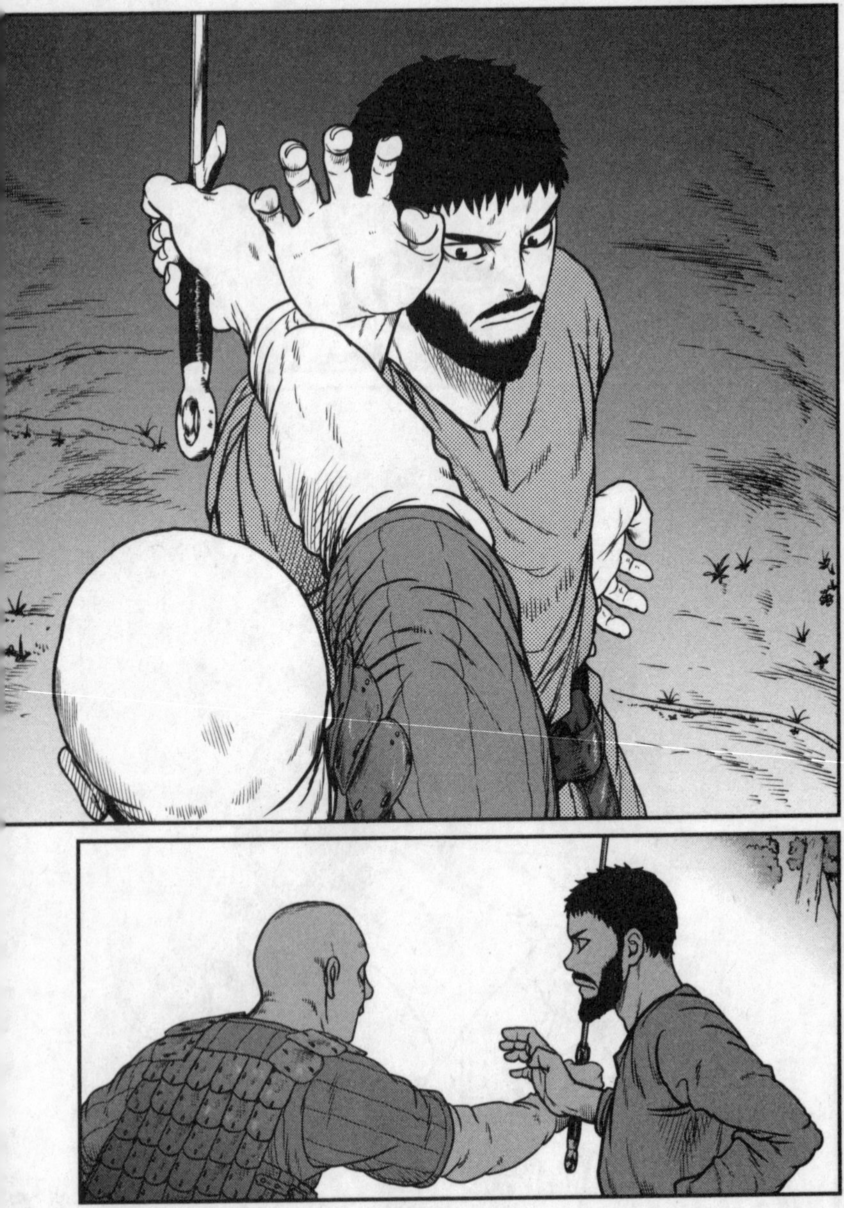

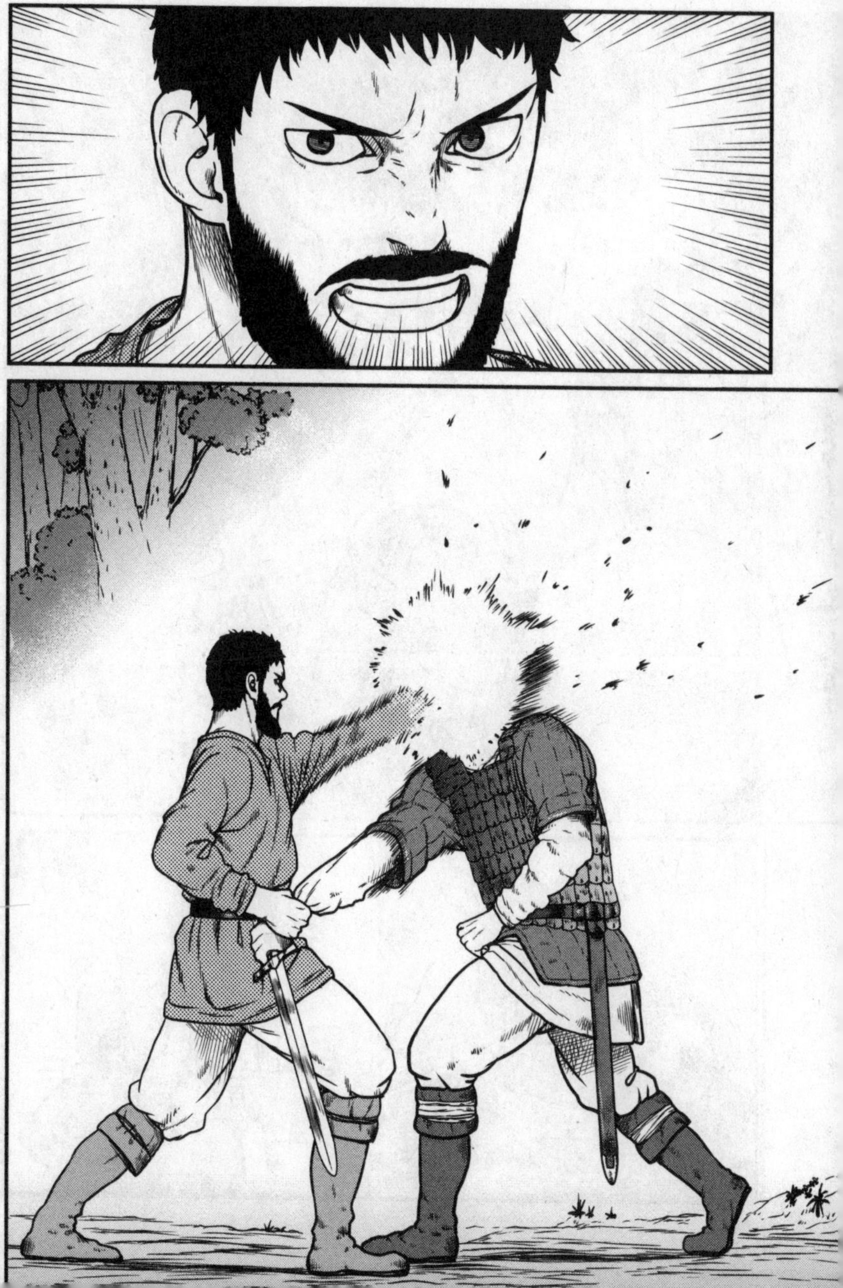

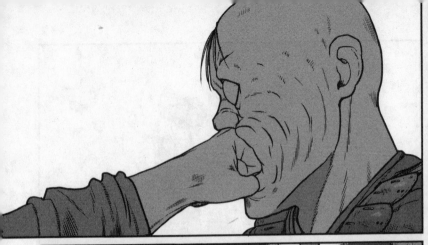

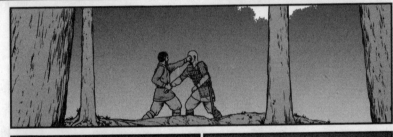

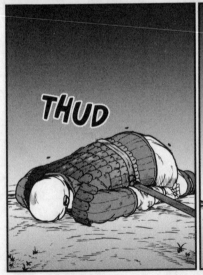

THUD

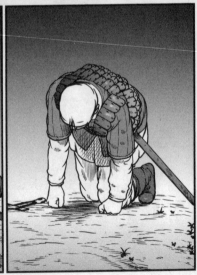

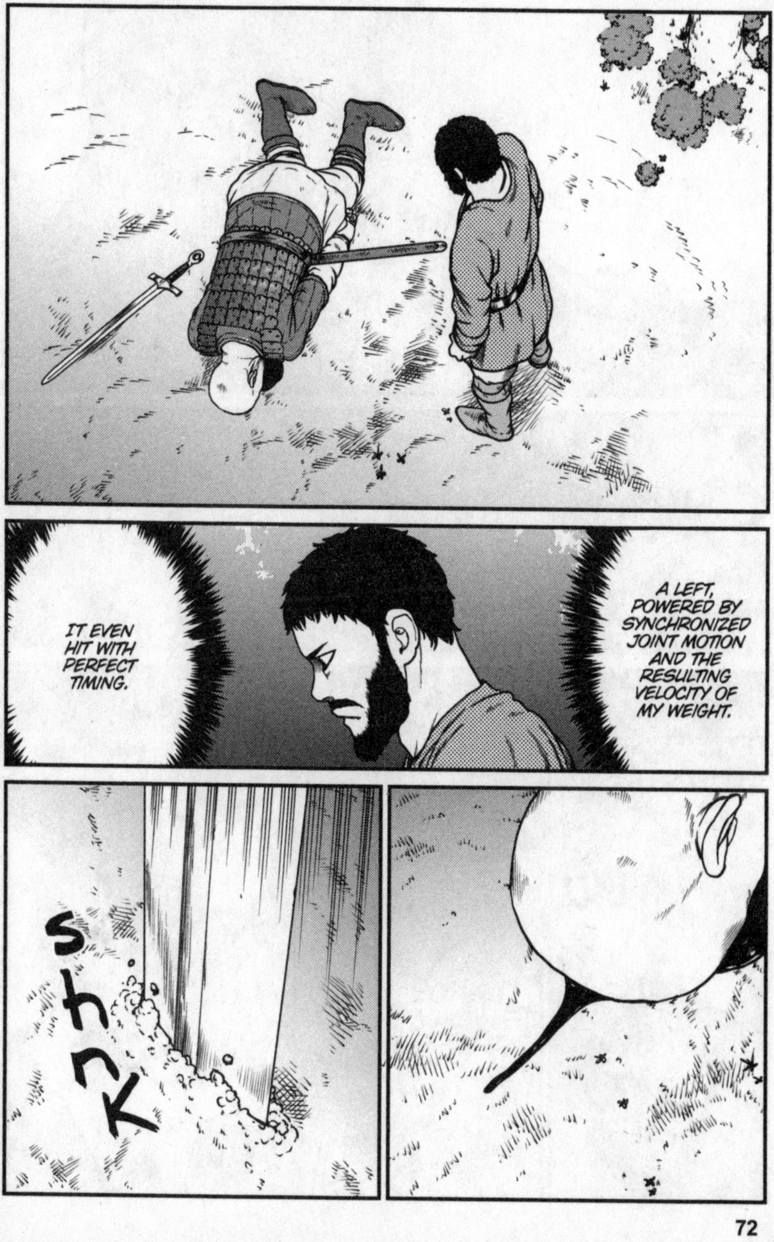
A LEFT, POWERED BY SYNCHRONIZED JOINT MOTION AND THE RESULTING VELOCITY OF MY WEIGHT.
IT EVEN HIT WITH PERFECT TIMING.

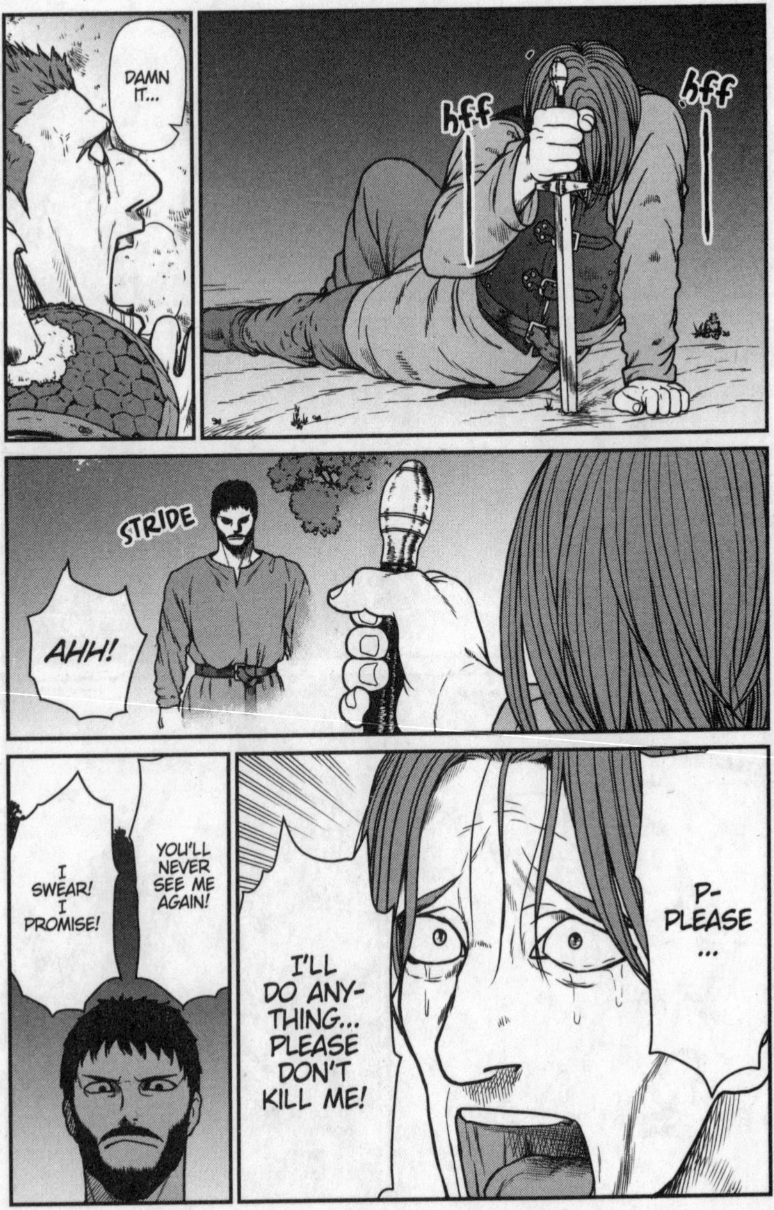
hff
hff
DAMN IT...
STRIDE
AHH!
P-PLEASE...
I'LL DO ANYTHING... PLEASE DON'T KILL ME!
YOU'LL NEVER SEE ME AGAIN!
I SWEAR! I PROMISE!

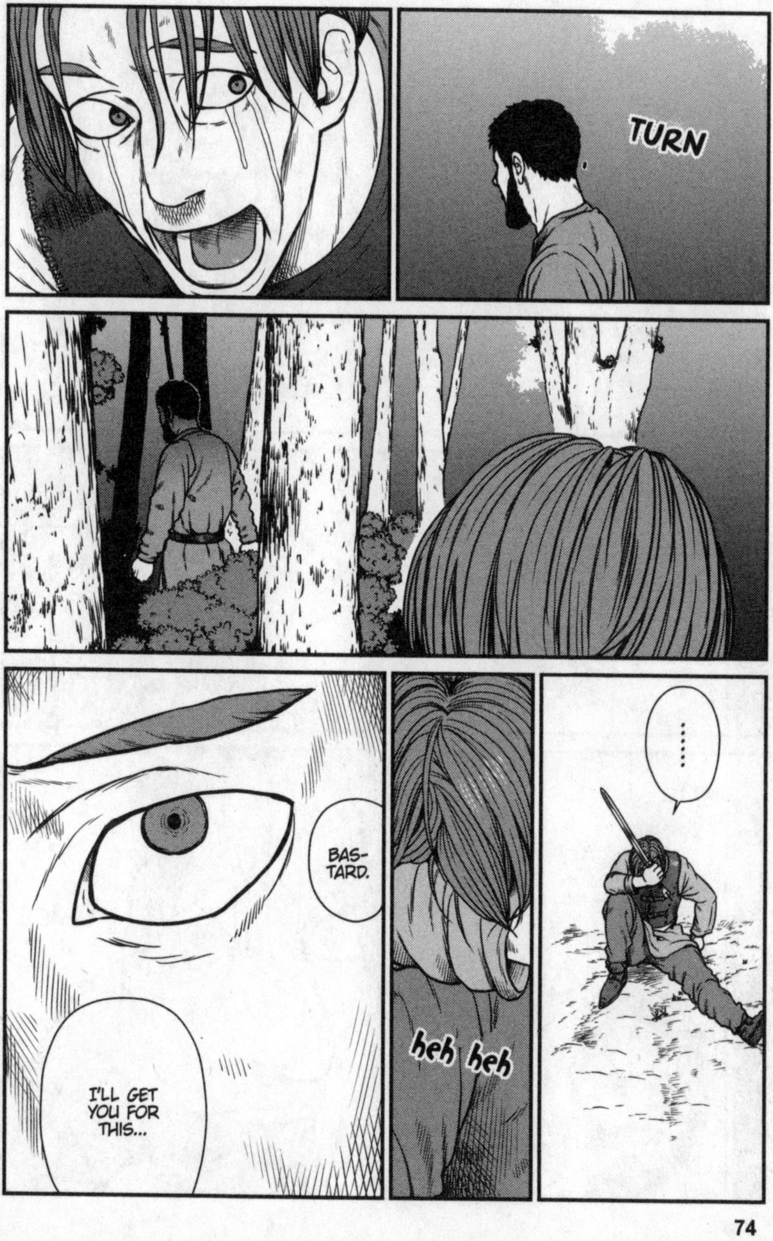
TURN
......
heh heh
BAS-TARD.
I'LL GET YOU FOR THIS...

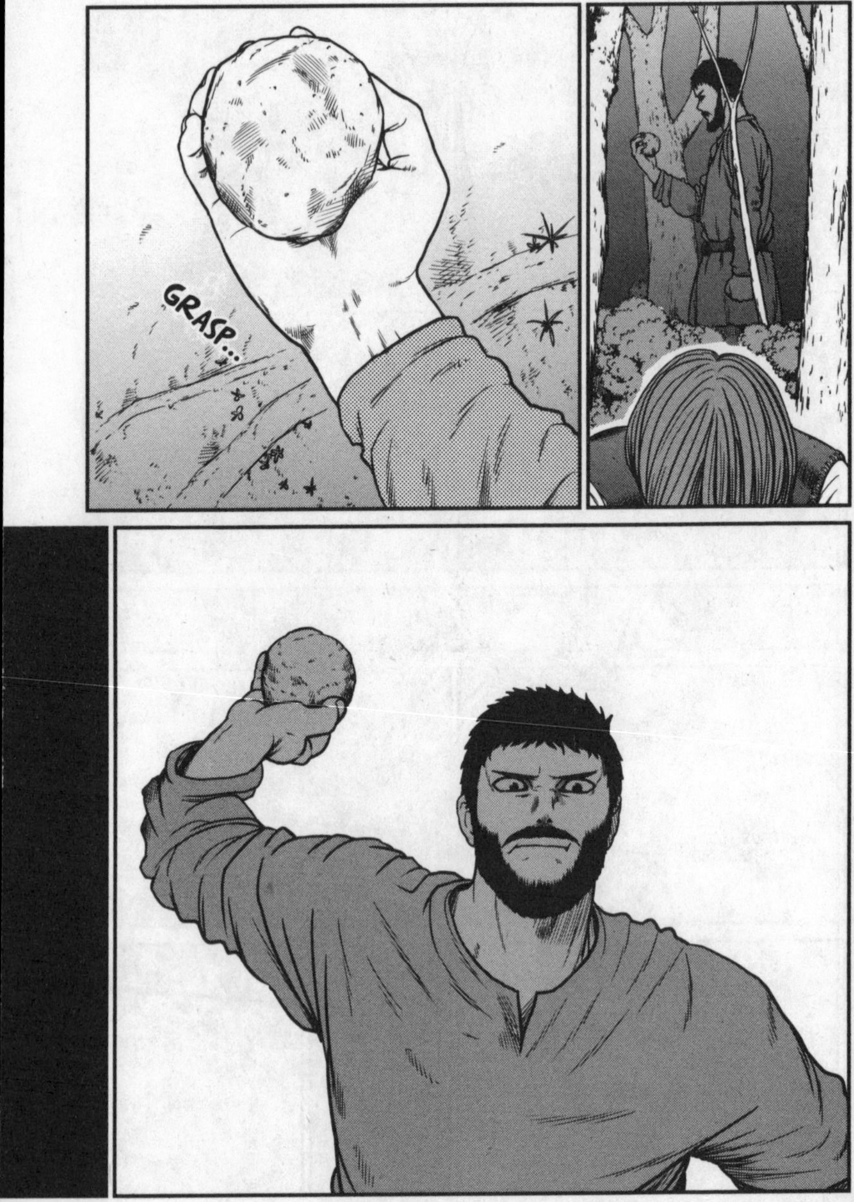
GRASP...

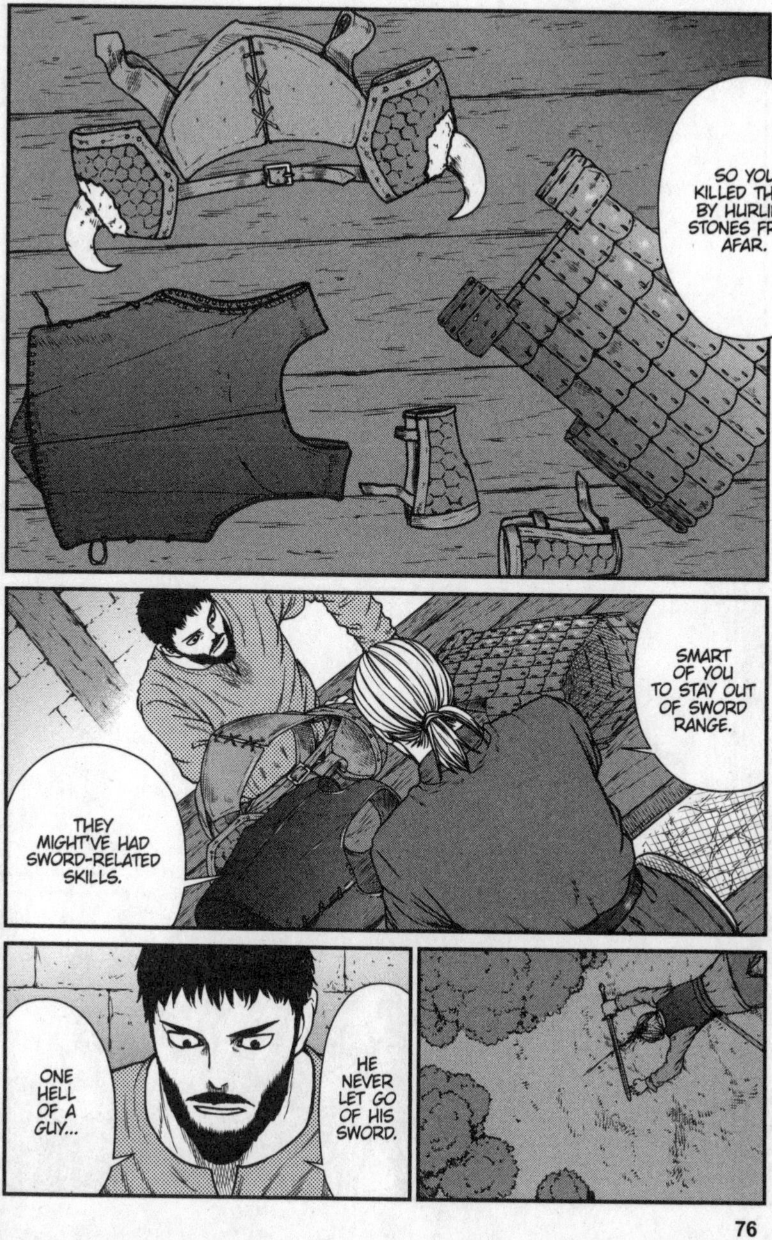
SO YOU KILLED THEM BY HURLING STONES FROM AFAR.
SMART OF YOU TO STAY OUT OF SWORD RANGE.
THEY MIGHT'VE HAD SWORD-RELATED SKILLS.
HE NEVER LET GO OF HIS SWORD.
ONE HELL OF A GUY...

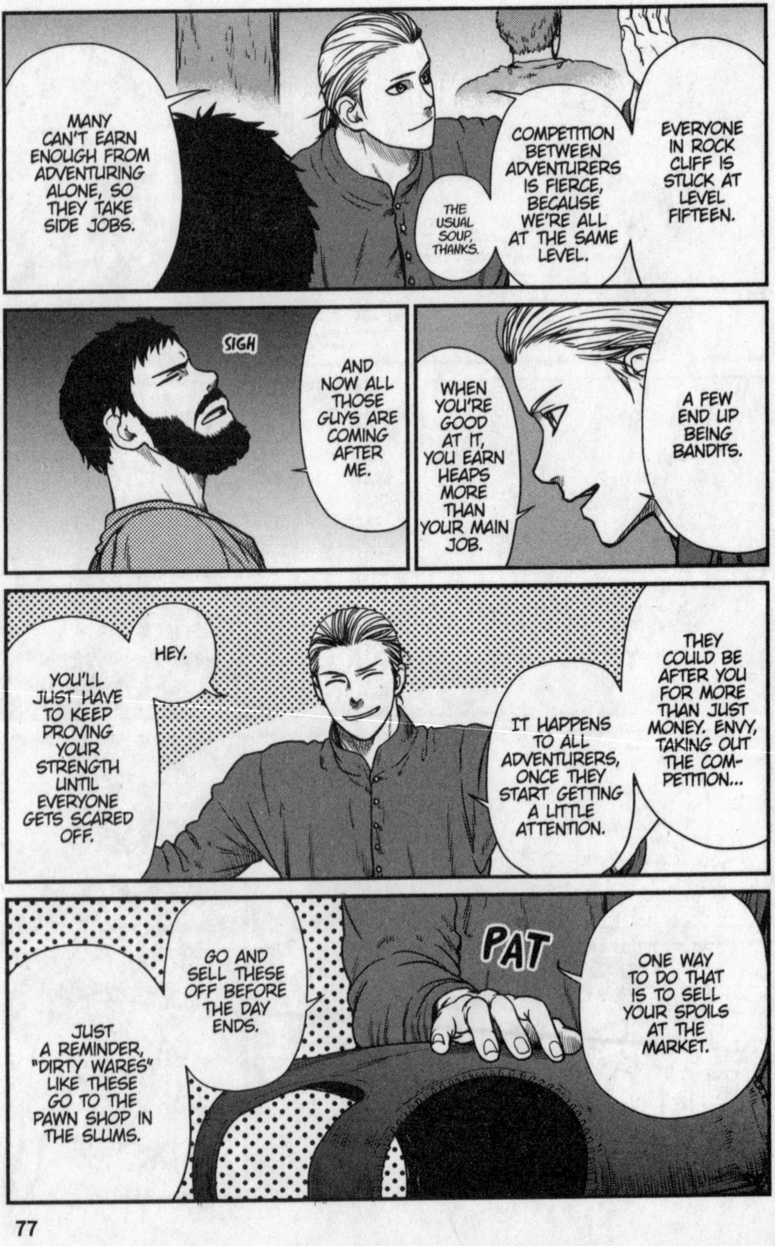
EVERYONE IN ROCK CLIFF IS STUCK AT LEVEL FIFTEEN.
COMPETITION BETWEEN ADVENTURERS IS FIERCE, BECAUSE WE'RE ALL AT THE SAME LEVEL.
THE USUAL SOUP, THANKS.
MANY CAN'T EARN ENOUGH FROM ADVENTURING ALONE, SO THEY TAKE SIDE JOBS.
A FEW END UP BEING BANDITS.
WHEN YOU'RE GOOD AT IT, YOU EARN HEAPS MORE THAN YOUR MAIN JOB.
AND NOW ALL THOSE GUYS ARE COMING AFTER ME.
SIGH
THEY COULD BE AFTER YOU FOR MORE THAN JUST MONEY. ENVY, TAKING OUT THE COM-PETITION...
IT HAPPENS TO ALL ADVENTURERS, ONCE THEY START GETTING A LITTLE ATTENTION.
HEY.
YOU'LL JUST HAVE TO KEEP PROVING YOUR STRENGTH UNTIL EVERYONE GETS SCARED OFF.
ONE WAY TO DO THAT IS TO SELL YOUR SPOILS AT THE MARKET.
PAT
GO AND SELL THESE OFF BEFORE THE DAY ENDS.
JUST A REMINDER, "DIRTY WARES" LIKE THESE GO TO THE PAWN SHOP IN THE SLUMS.

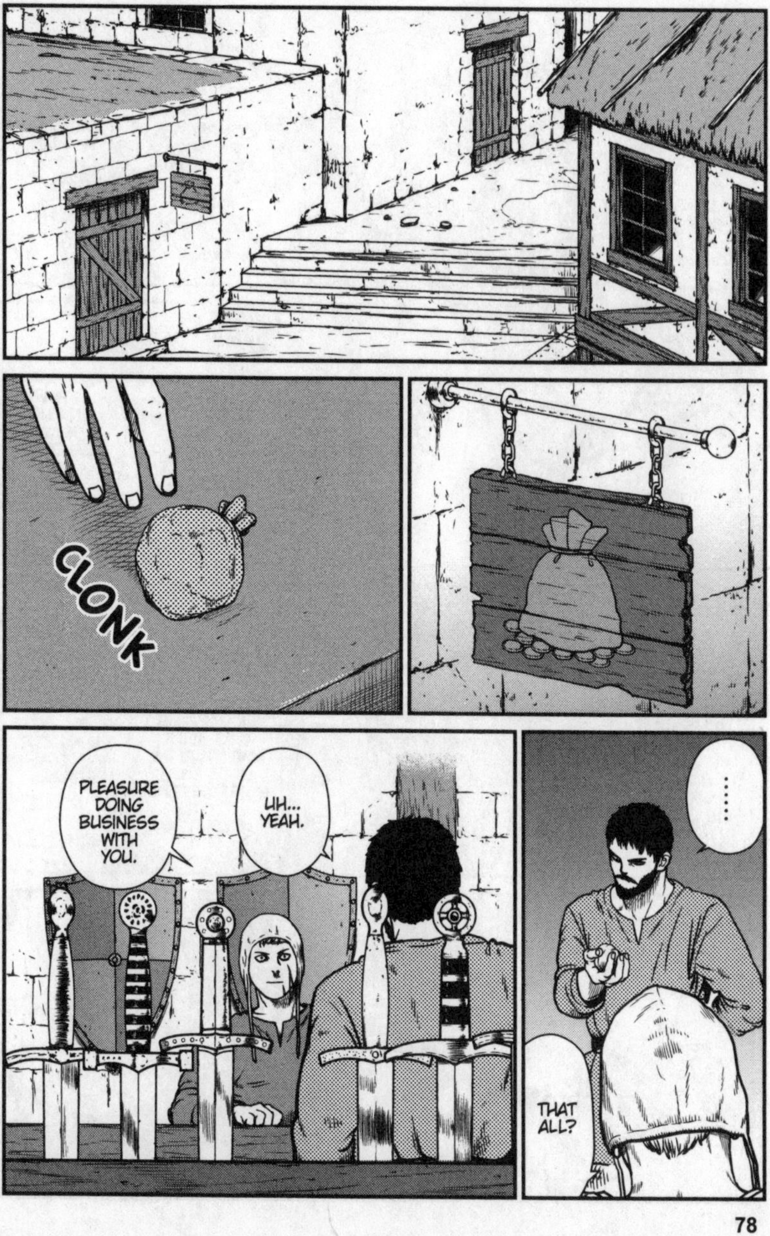
CLONK
……
THAT ALL?
UH... YEAH.
PLEASURE DOING BUSINESS WITH YOU.

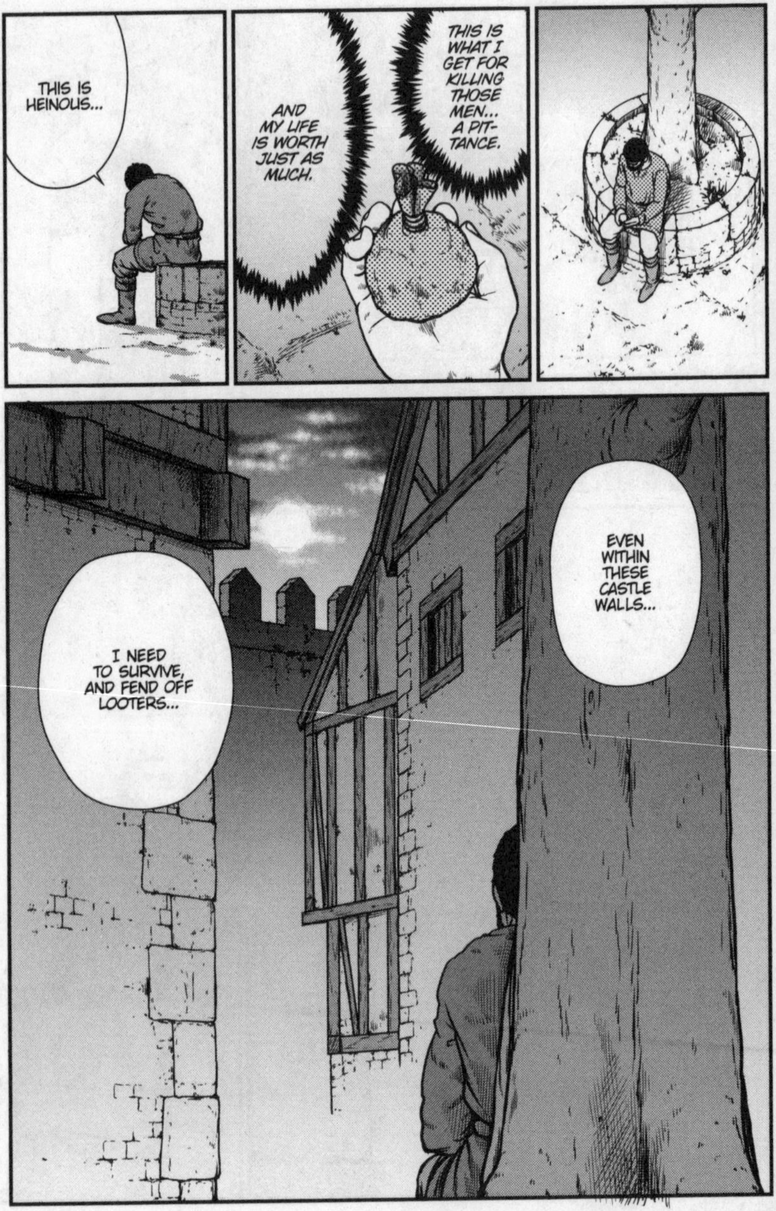
THIS IS WHAT I GET FOR KILLING THOSE MEN... A PIT-TANCE.
AND MY LIFE IS WORTH JUST AS MUCH.
THIS IS HEINOUS...
EVEN WITHIN THESE CASTLE WALLS...
I NEED TO SURVIVE, AND FEND OFF LOOTERS...

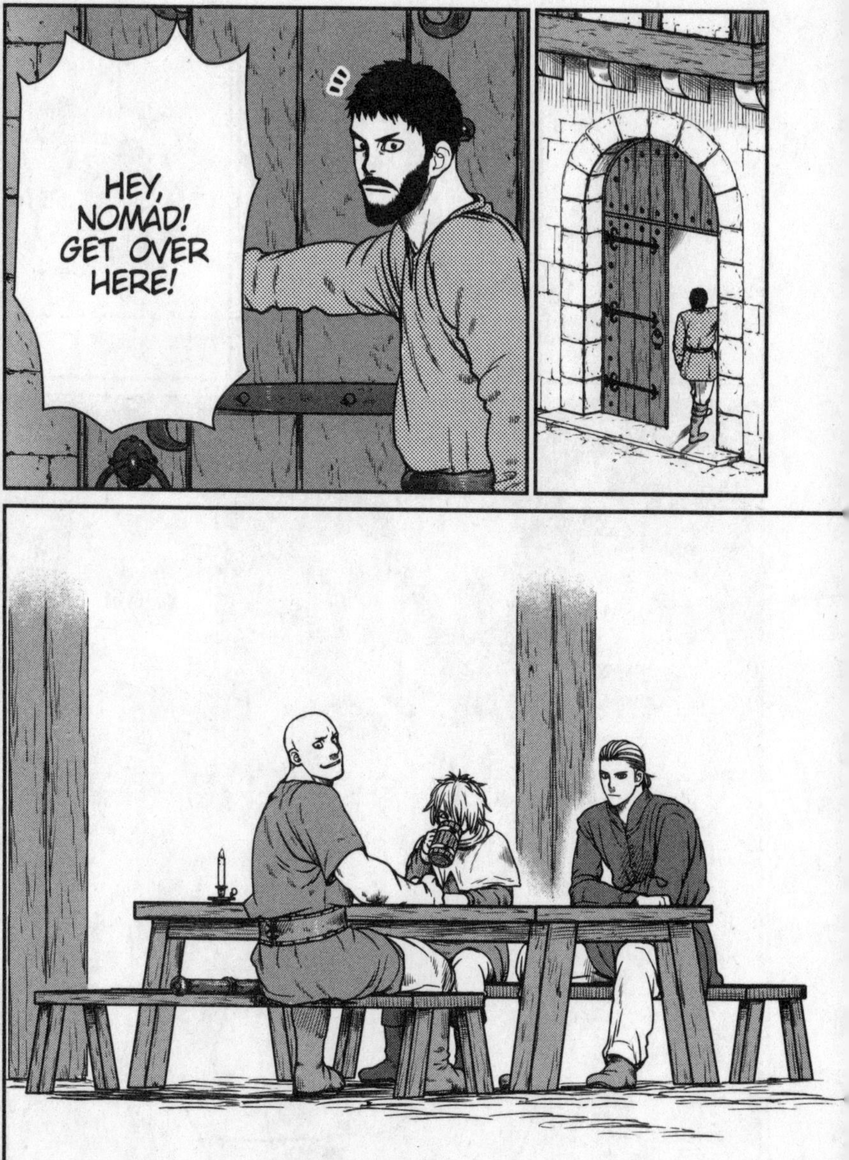
!!!
HEY, NOMAD! GET OVER HERE!

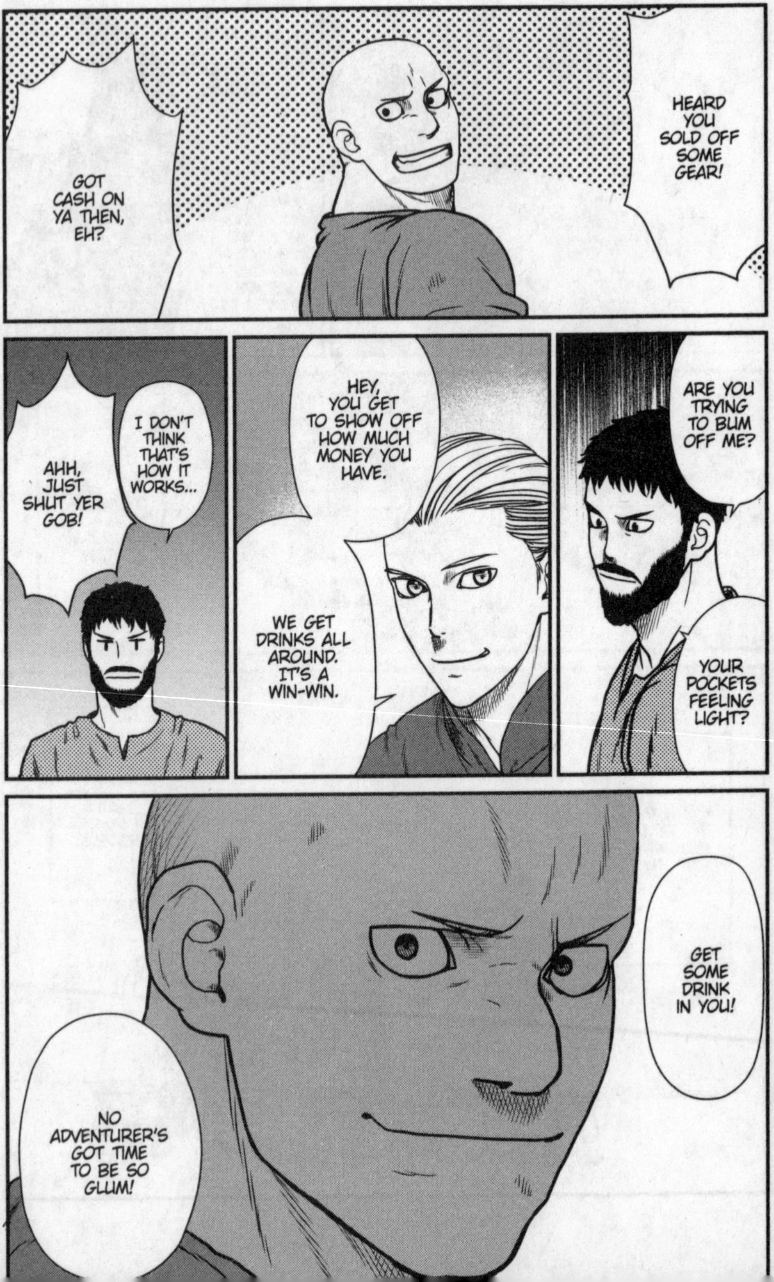
HEARD YOU SOLD OFF SOME GEAR!
GOT CASH ON YA THEN, EH?
ARE YOU TRYING TO BUM OFF ME?
YOUR POCKETS FEELING LIGHT?
HEY, YOU GET TO SHOW OFF HOW MUCH MONEY YOU HAVE.
WE GET DRINKS ALL AROUND. IT'S A WIN-WIN.
I DON'T THINK THAT'S HOW IT WORKS...
AHH, JUST SHUT YER GOB!
GET SOME DRINK IN YOU!
NO ADVENTURER'S GOT TIME TO BE SO GLUM!

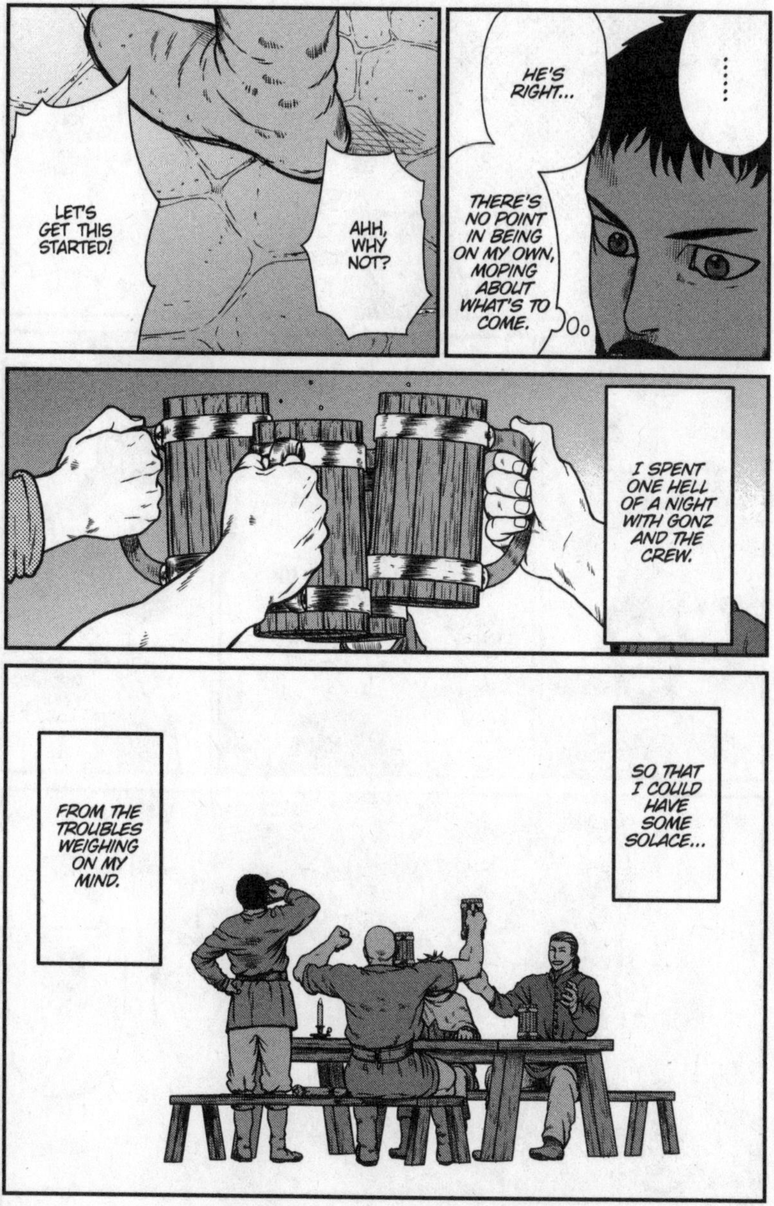
......
HE'S RIGHT...
THERE'S NO POINT IN BEING ON MY OWN, MOPING ABOUT WHAT'S TO COME.
AHH, WHY NOT?
LET'S GET THIS STARTED!
I SPENT ONE HELL OF A NIGHT WITH GONZ AND THE CREW.
SO THAT I COULD HAVE SOME SOLACE...
FROM THE TROUBLES WEIGHING ON MY MIND.

SPECIAL COLUMN BY AUTHOR YAZIN

KARATE SURVIVOR IN ANOTHER WORLD

INTERMISSION

SAVAGE RULES 15

THE EMPTY-HANDED FIGHTER VS THE ARMED COMBATANT

Weapons, especially ranged weapons, allow for speedier attacks than bare hands. The hands of a human are too slow to deal with a swiftly moving weapon. I've seen several works of fiction espouse this principle by making simple comparisons between the two. A punch travels at approximately thirty km/h while a swing from a baseball bat or katana can exceed one hundred km/h. That's more than three times the speed of the former. You wouldn't be blamed for thinking fighting unarmed makes you a lot slower.

However, the distance that the weapon must travel to impact its target is also extended by two to three times. If the faster weapon has to travel a further distance, then the practical difference between the two is reduced. Weapons also need time to accelerate. Compare a swing of a bat with a short jab—it is clear which reaches their respective maximum speed faster.

Furthermore, melee weapons are a prominent extension of the arm. Their mode of attack is obvious. Contrast this to a barehanded fighter, where the opponent must contend with multiple forms of attacks, from the head, shoulders, fists, elbows, knees, and feet, in addition to grabs and tackles that they must be wary of. The opponent's attention is spread thin, and their reaction and response will be delayed. It might be even more difficult to prevent a barehanded fighter from attacking than it is an armed one.

I once had a friend who did kendo. I challenged him to try to hit a *men strike* (a long downward strike to the head) on me. I underestimated his wide range and the speed of the flexing bamboo sword and received a right good wallop. But simultaneously, he also struggled to respond to the multitude of combinations from an unarmed combatant. And through practice, we both became able to dodge and fend off the other's attacks, even if a bit awkwardly. In the end, success came down to familiarity, not speed.

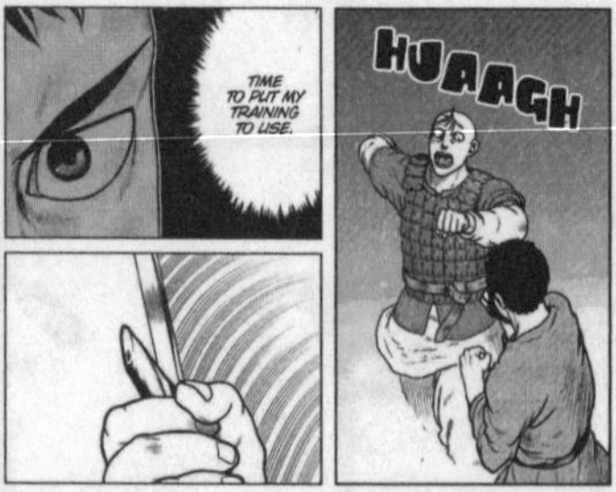
HUAAAGH
TIME TO PUT MY TRAINING TO USE.

But what about the difference in lethality of a weapon compared to bare hands? Indeed, weapons have a huge advantage in this respect. First of all, weapons allow you to position yourself further from your opponent. The advantage of a wide reach is immense, and it can be a challenge to fight against an opponent who can attack from a safe distance with a weapon.

Furthermore, weapons such as sharp blades are innately deadly. You can fight carefully around a bamboo sword to close the distance on your opponent, so long as you stay clear of their jabs and are prepared to take a few hits. However, a single hit from an actual blade can prove lethal.

There is also the mental pressure of fighting against bladed weapons, which can significantly affect performance. I can certainly attest to the brutal ruthlessness of blades against flesh. (Your writer once grasped a knife's edge by accident and had to have eleven stitches put in.)

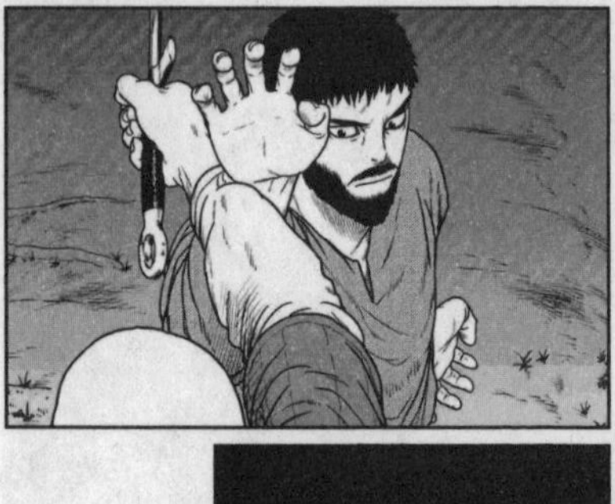

In conclusion, unless your body has been leveled up to monster standards like Nomad's, I cannot recommend you fight armed opponents barehanded. It is highly unlikely to end well for you.

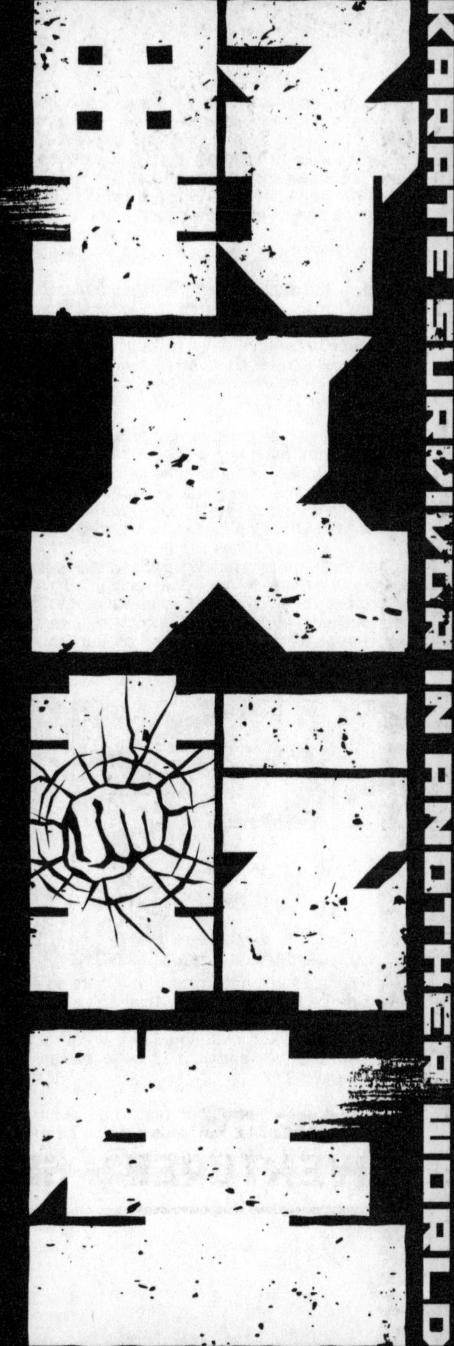
KARATE SURVIVOR IN ANOTHER WORLD

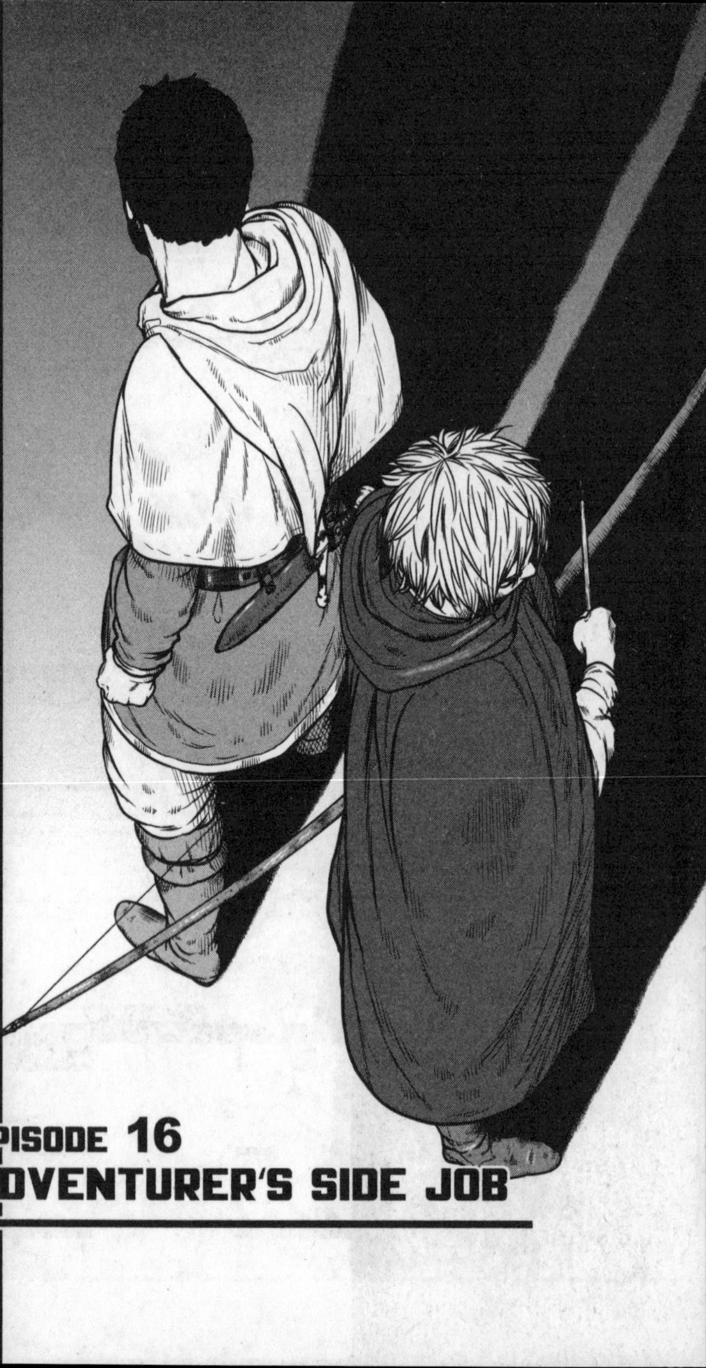

EPISODE 16
ADVENTURER'S SIDE JOB

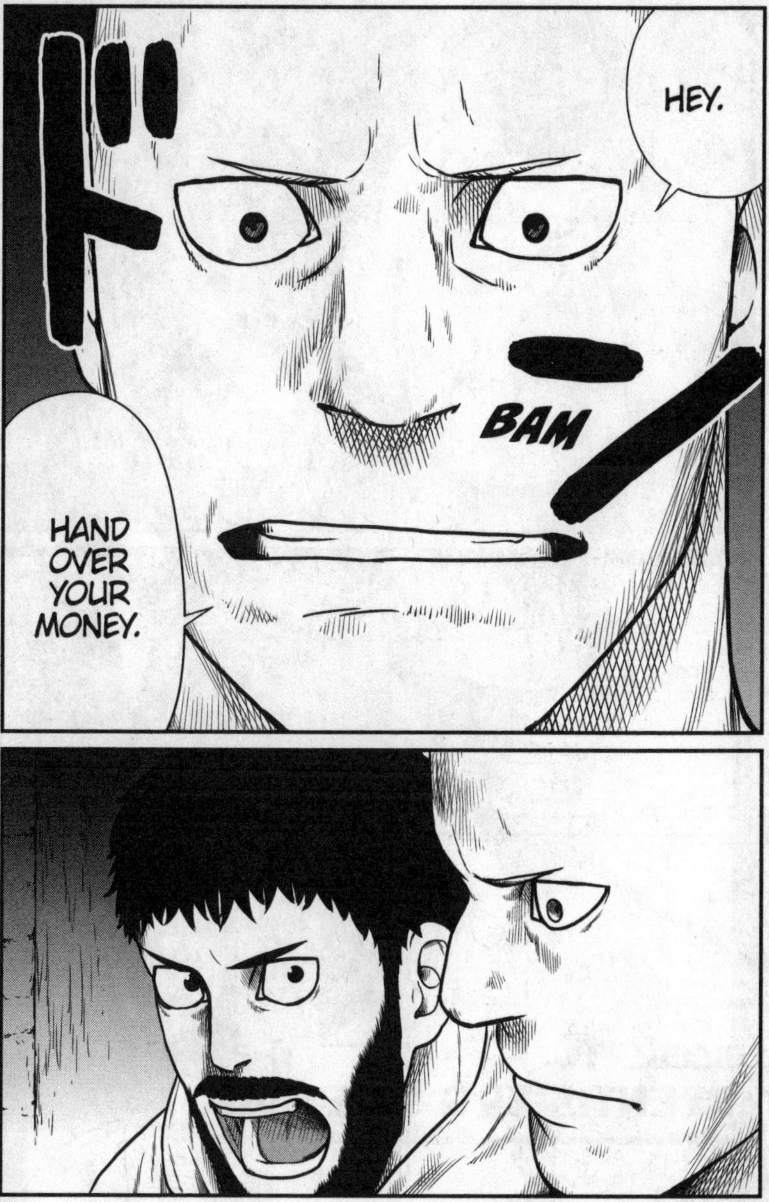
HEY.
BAM
HAND OVER YOUR MONEY.

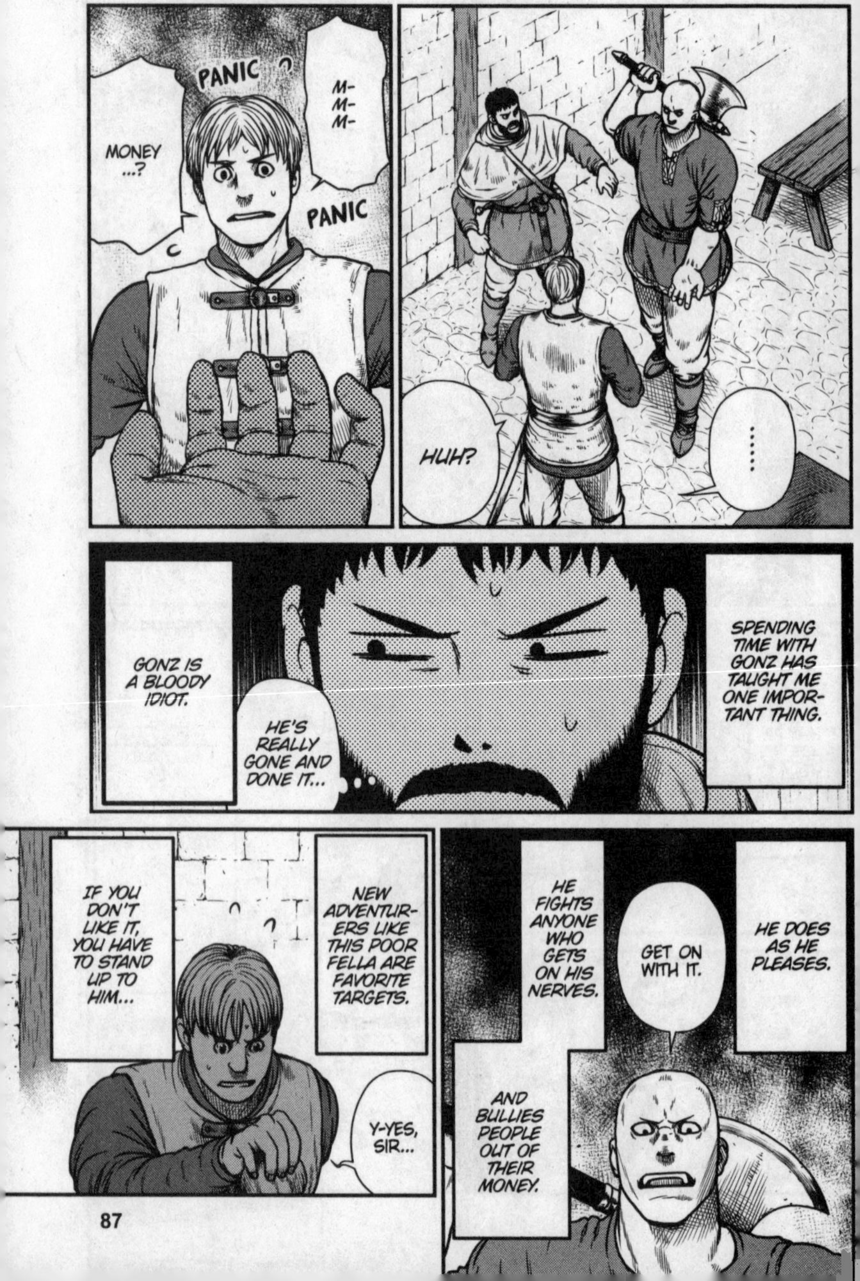
......
HUH?
M-
M-
M-
PANIC
MONEY ...?
PANIC
SPENDING TIME WITH GONZ HAS TAUGHT ME ONE IMPORTANT THING.
HE'S REALLY GONE AND DONE IT...
GONZ IS A BLOODY IDIOT.
HE DOES AS HE PLEASES.
GET ON WITH IT.
HE FIGHTS ANYONE WHO GETS ON HIS NERVES.
AND BULLIES PEOPLE OUT OF THEIR MONEY.
NEW ADVENTURERS LIKE THIS POOR FELLA ARE FAVORITE TARGETS.
IF YOU DON'T LIKE IT, YOU HAVE TO STAND UP TO HIM...
Y-YES, SIR...

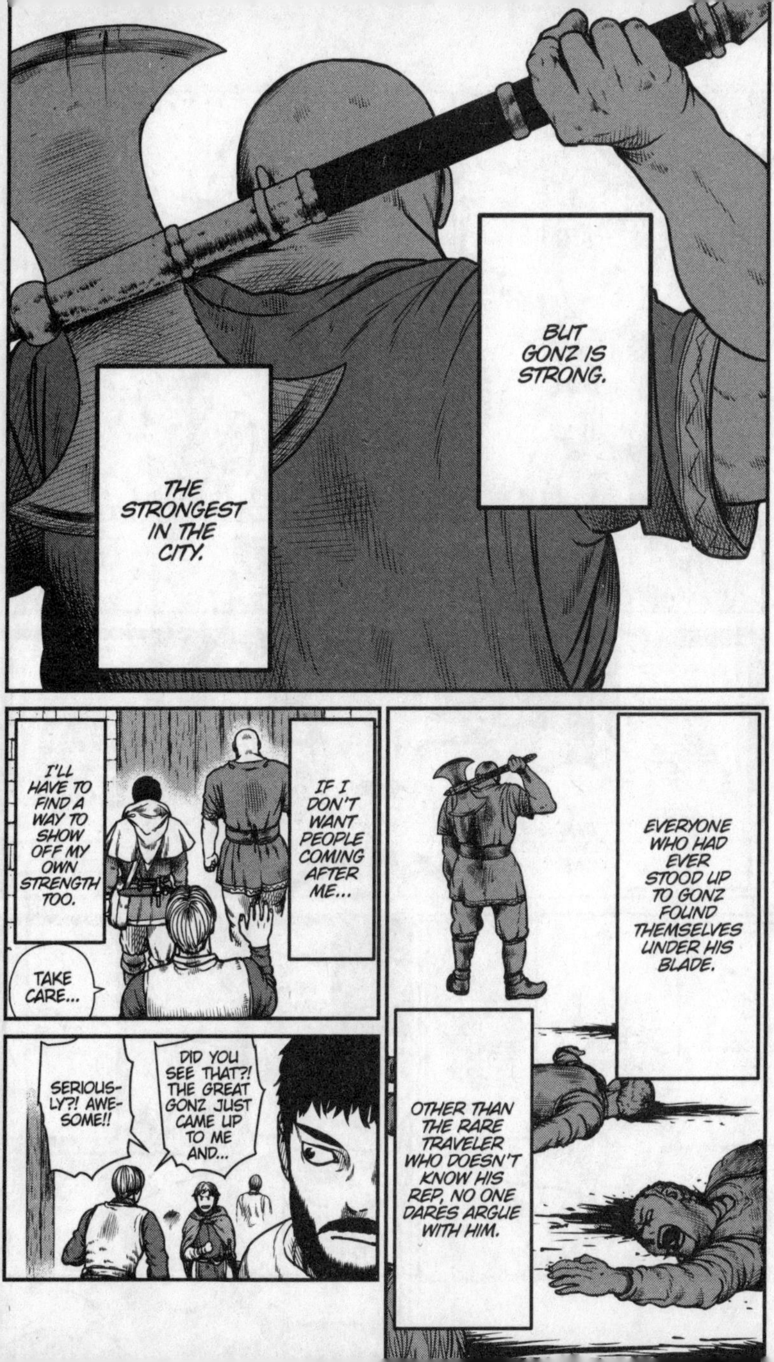
BUT GONZ IS STRONG.
THE STRONGEST IN THE CITY.
EVERYONE WHO HAD EVER STOOD UP TO GONZ FOUND THEMSELVES UNDER HIS BLADE.
OTHER THAN THE RARE TRAVELER WHO DOESN'T KNOW HIS REP, NO ONE DARES ARGUE WITH HIM.
IF I DON'T WANT PEOPLE COMING AFTER ME...
I'LL HAVE TO FIND A WAY TO SHOW OFF MY OWN STRENGTH TOO.
TAKE CARE...
DID YOU SEE THAT?! THE GREAT GONZ JUST CAME UP TO ME AND...
SERIOUS-LY?! AWE-SOME!!

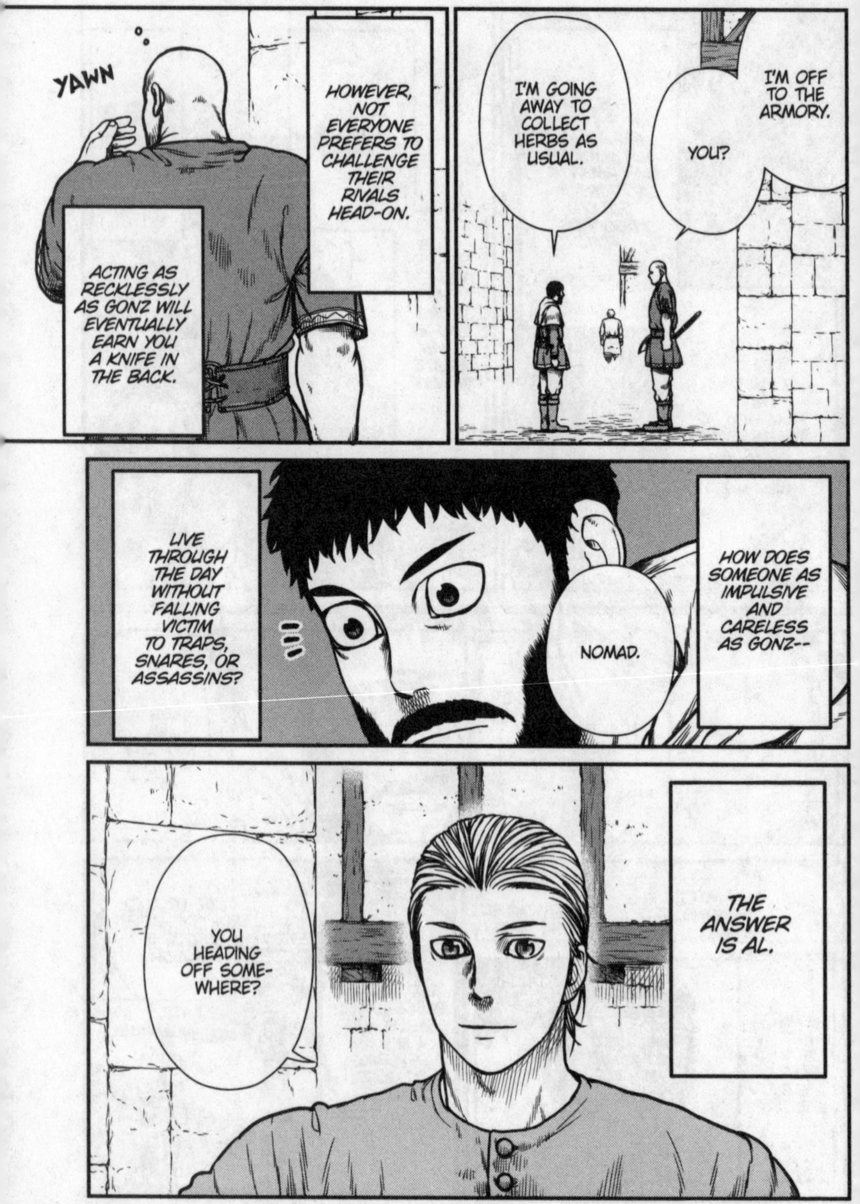
I'M OFF TO THE ARMORY.
YOU?
I'M GOING AWAY TO COLLECT HERBS AS USUAL.
HOWEVER, NOT EVERYONE PREFERS TO CHALLENGE THEIR RIVALS HEAD-ON.
YAWN
ACTING AS RECKLESSLY AS GONZ WILL EVENTUALLY EARN YOU A KNIFE IN THE BACK.
HOW DOES SOMEONE AS IMPULSIVE AND CARELESS AS GONZ--
NOMAD.
LIVE THROUGH THE DAY WITHOUT FALLING VICTIM TO TRAPS, SNARES, OR ASSASSINS?
THE ANSWER IS AL.
YOU HEADING OFF SOME-WHERE?

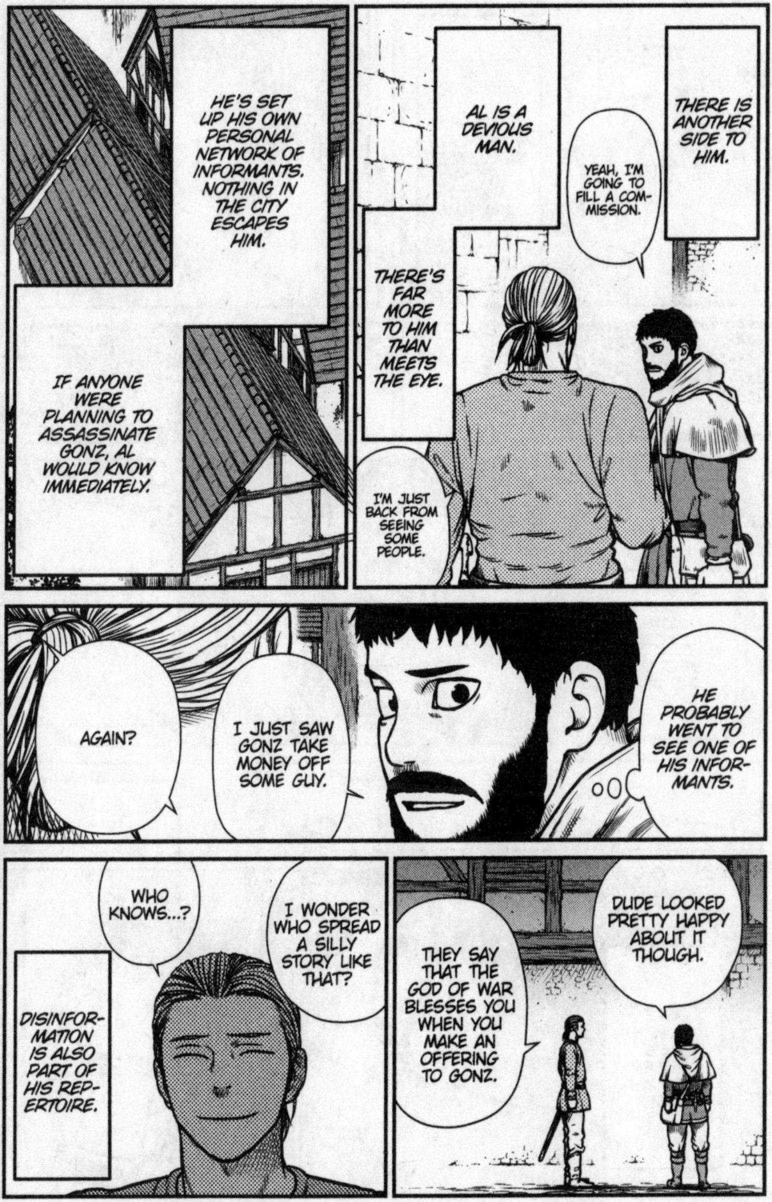
THERE IS ANOTHER SIDE TO HIM.
YEAH, I'M GOING TO FILL A COMMISSION.
AL IS A DEVIOUS MAN.
THERE'S FAR MORE TO HIM THAN MEETS THE EYE.
I'M JUST BACK FROM SEEING SOME PEOPLE.
HE'S SET UP HIS OWN PERSONAL NETWORK OF INFORMANTS. NOTHING IN THE CITY ESCAPES HIM.
IF ANYONE WERE PLANNING TO ASSASSINATE GONZ, AL WOULD KNOW IMMEDIATELY.
HE PROBABLY WENT TO SEE ONE OF HIS INFORMANTS.
I JUST SAW GONZ TAKE MONEY OFF SOME GUY.
AGAIN?
DUDE LOOKED PRETTY HAPPY ABOUT IT THOUGH.
THEY SAY THAT THE GOD OF WAR BLESSES YOU WHEN YOU MAKE AN OFFERING TO GONZ.
I WONDER WHO SPREAD A SILLY STORY LIKE THAT?
WHO KNOWS...?
DISINFORMATION IS ALSO PART OF HIS REPERTOIRE.

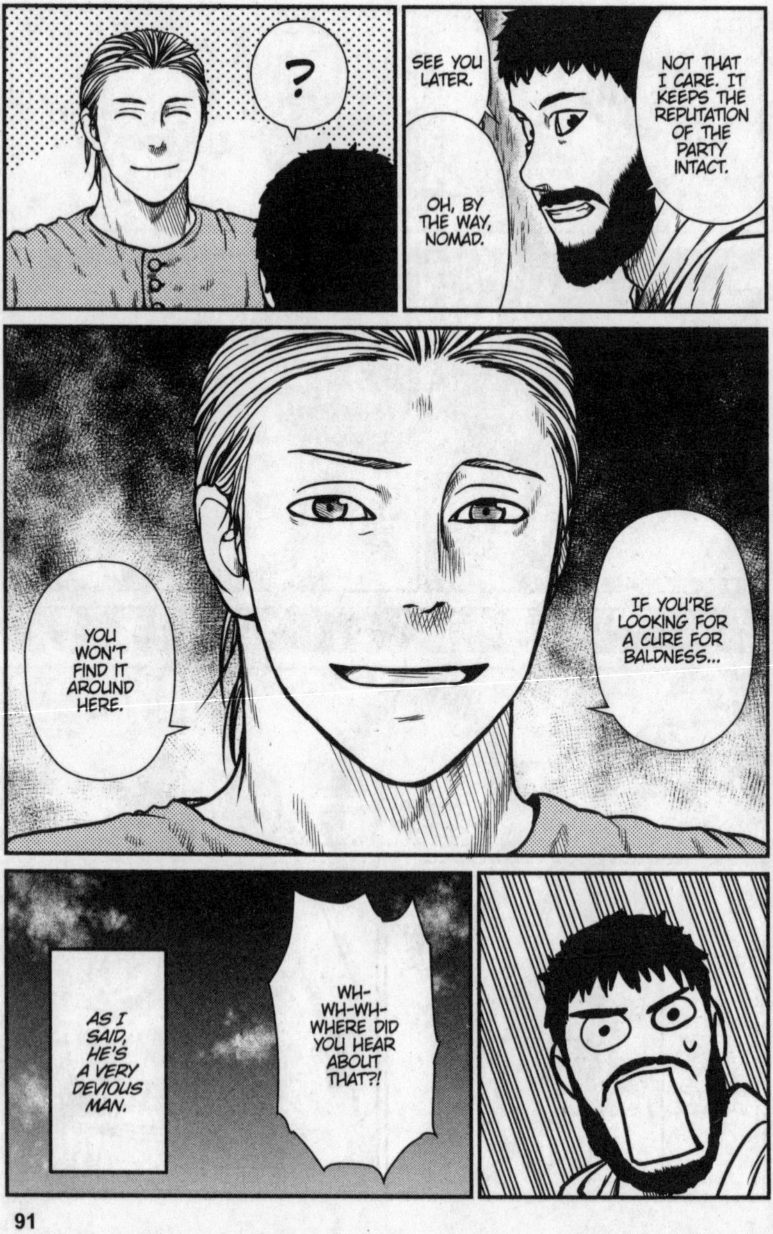
NOT THAT I CARE. IT KEEPS THE REPUTATION OF THE PARTY INTACT.
SEE YOU LATER.
OH, BY THE WAY, NOMAD.
?
IF YOU'RE LOOKING FOR A CURE FOR BALDNESS...
YOU WON'T FIND IT AROUND HERE.
WH-WH-WH-WHERE DID YOU HEAR ABOUT THAT?!
AS I SAID, HE'S A VERY DEVIOUS MAN.

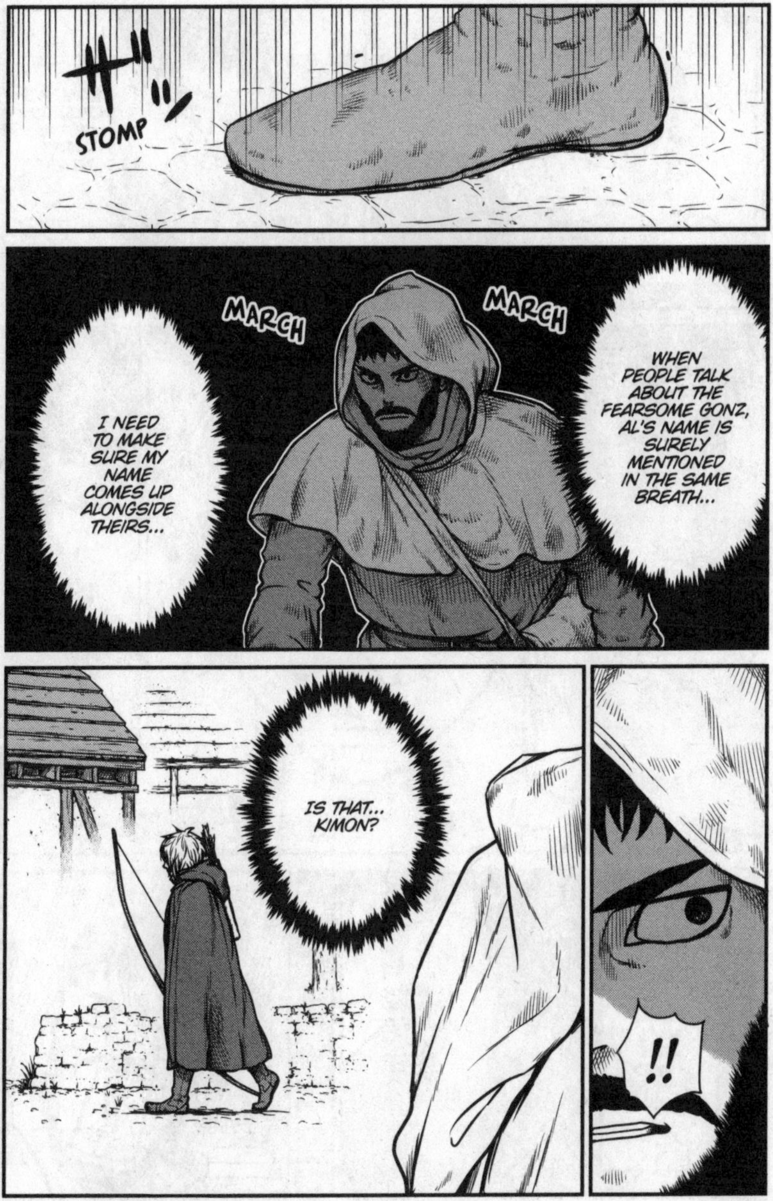
STOMP
MARCH
MARCH
WHEN PEOPLE TALK ABOUT THE FEARSOME GONZ, AL'S NAME IS SURELY MENTIONED IN THE SAME BREATH...
I NEED TO MAKE SURE MY NAME COMES UP ALONGSIDE THEIRS...
!!
IS THAT... KIMON?

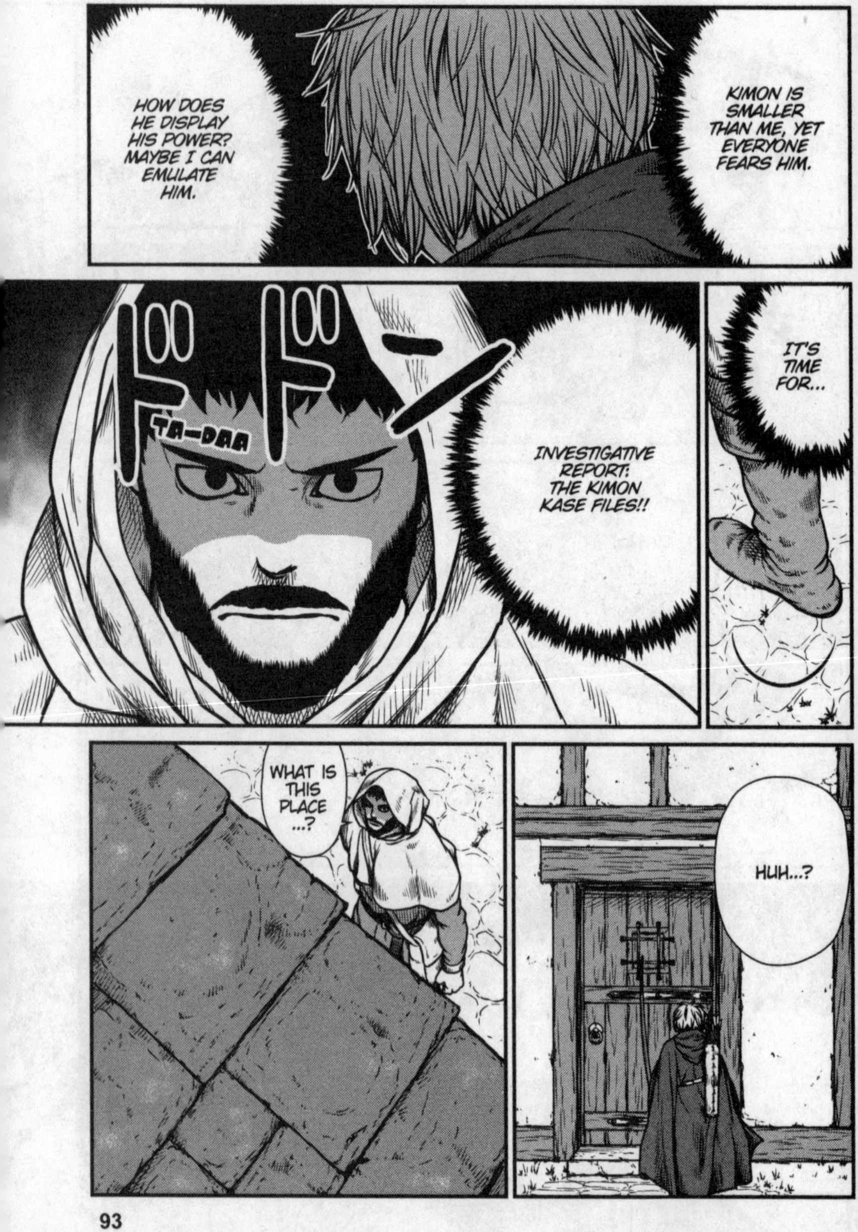
KIMON IS SMALLER THAN ME, YET EVERYONE FEARS HIM.
HOW DOES HE DISPLAY HIS POWER? MAYBE I CAN EMULATE HIM.
IT'S TIME FOR...
INVESTIGATIVE REPORT: THE KIMON KASE FILES!!
ドドー
TA-DAA
HUH...?
WHAT IS THIS PLACE ...?

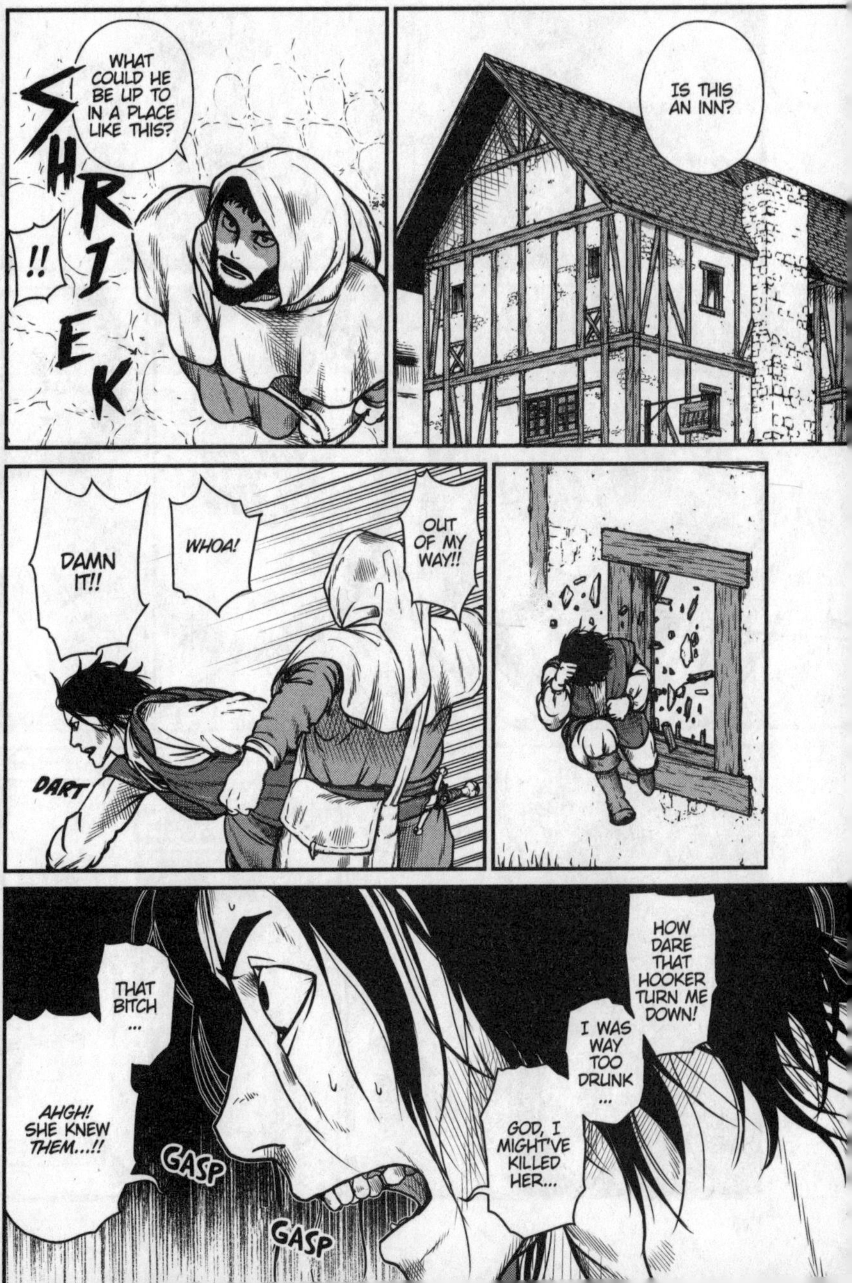
IS THIS AN INN?
WHAT COULD HE BE UP TO IN A PLACE LIKE THIS?
SHRIEK
!!
OUT OF MY WAY!!
WHOA!
DAMN IT!!
DART
HOW DARE THAT HOOKER TURN ME DOWN!
I WAS WAY TOO DRUNK ...
THAT BITCH ...
GOD, I MIGHT'VE KILLED HER...
AHGH! SHE KNEW THEM...!!
GASP
GASP

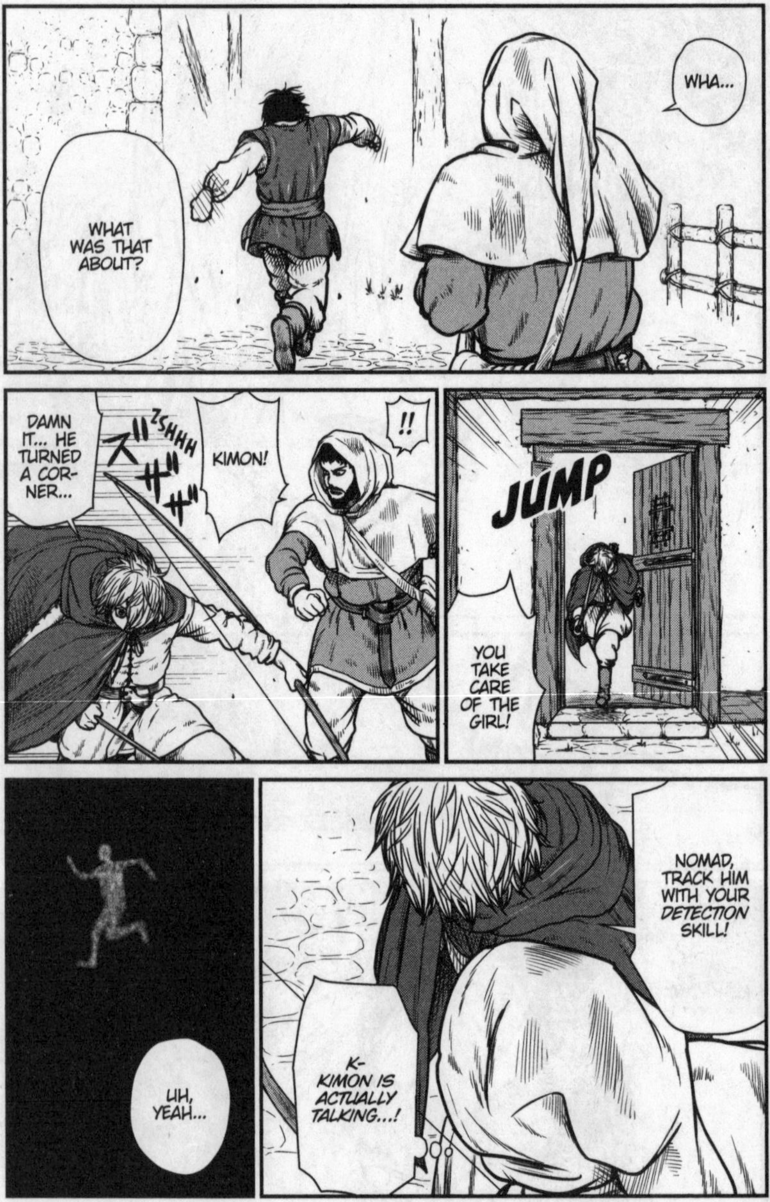
WHA...
WHAT WAS THAT ABOUT?
JUMP
YOU TAKE CARE OF THE GIRL!
!!
KIMON!
ZSHHH
DAMN IT... HE TURNED A COR-NER...
NOMAD, TRACK HIM WITH YOUR *DETECTION* SKILL!
K-KIMON IS ACTUALLY TALKING...!
UH, YEAH...

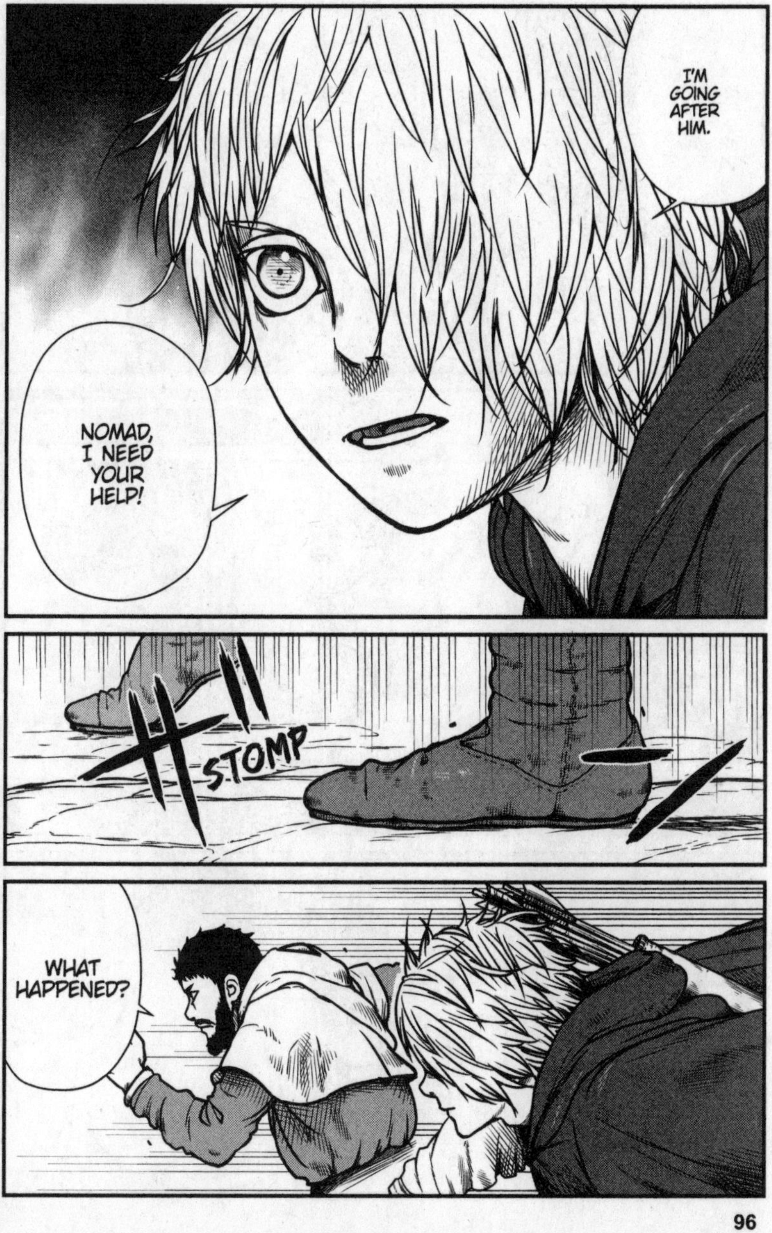
I'M GOING AFTER HIM.
NOMAD, I NEED YOUR HELP!
STOMP
WHAT HAPPENED?

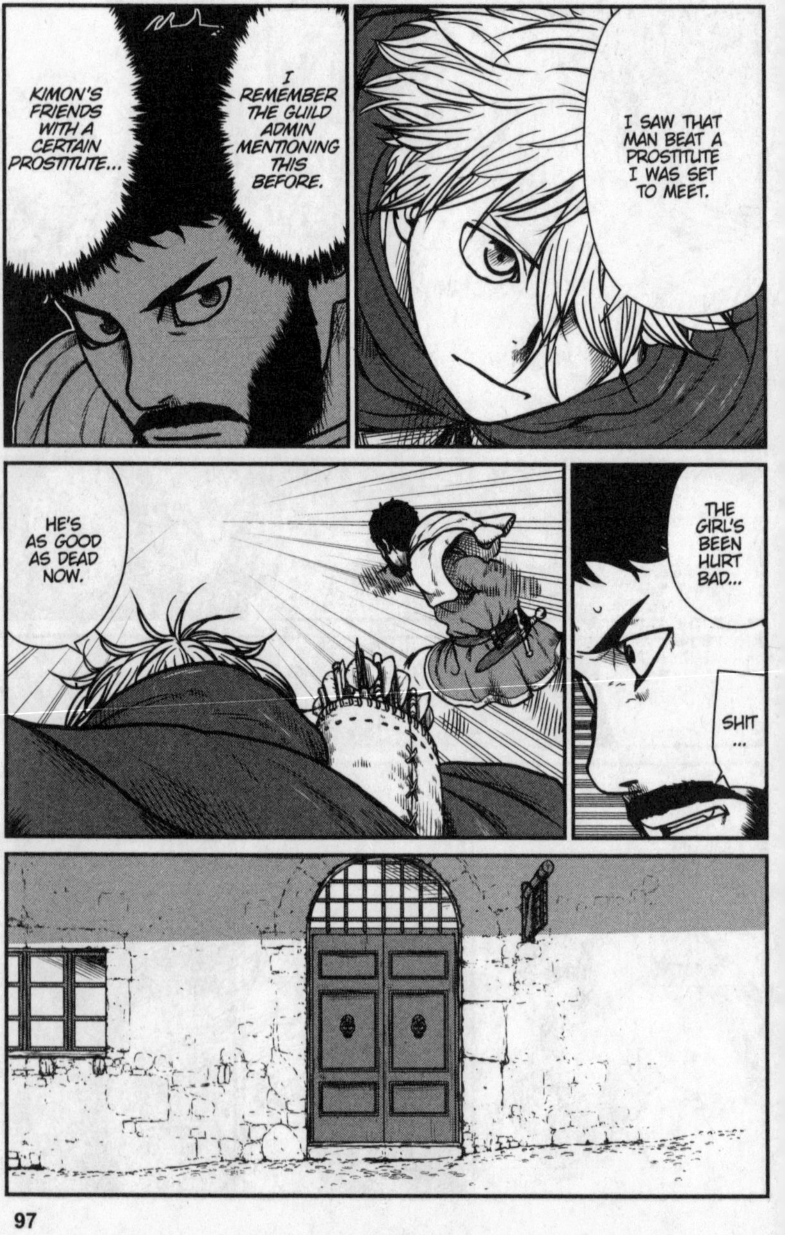
I SAW THAT MAN BEAT A PROSTITUTE I WAS SET TO MEET.
I REMEMBER THE GUILD ADMIN MENTIONING THIS BEFORE.
KIMON'S FRIENDS WITH A CERTAIN PROSTITUTE...
THE GIRL'S BEEN HURT BAD...
SHIT ...
HE'S AS GOOD AS DEAD NOW.

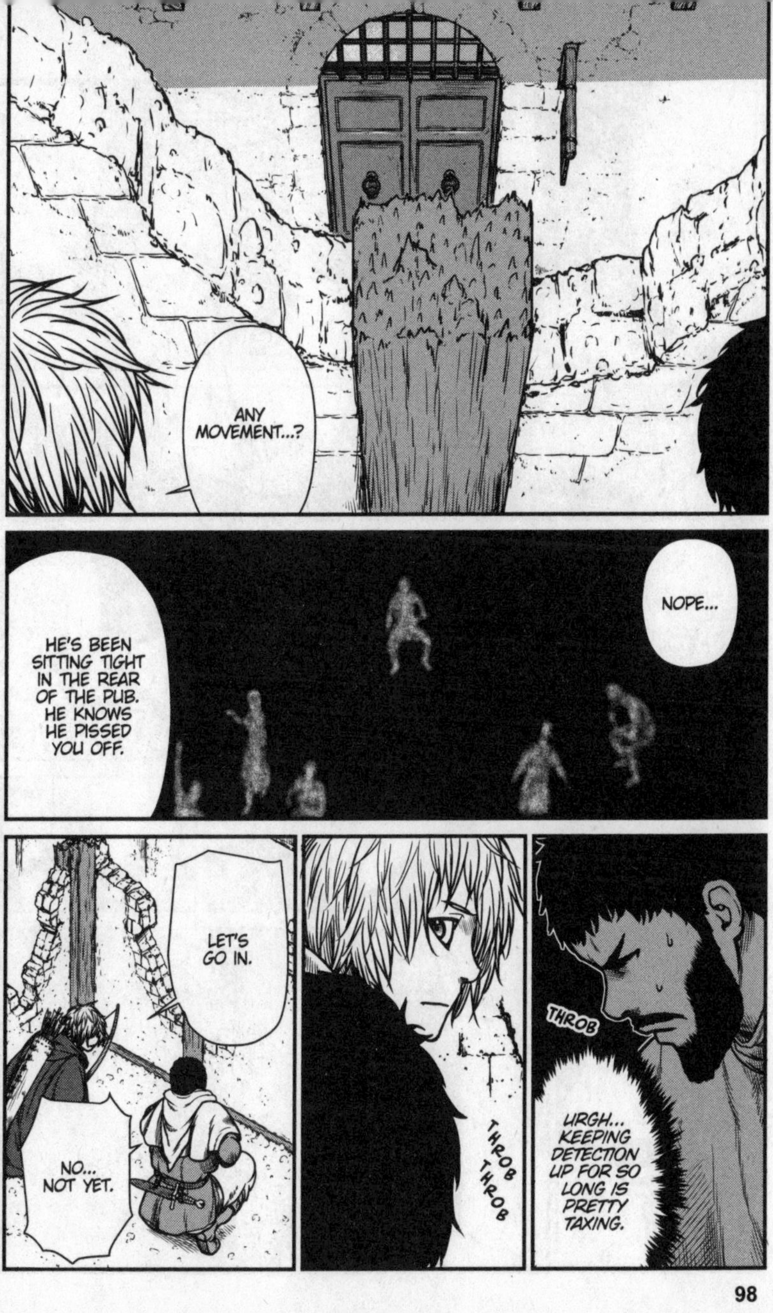
ANY MOVEMENT...?
NOPE...
HE'S BEEN SITTING TIGHT IN THE REAR OF THE PUB. HE KNOWS HE PISSED YOU OFF.
THROB
URGH... KEEPING DETECTION UP FOR SO LONG IS PRETTY TAXING.
THROB THROB
LET'S GO IN.
NO... NOT YET.

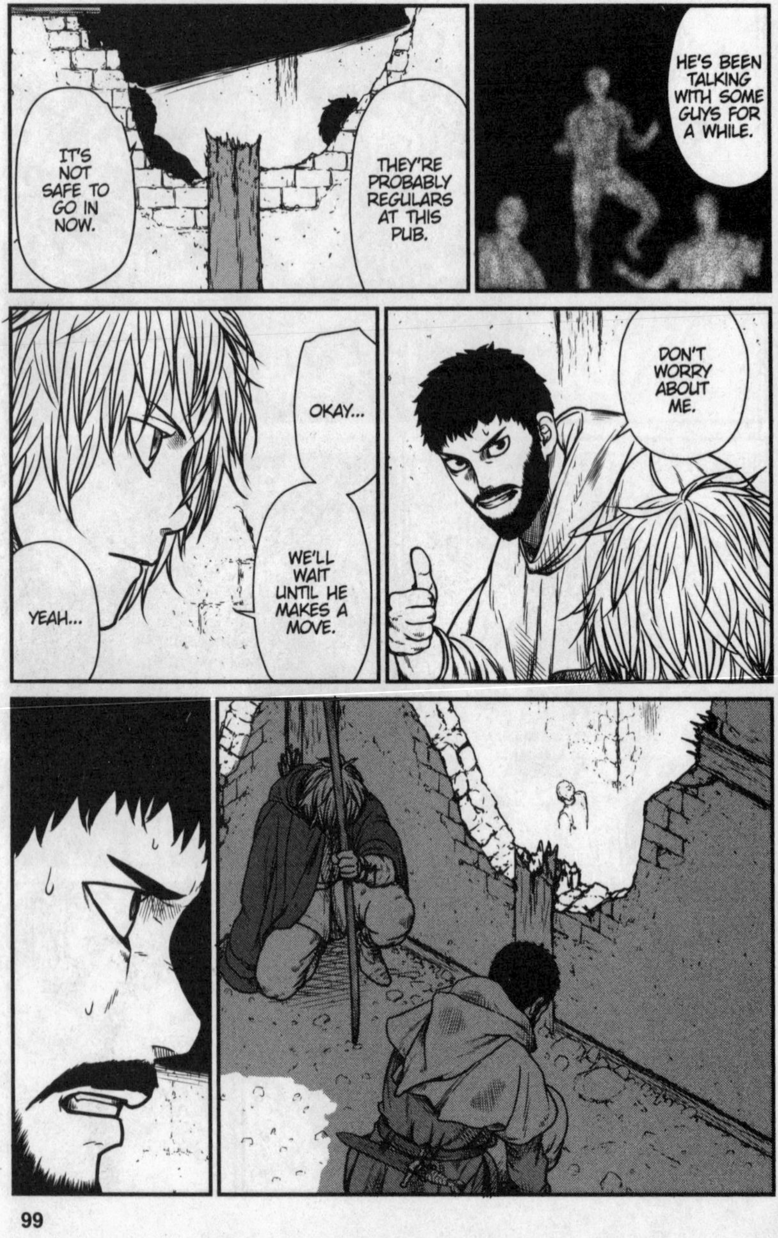
HE'S BEEN TALKING WITH SOME GUYS FOR A WHILE.
THEY'RE PROBABLY REGULARS AT THIS PUB.
IT'S NOT SAFE TO GO IN NOW.
DON'T WORRY ABOUT ME.
OKAY...
WE'LL WAIT UNTIL HE MAKES A MOVE.
YEAH...

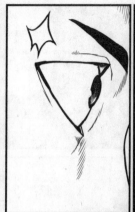

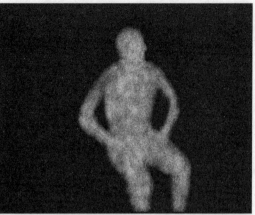

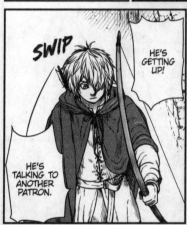

HE'S GETTING UP!
SWIP
HE'S TALKING TO ANOTHER PATRON.
!!
HE'S HEADING TO THE COUNTER!
WATCH THE TOP OF THE DOOR! COMING IN FROM LEFT TO RIGHT!!

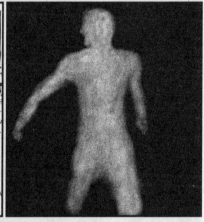

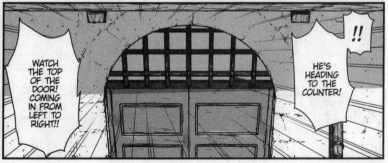

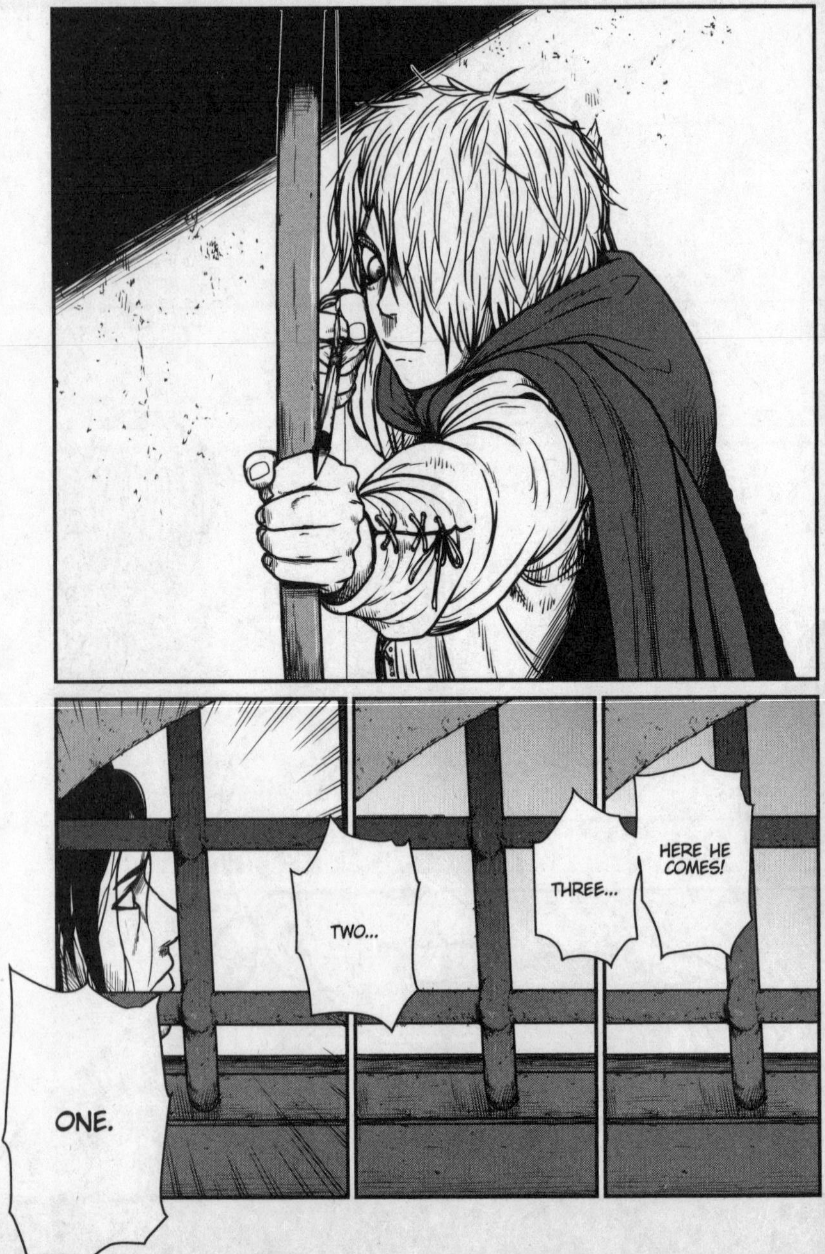
HERE HE COMES!
THREE...
TWO...
ONE.

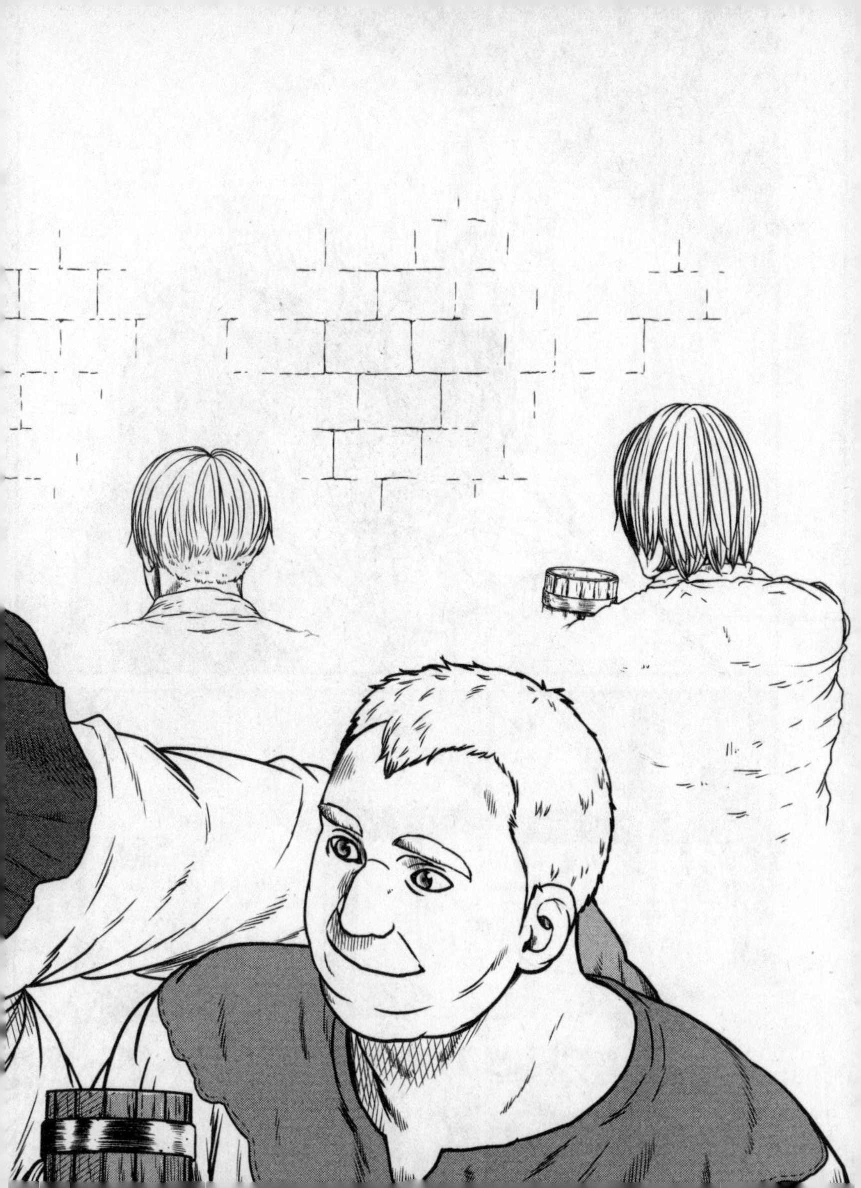

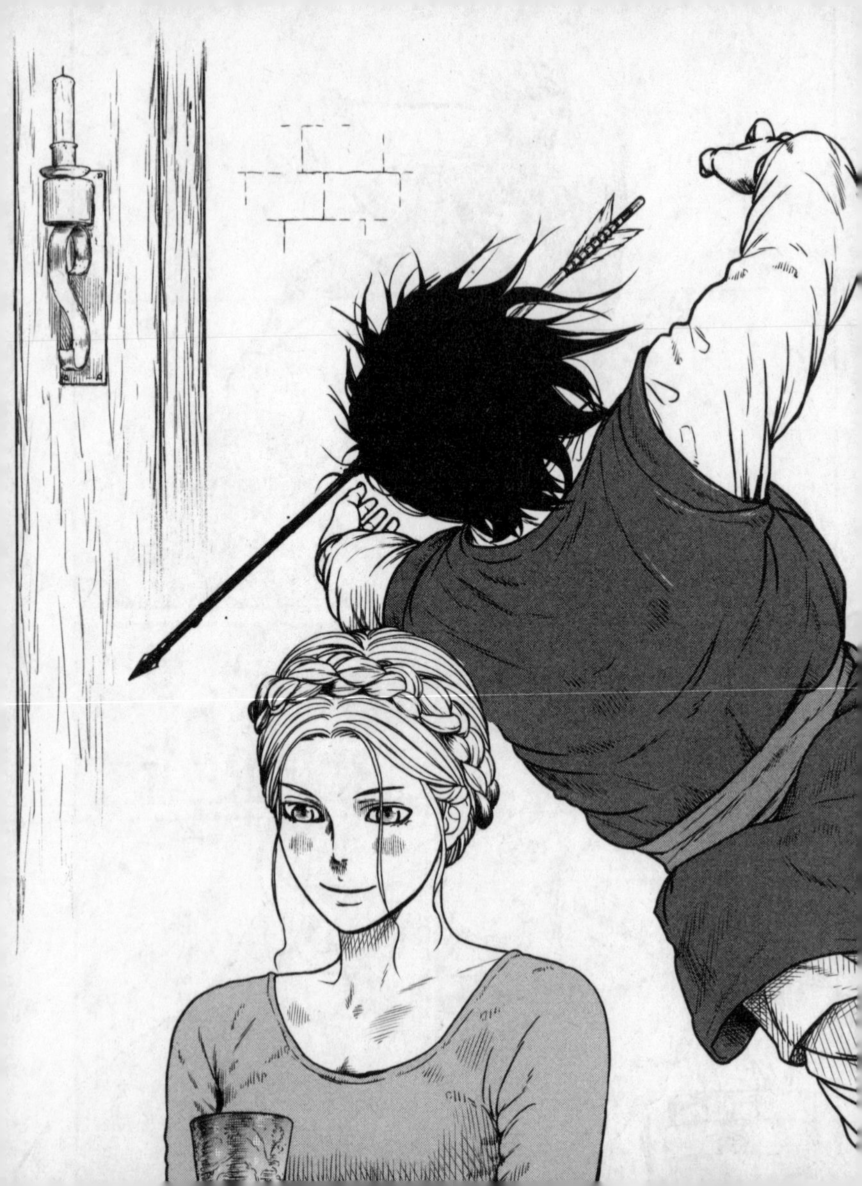

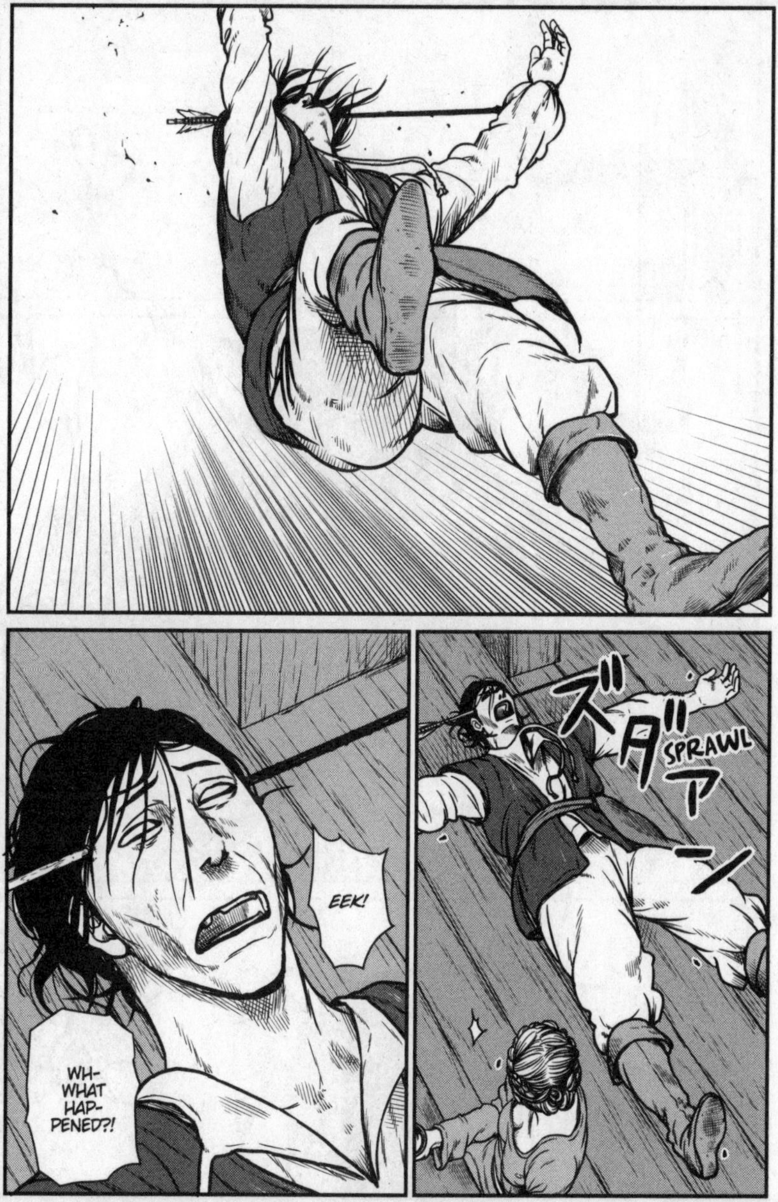
ズダァーン
SPRAWL
EEK!
WH-
WHAT
HAP-
PENED?!

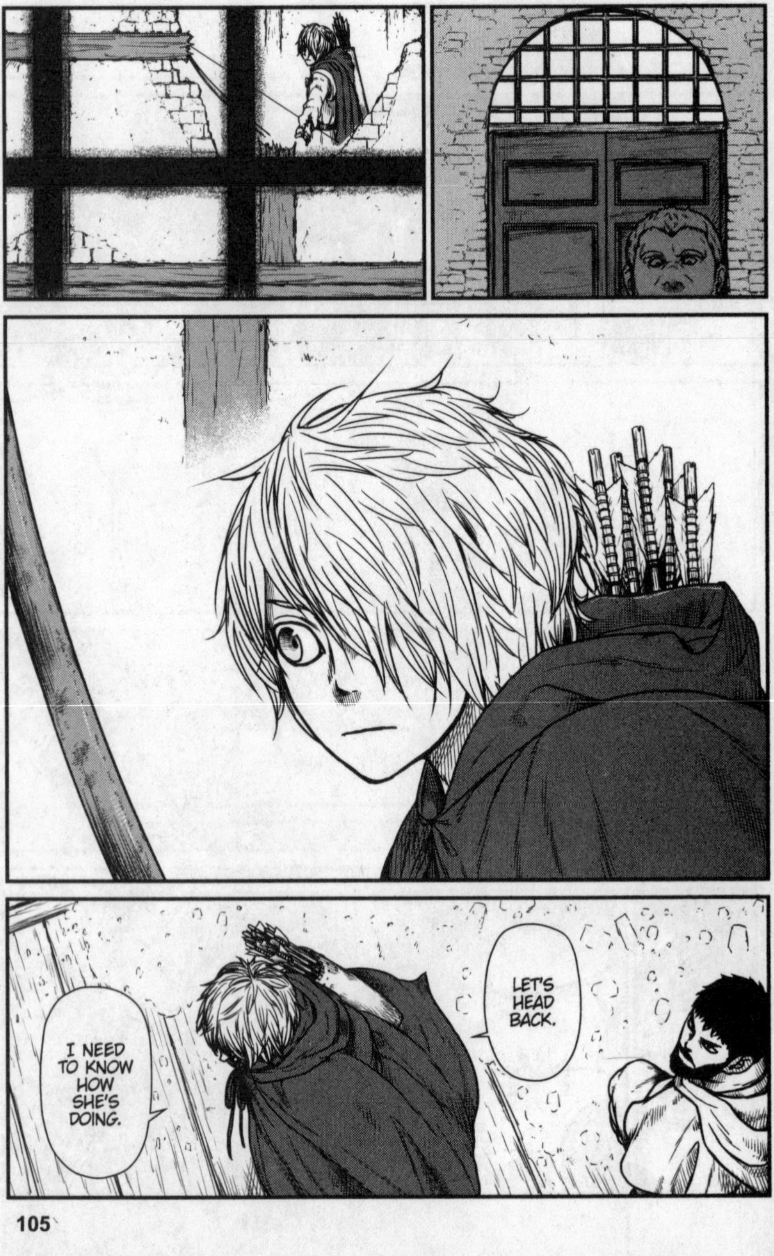
LET'S HEAD BACK.
I NEED TO KNOW HOW SHE'S DOING.

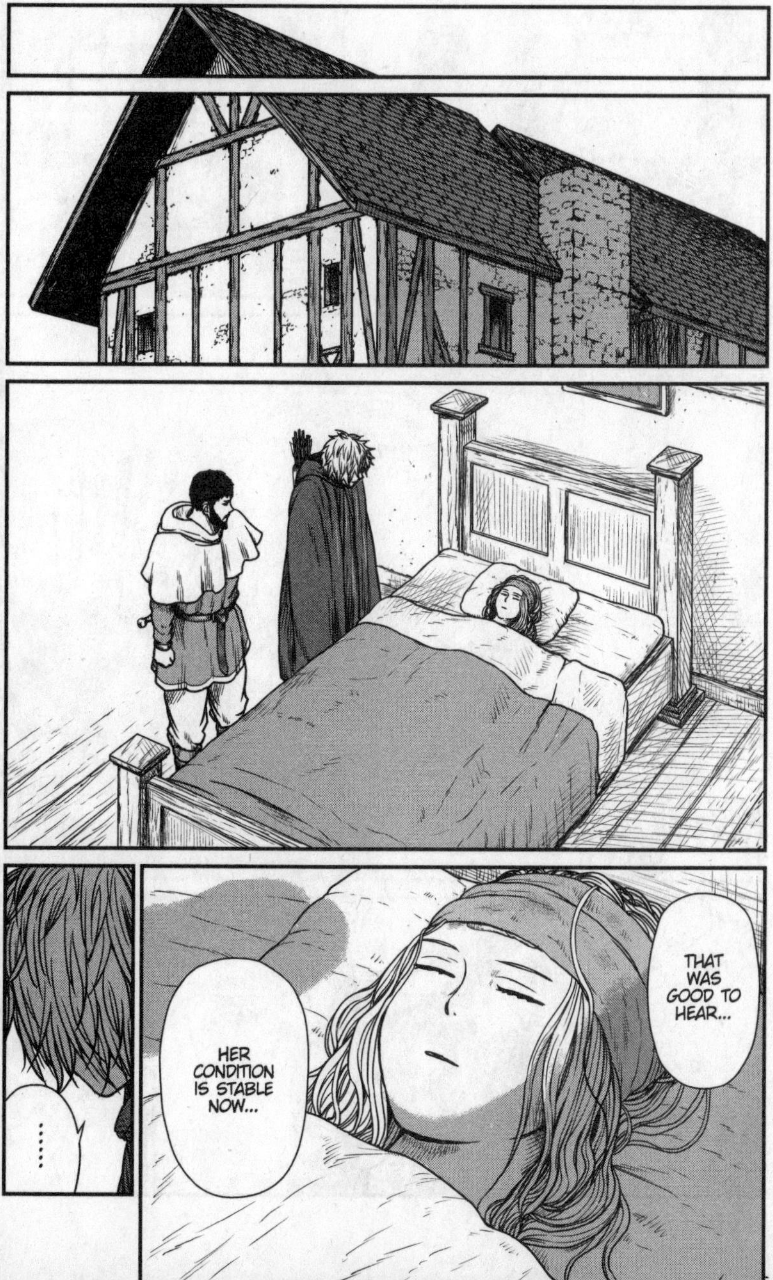
THAT WAS GOOD TO HEAR...
HER CONDITION IS STABLE NOW...
......

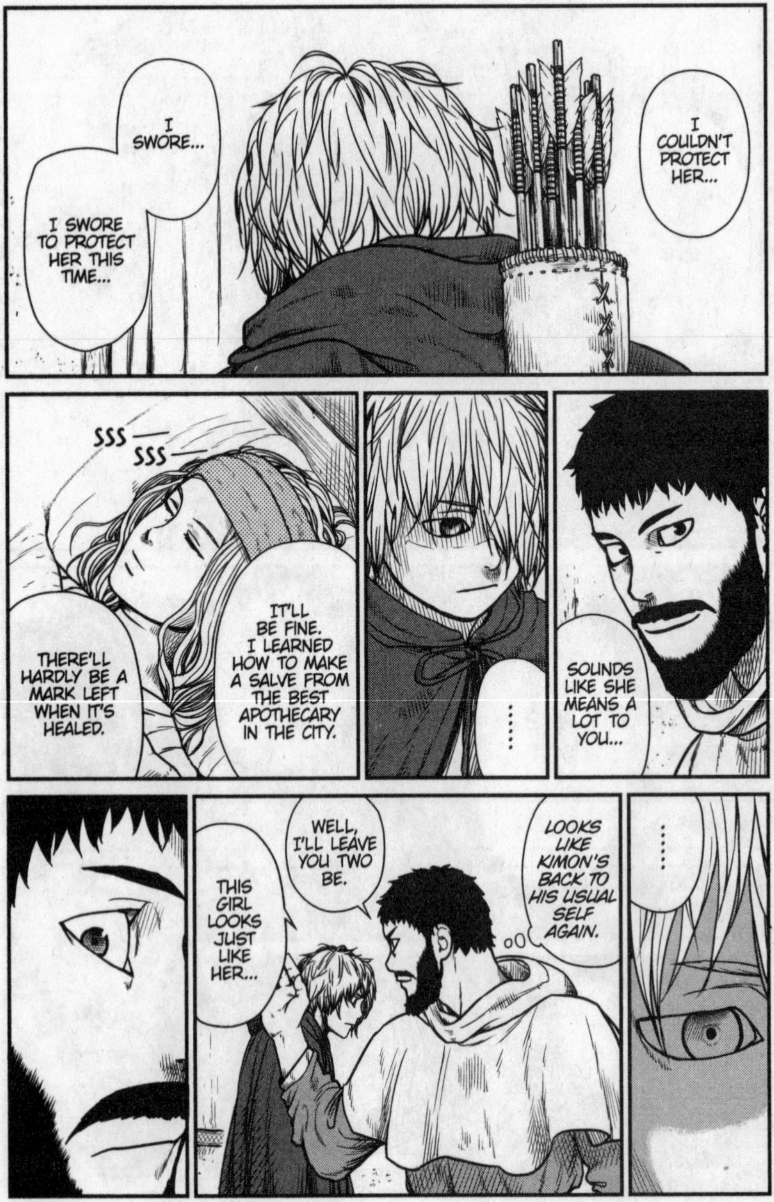
I SWORE...
I SWORE TO PROTECT HER THIS TIME...
I COULDN'T PROTECT HER...
SOUNDS LIKE SHE MEANS A LOT TO YOU...
......
SSS— SSS—
IT'LL BE FINE. I LEARNED HOW TO MAKE A SALVE FROM THE BEST APOTHECARY IN THE CITY.
THERE'LL HARDLY BE A MARK LEFT WHEN IT'S HEALED.
......
LOOKS LIKE KIMON'S BACK TO HIS USUAL SELF AGAIN.
WELL, I'LL LEAVE YOU TWO BE.
THIS GIRL LOOKS JUST LIKE HER...

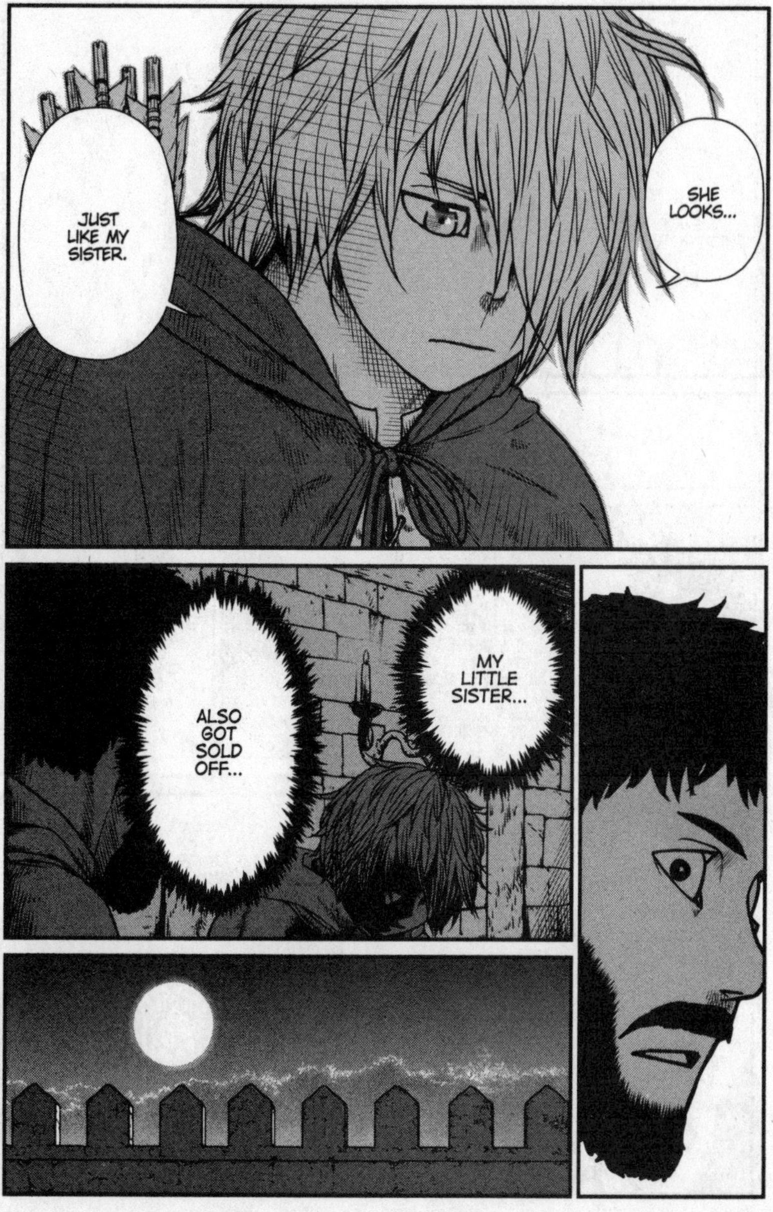
SHE LOOKS...
JUST LIKE MY SISTER.
MY LITTLE SISTER...
ALSO GOT SOLD OFF...

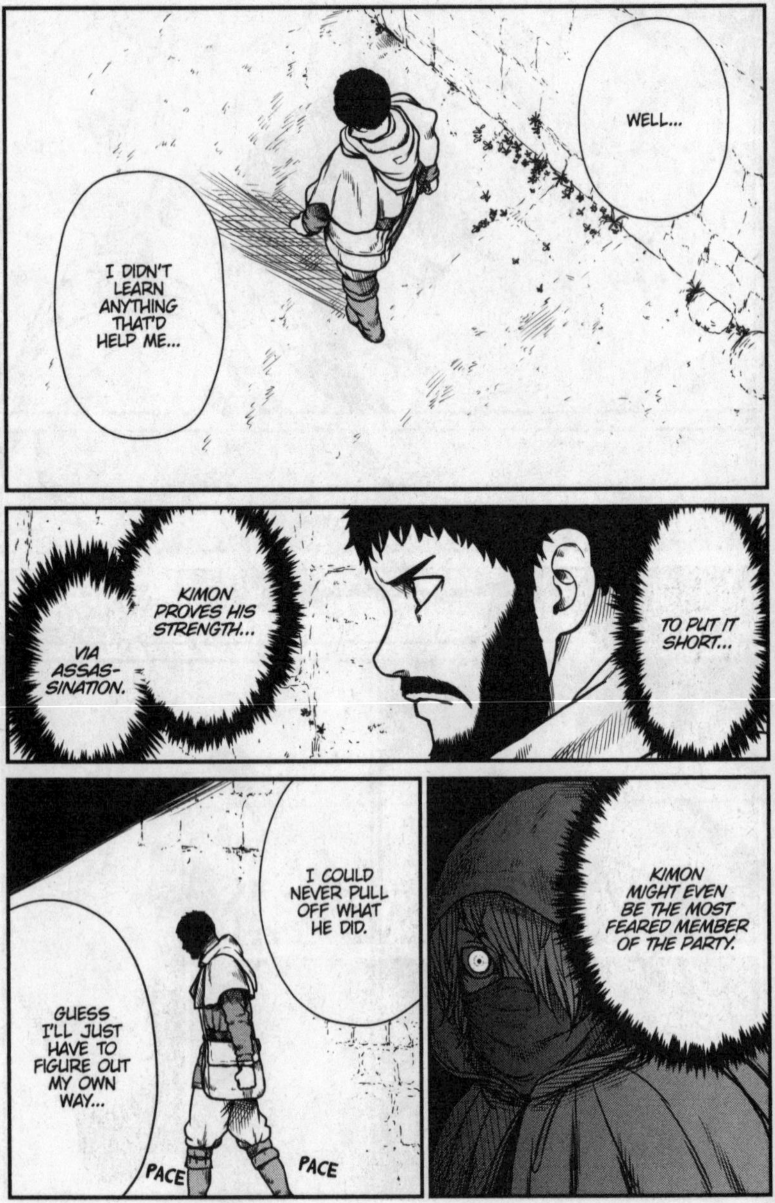
WELL...
I DIDN'T LEARN ANYTHING THAT'D HELP ME...
TO PUT IT SHORT...
KIMON PROVES HIS STRENGTH...
VIA ASSAS-SINATION.
KIMON MIGHT EVEN BE THE MOST FEARED MEMBER OF THE PARTY.
I COULD NEVER PULL OFF WHAT HE DID.
GUESS I'LL JUST HAVE TO FIGURE OUT MY OWN WAY...
PACE
PACE

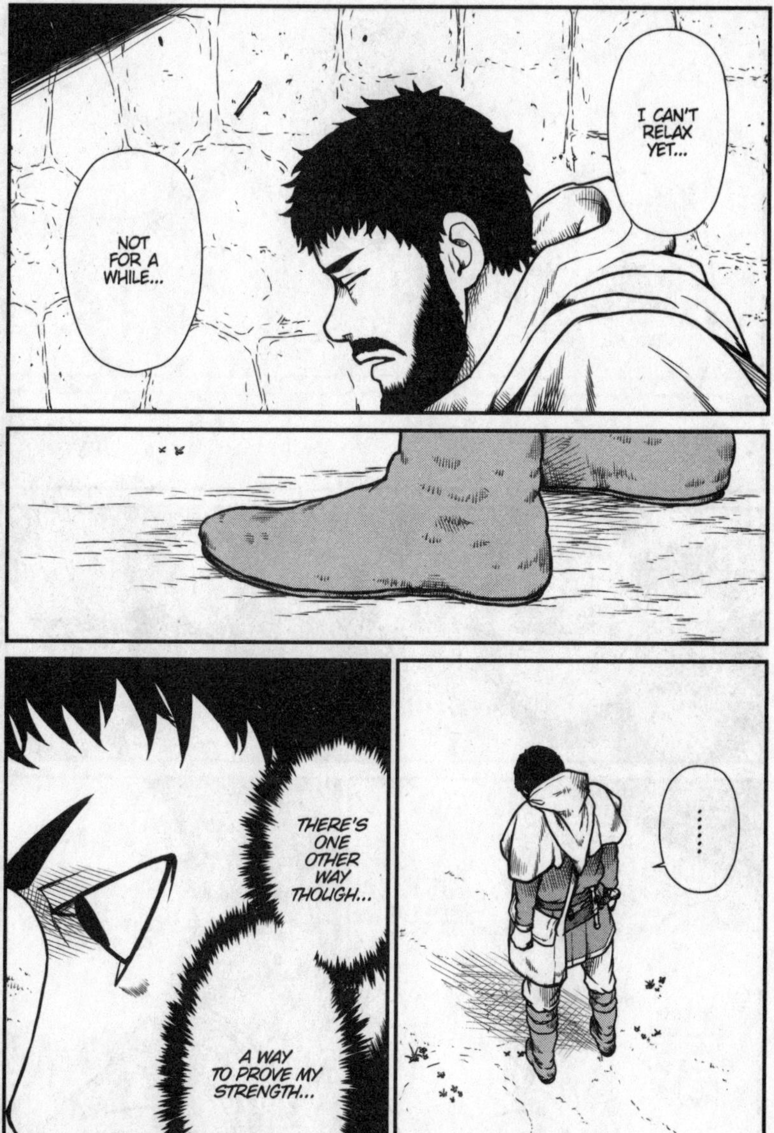
I CAN'T RELAX YET...
NOT FOR A WHILE...
......
THERE'S ONE OTHER WAY THOUGH...
A WAY TO PROVE MY STRENGTH...

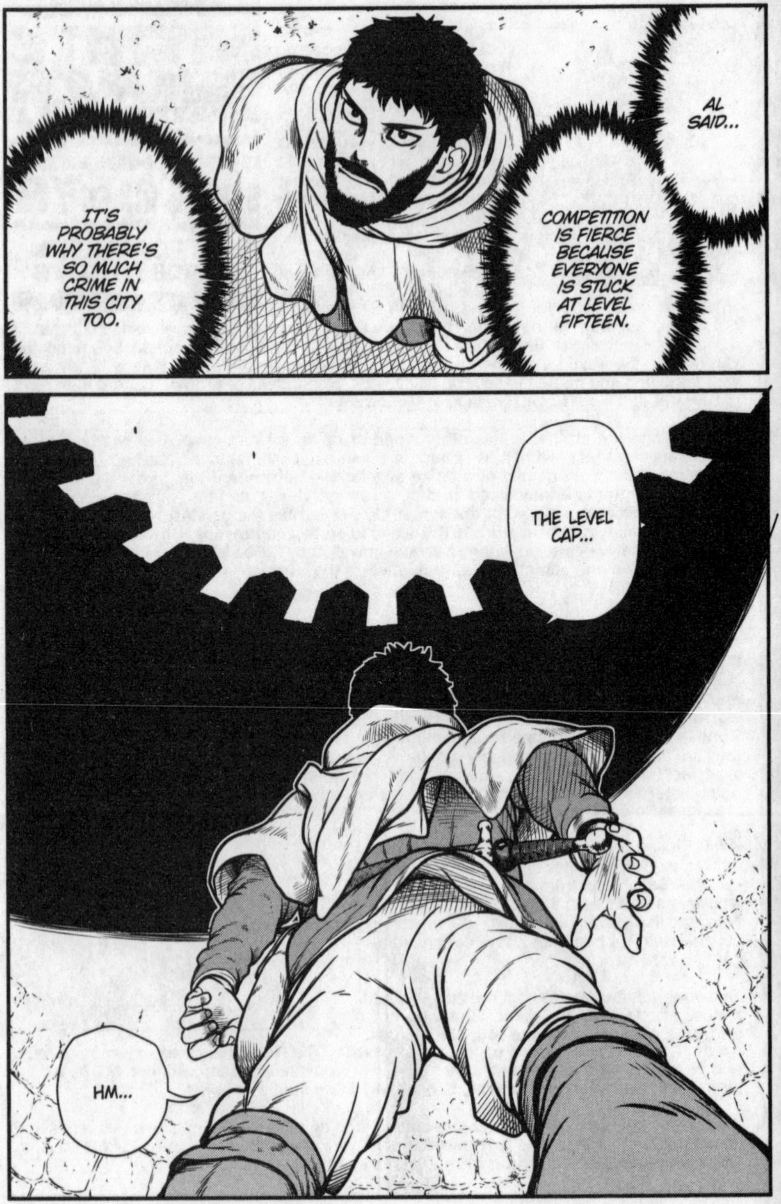
AL SAID...
COMPETITION IS FIERCE BECAUSE EVERYONE IS STUCK AT LEVEL FIFTEEN.
IT'S PROBABLY WHY THERE'S SO MUCH CRIME IN THIS CITY TOO.
THE LEVEL CAP...
HM...

SPECIAL COLUMN BY
AUTHOR. YAZIN

KARATE SURVIVOR IN ANOTHER WORLD

INTERMISSION
SAVAGE RULES 16
THE TRIBULATION OF PROSTITUTES

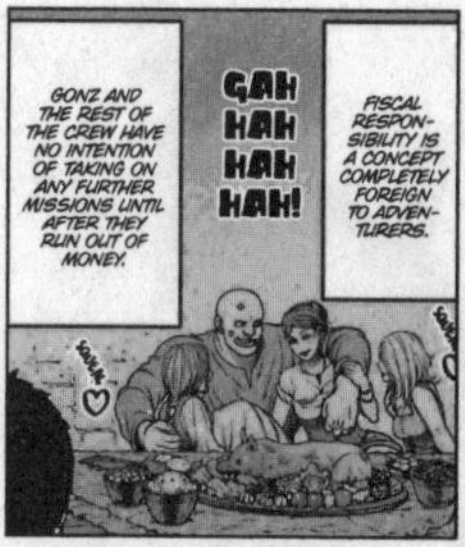
FISCAL RESPONSIBILITY IS A CONCEPT COMPLETELY FOREIGN TO ADVENTURERS.
GAH HAH HAH HAH!
GONZ AND THE REST OF THE CREW HAVE NO INTENTION OF TAKING ON ANY FURTHER MISSIONS UNTIL AFTER THEY RUN OUT OF MONEY.

There are several categories of sex workers, ranging from high-class courtesans to the so-called streetwalkers.

High-class courtesans explicitly separate themselves from other sex workers. They present attractively, offer clients a level of sophistication, and have perfected the techniques and art of hospitality. They embody what men would consider the ideal women. Their clients are largely nobles and major merchants, and their earnings are far greater than that of the average citizen. In Japan, we had the *Oiran* of the Yoshiwara district. Among the Oiran were the *Tayuu*, regarded as the most prestigious of the courtesans. They were well-educated and trained in several disciplines. Regardless of era and nation, men have always needed a glamorous prize to strive towards.

The ladies of the brothel in this other world are able to work in relative safety. People avoid troubling these women, as many of these establishments are backed by either a government-sanctioned guild or a crime syndicate. I have heard that in our world, if you hurt a sex worker in a franchised brothel, a scary man will barge in, take a photocopy of your driver's license, and soon enough, a slew of terrible things start happening to you. There is a similar system in place in this world to protect courtesans. However, sex work is not a completely secure job. If they become unwell, they will be abandoned with no mercy. A courtesan's life is still comfortable relative to the average person, but the conditions remain brutal.

On the opposite end are streetwalkers, the lowest class of sex workers. These women wander the streets in search of clients. Their job is very risky, as they complete their work in the place of their client's choosing. They are in a very vulnerable position, and their clients might turn violent or escape without paying at any time. Some may even be murdered and have their money stolen. (The infamous Jack the Ripper made a victim of several sex workers.) For this reason, streetwalkers may choose to work with a procurer or pimp. In this world, pimping is often done by adventurers as a side job. In exchange for a commission, they are tasked with resolving any problems the women may have with the clients. The job is perfect for adventurers, as arguments can easily escalate and adventurers are certainly no strangers to violence. Oftentimes, clients are adventurers too, so the two professions are closely intertwined.

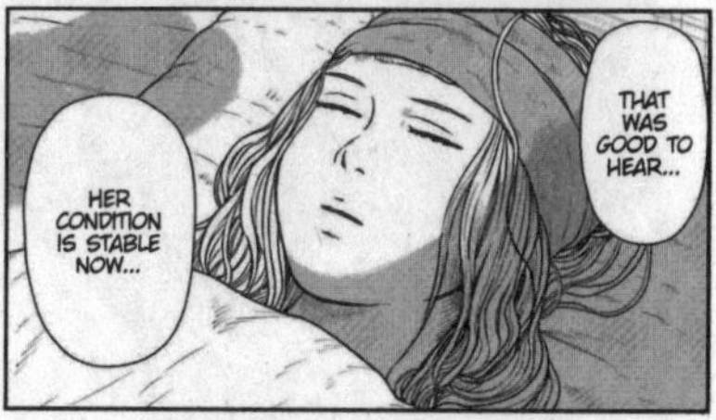
THAT WAS GOOD TO HEAR...
HER CONDITION IS STABLE NOW...

Kimon killed a man in revenge for a sex worker, but he himself is not a pimp.
He was separated from his younger sister, who was sold off as a slave. Her screams for help and his powerlessness to do anything cut deep into his heart, and have continued to haunt him since.

One day, he found a prostitute that looked almost exactly like his sister. She was not attracting many clients. She was standing at a corner, severely emaciated and close to collapse. The sight of her pained Kimon greatly, and he felt the urge to feed and care for her. He would never sleep with her, but he would periodically pay for the opportunity to chat and share food with her.

Kimon only offered a moderate amount of aid, and never enough that she could leave sex work altogether. Kimon was fully aware that he was only helping her in lieu of his missing sister, attempting to fill a hole in his heart with empty gestures.

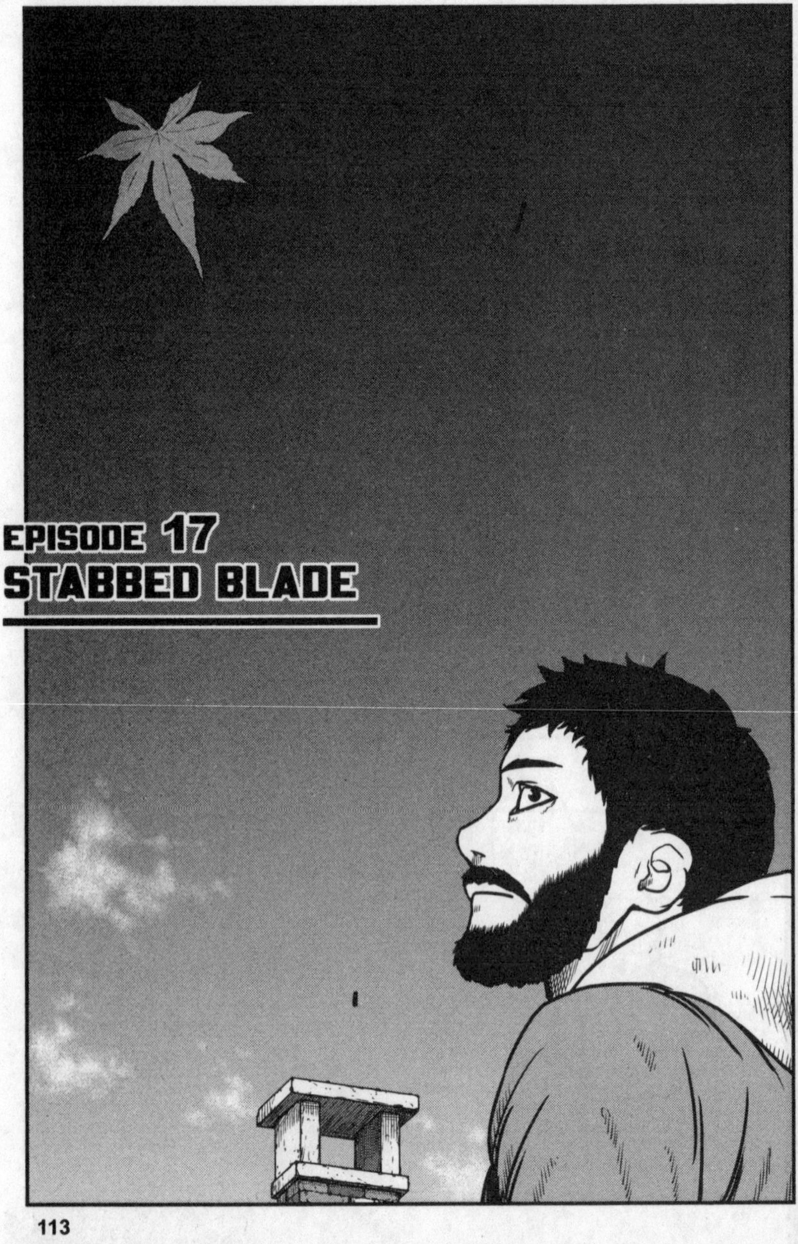
EPISODE 17
STABBED BLADE

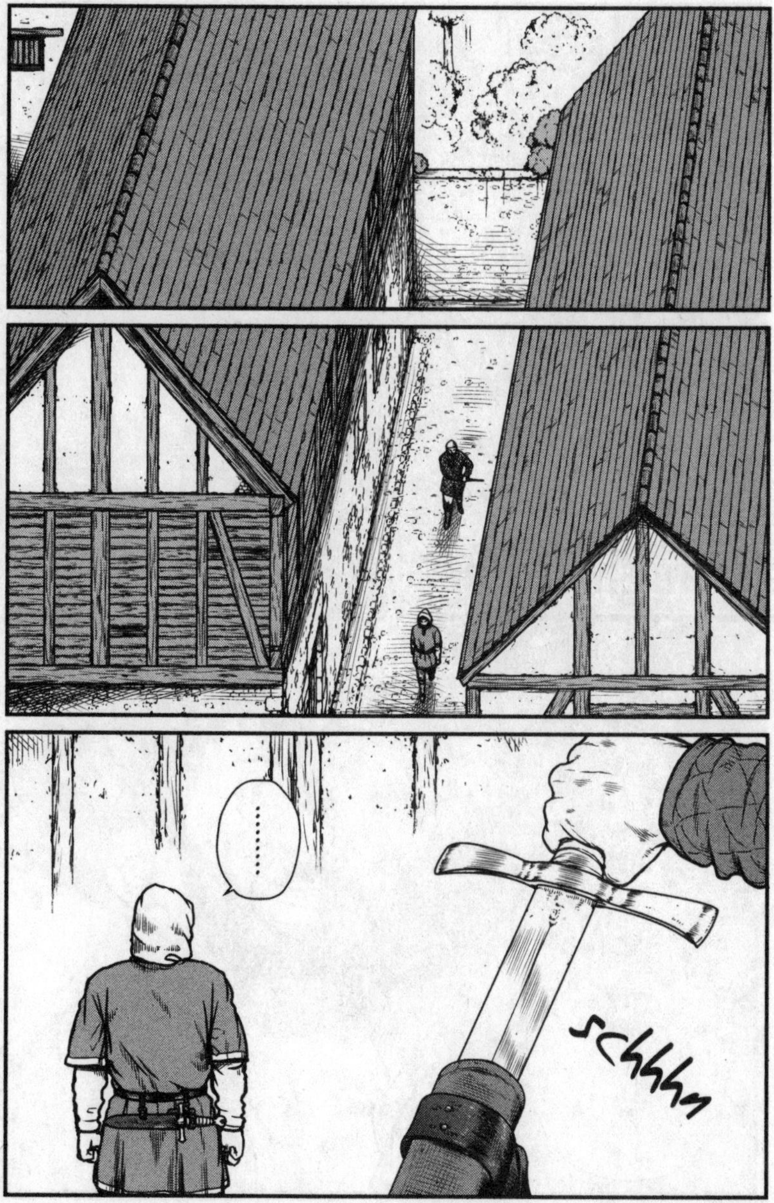
SCHHHN
......

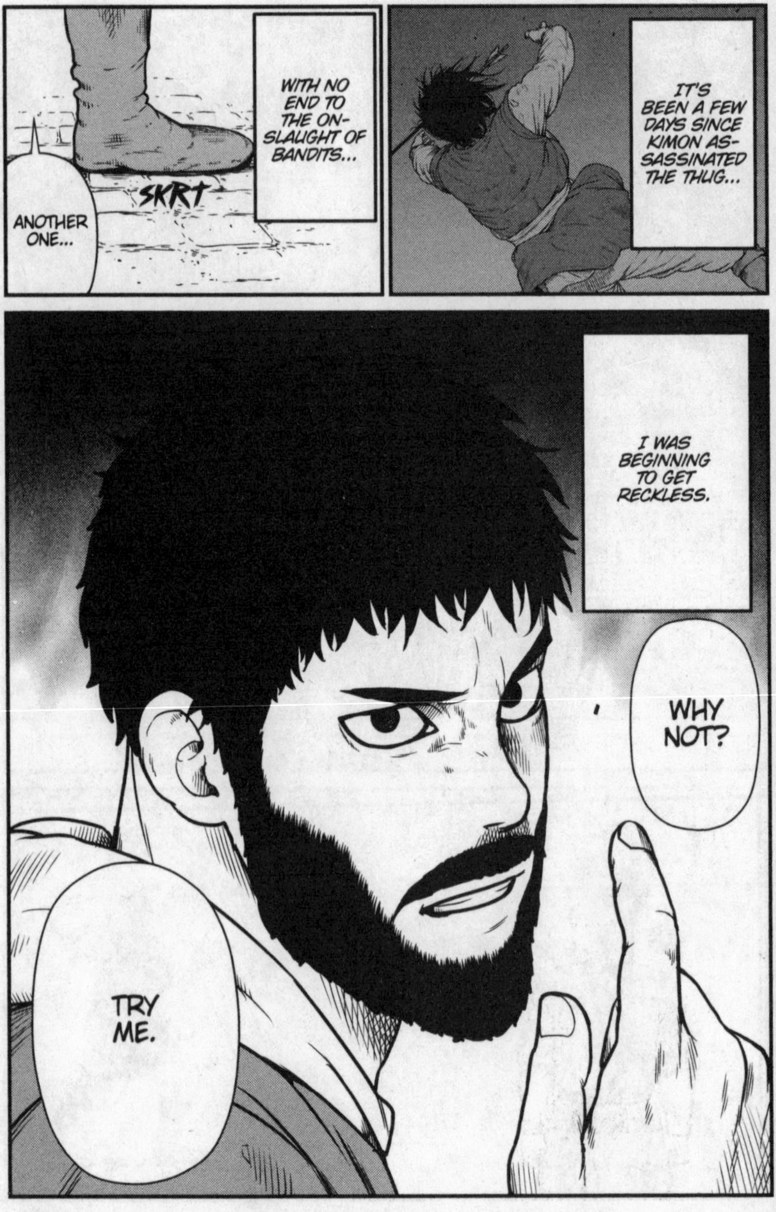
IT'S BEEN A FEW DAYS SINCE KIMON AS-SASSINATED THE THUG...
WITH NO END TO THE ON-SLAUGHT OF BANDITS...
SKRT
ANOTHER ONE...
I WAS BEGINNING TO GET RECKLESS.
WHY NOT?
TRY ME.

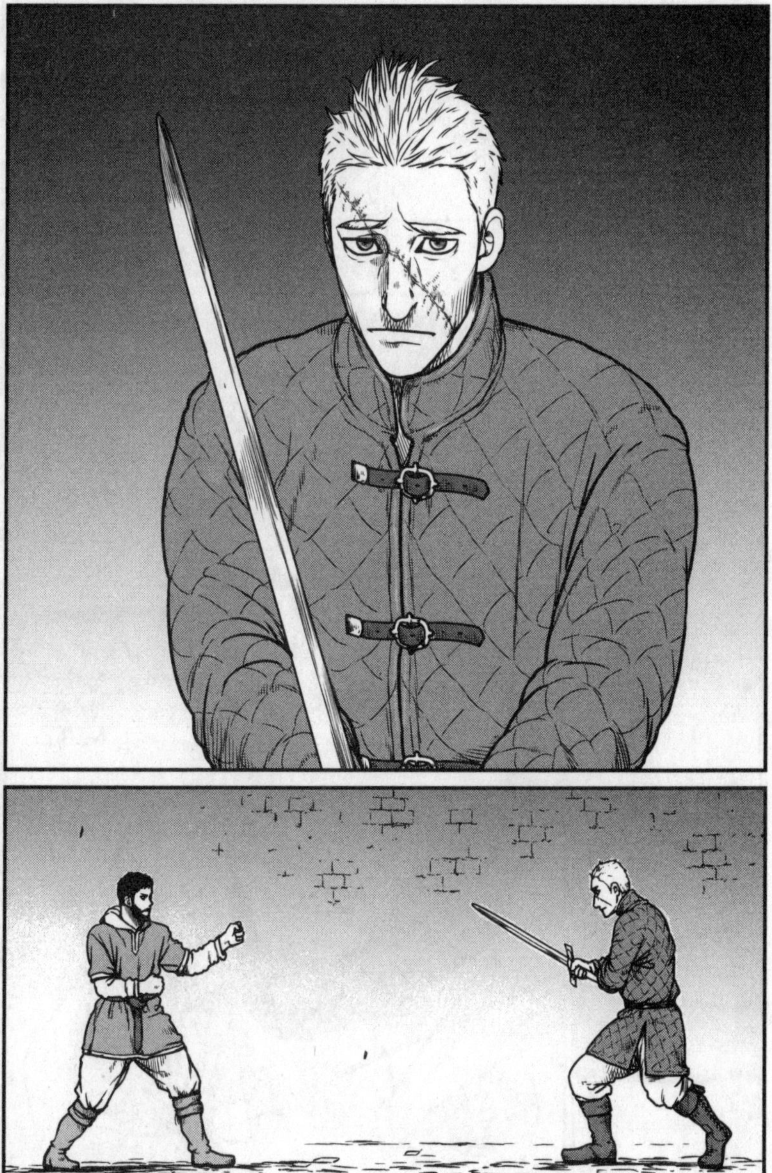

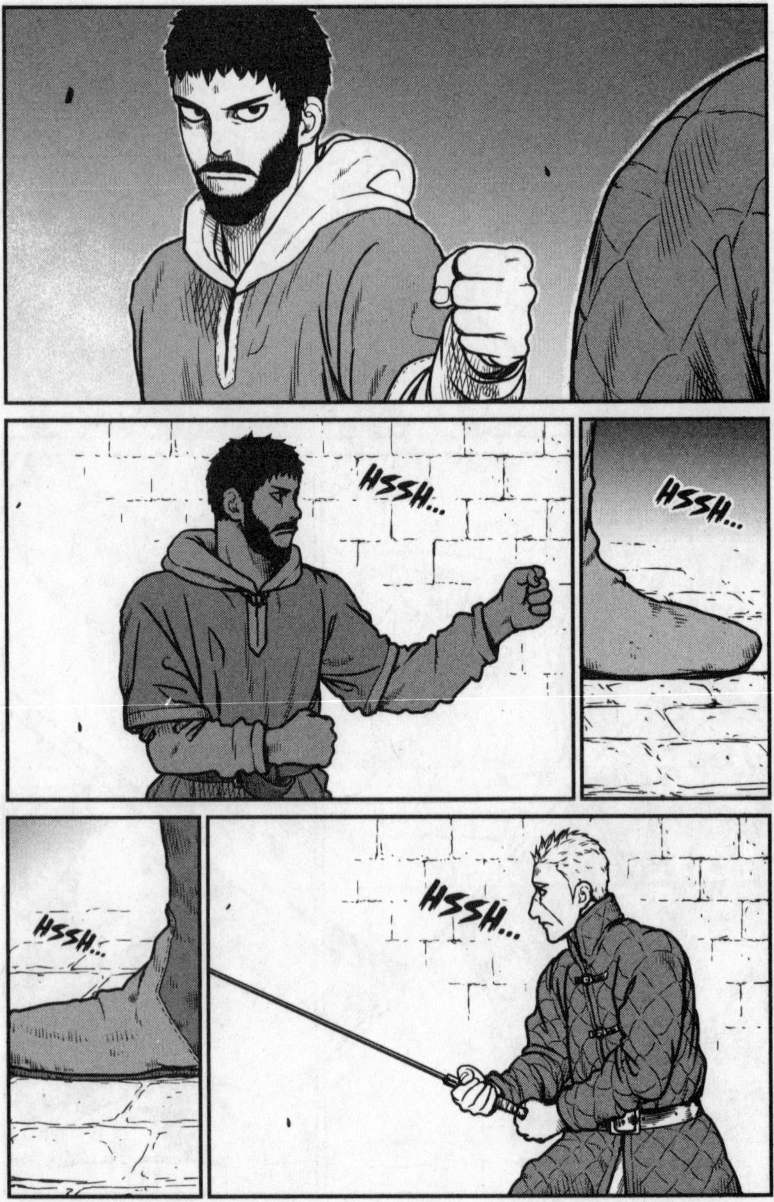
HSSH...
HSSH...
HSSH...
HSSH...

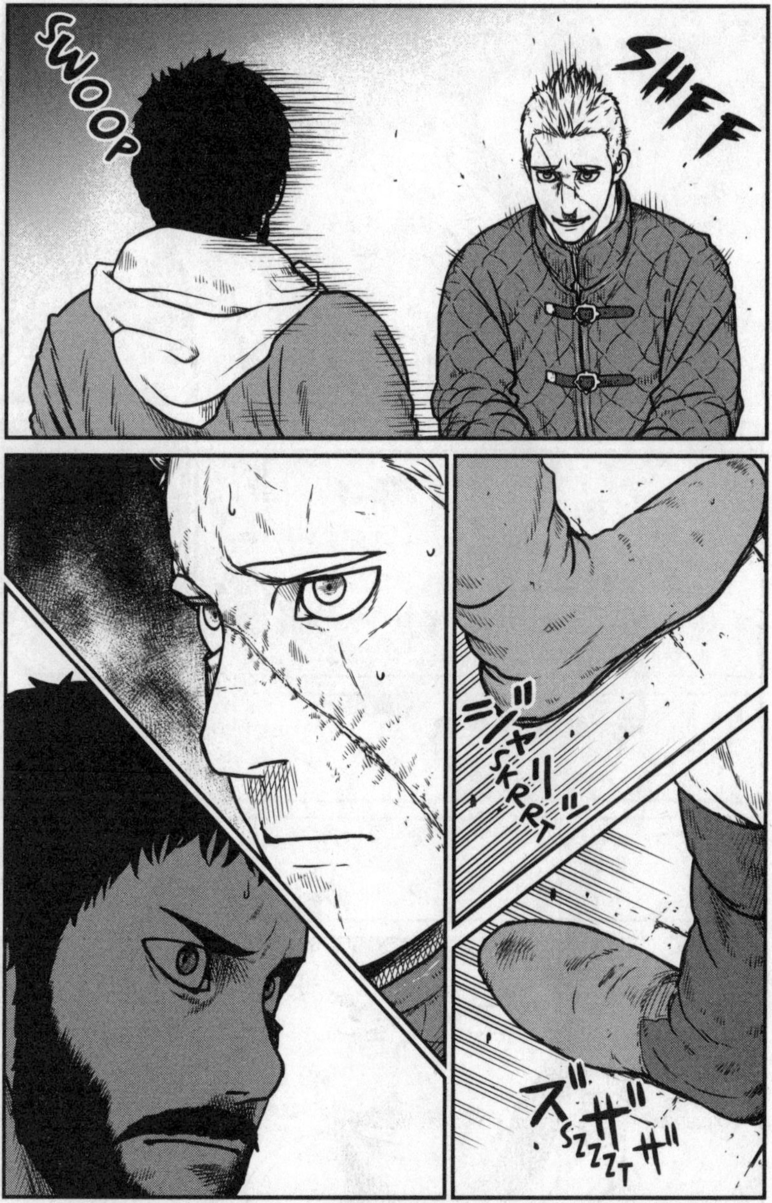
SHFF
SWOOP
ジャリ
SKRRT
ズザザ
SZZZZT

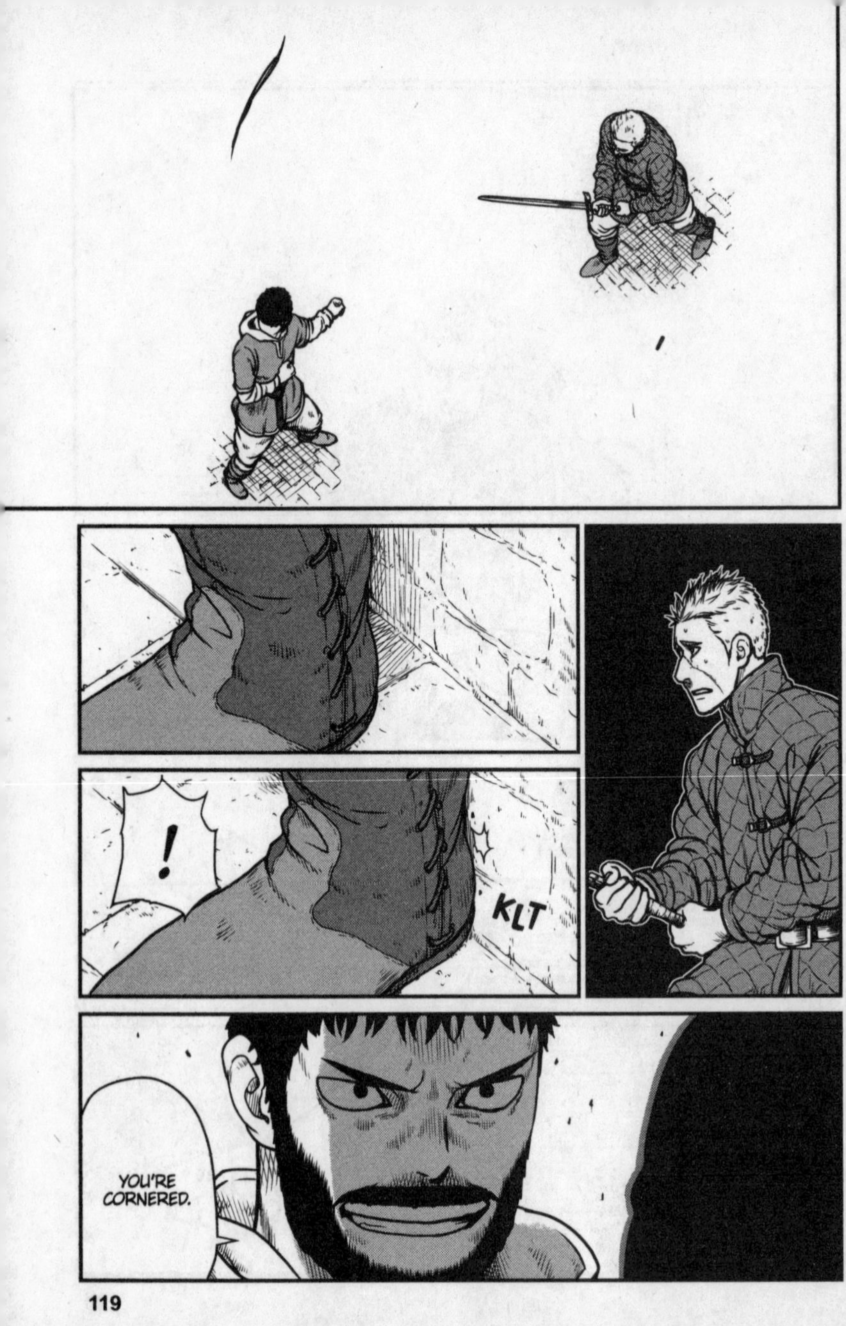
!
KLT
YOU'RE CORNERED.

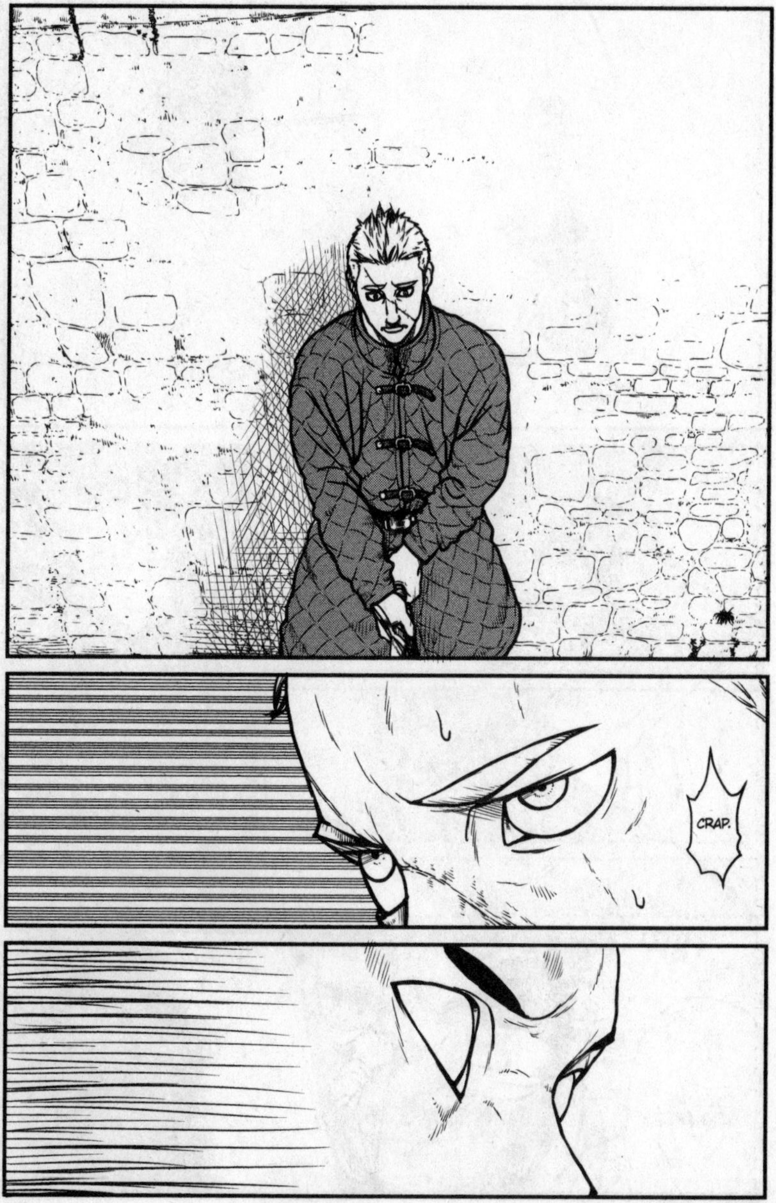
CRAP.

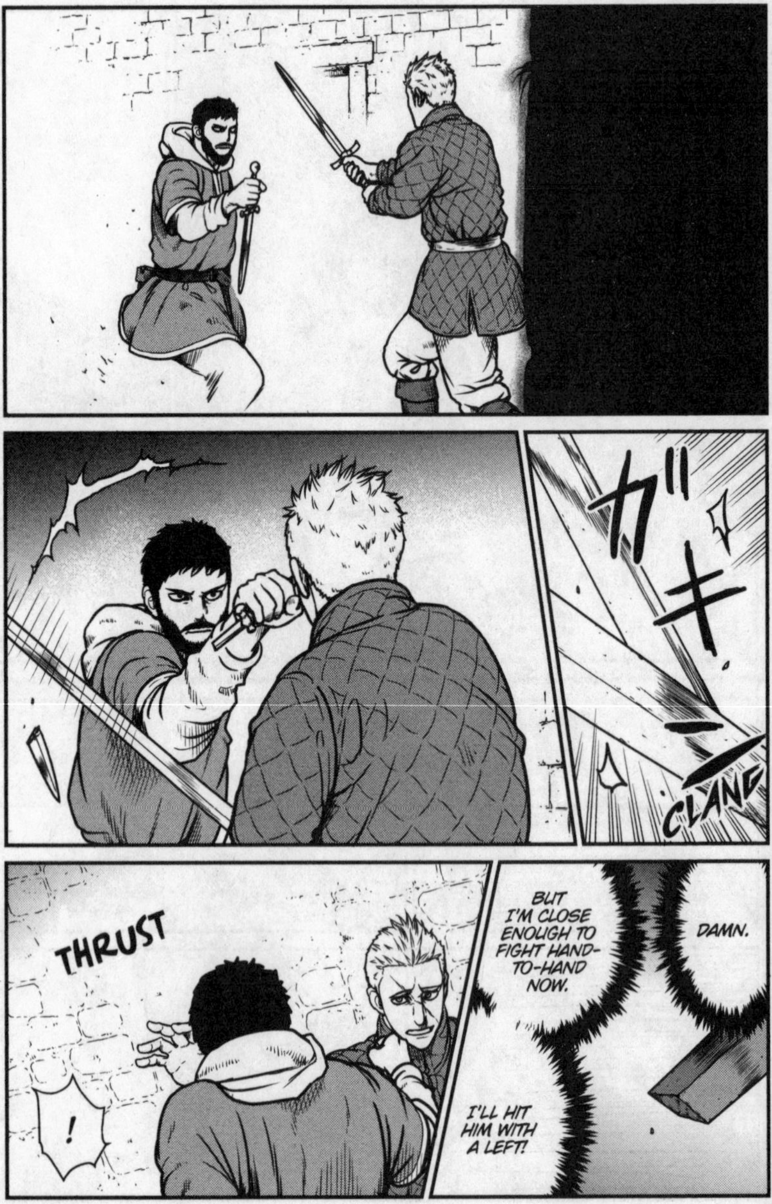
ガキ
CLANG
DAMN.
BUT I'M CLOSE ENOUGH TO FIGHT HAND-TO-HAND NOW.
I'LL HIT HIM WITH A LEFT!
THRUST
!

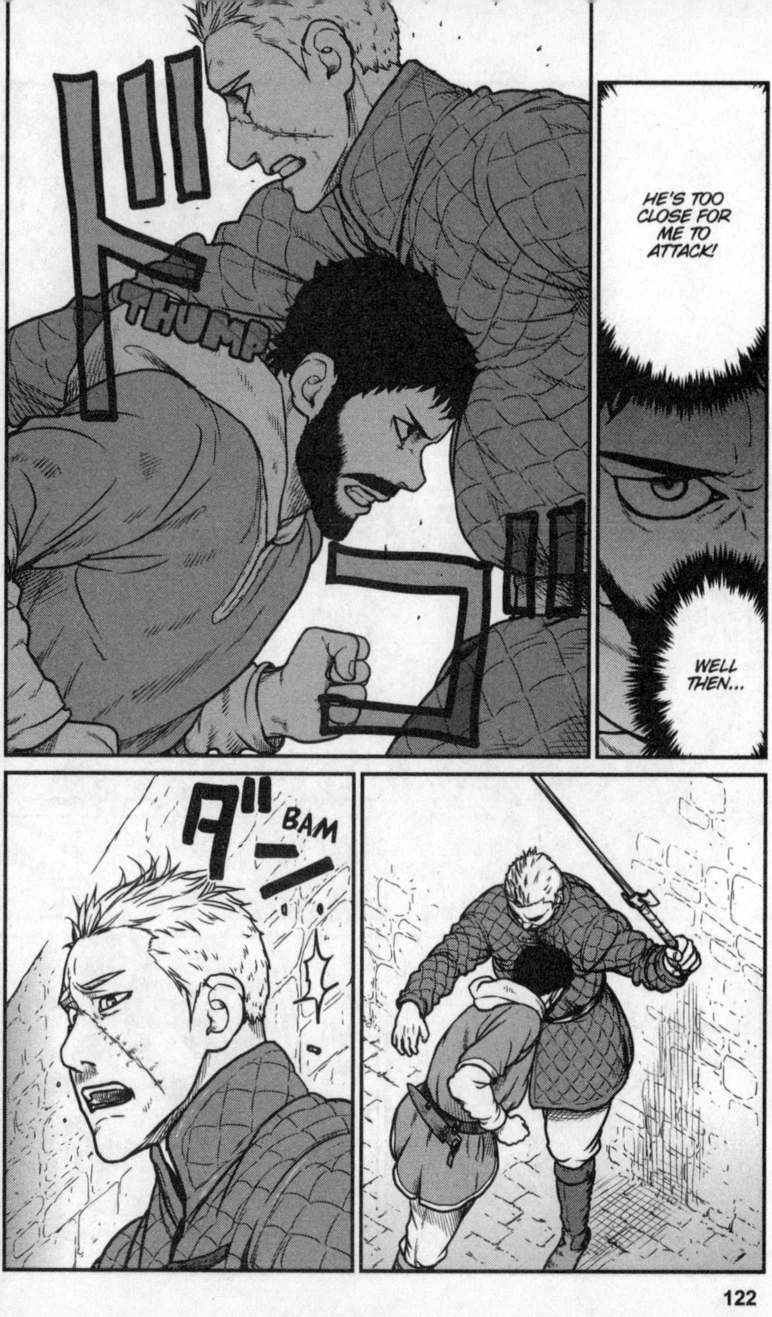
HE'S TOO CLOSE FOR ME TO ATTACK!
WELL THEN...
THUMP
BAM

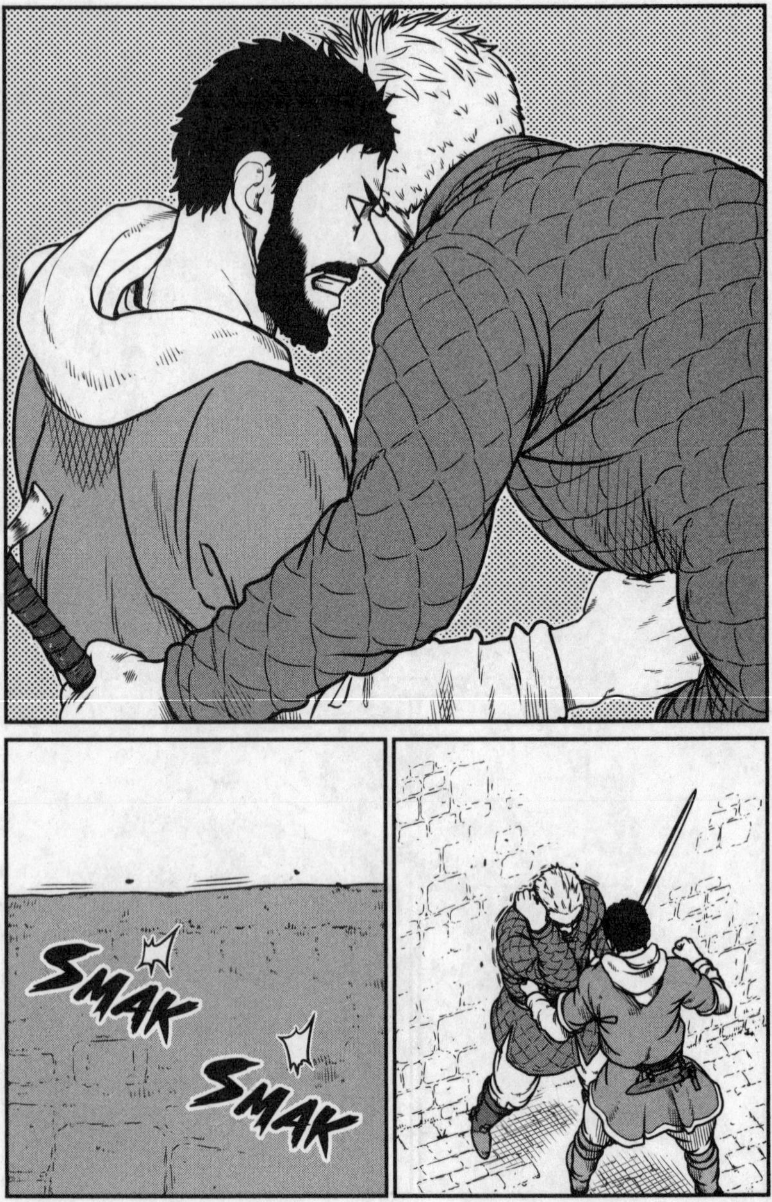
SMAK
SMAK

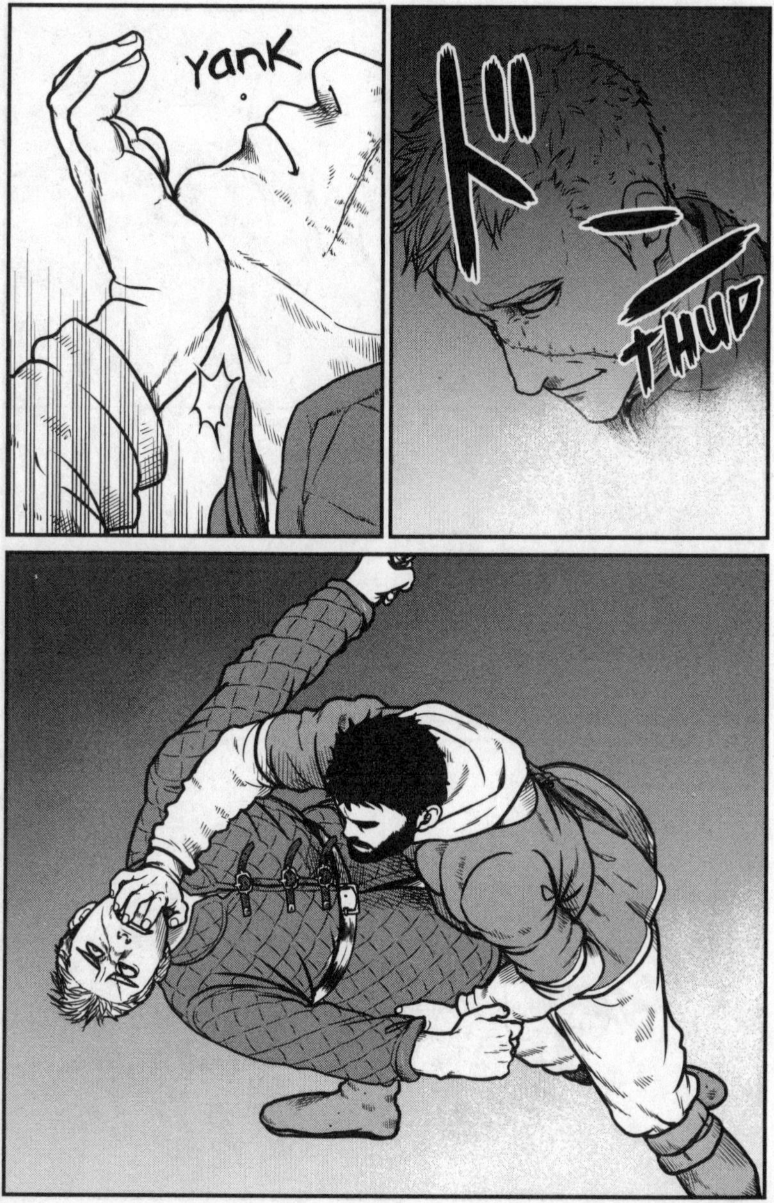
ドーン
THUD
yank

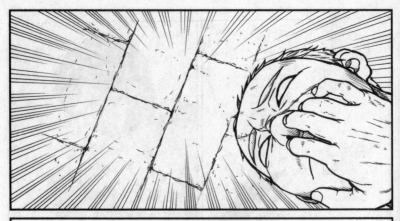

smash

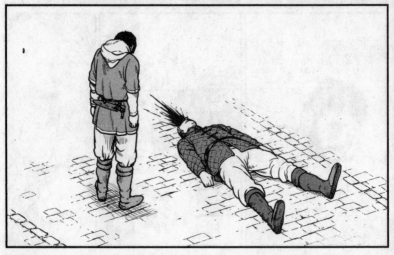

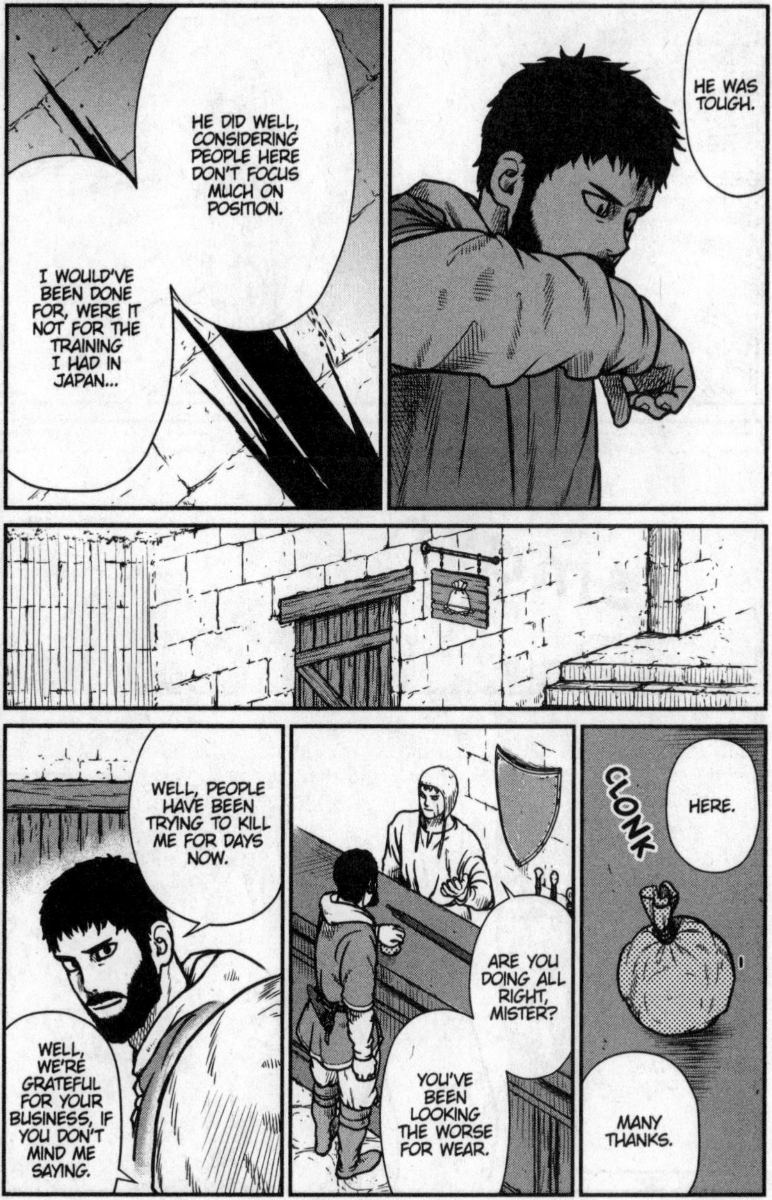
HE WAS TOUGH.
HE DID WELL, CONSIDERING PEOPLE HERE DON'T FOCUS MUCH ON POSITION.
I WOULD'VE BEEN DONE FOR, WERE IT NOT FOR THE TRAINING I HAD IN JAPAN...
HERE.
CLONK
MANY THANKS.
ARE YOU DOING ALL RIGHT, MISTER?
YOU'VE BEEN LOOKING THE WORSE FOR WEAR.
WELL, PEOPLE HAVE BEEN TRYING TO KILL ME FOR DAYS NOW.
WELL, WE'RE GRATEFUL FOR YOUR BUSINESS, IF YOU DON'T MIND ME SAYING.

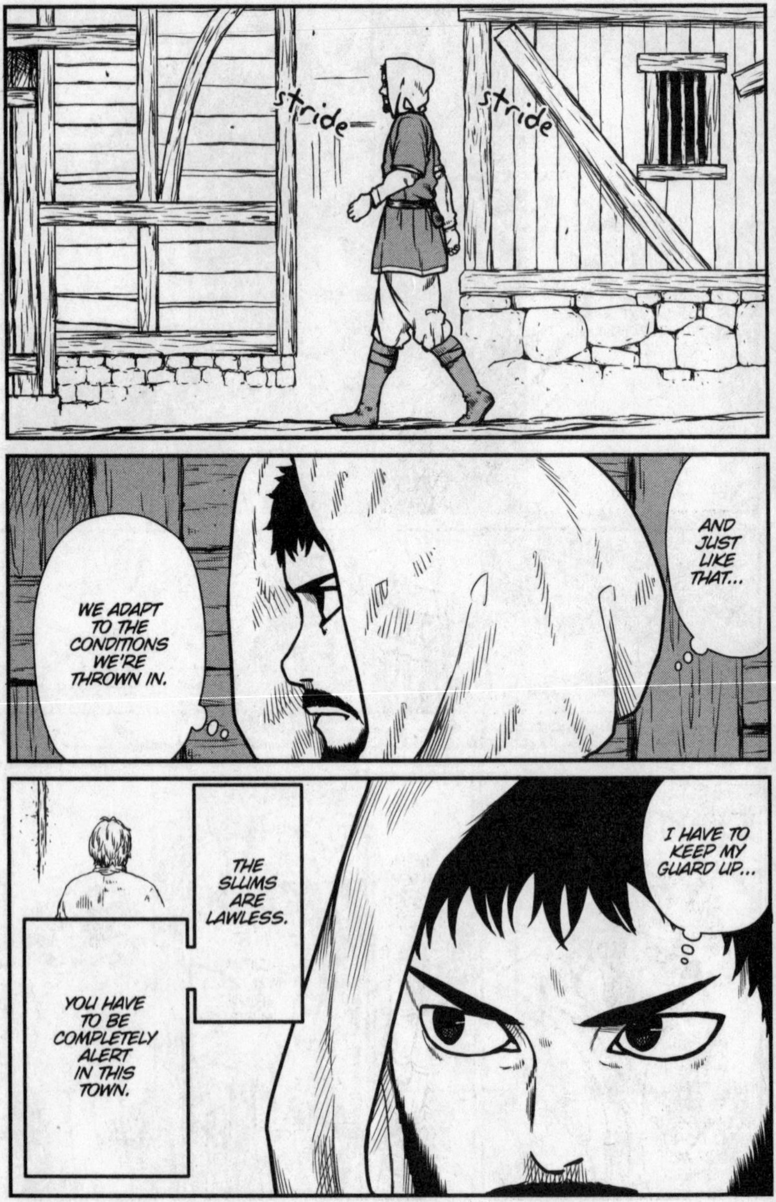
stride
stride
AND JUST LIKE THAT...
WE ADAPT TO THE CONDITIONS WE'RE THROWN IN.
I HAVE TO KEEP MY GUARD UP...
THE SLUMS ARE LAWLESS.
YOU HAVE TO BE COMPLETELY ALERT IN THIS TOWN.

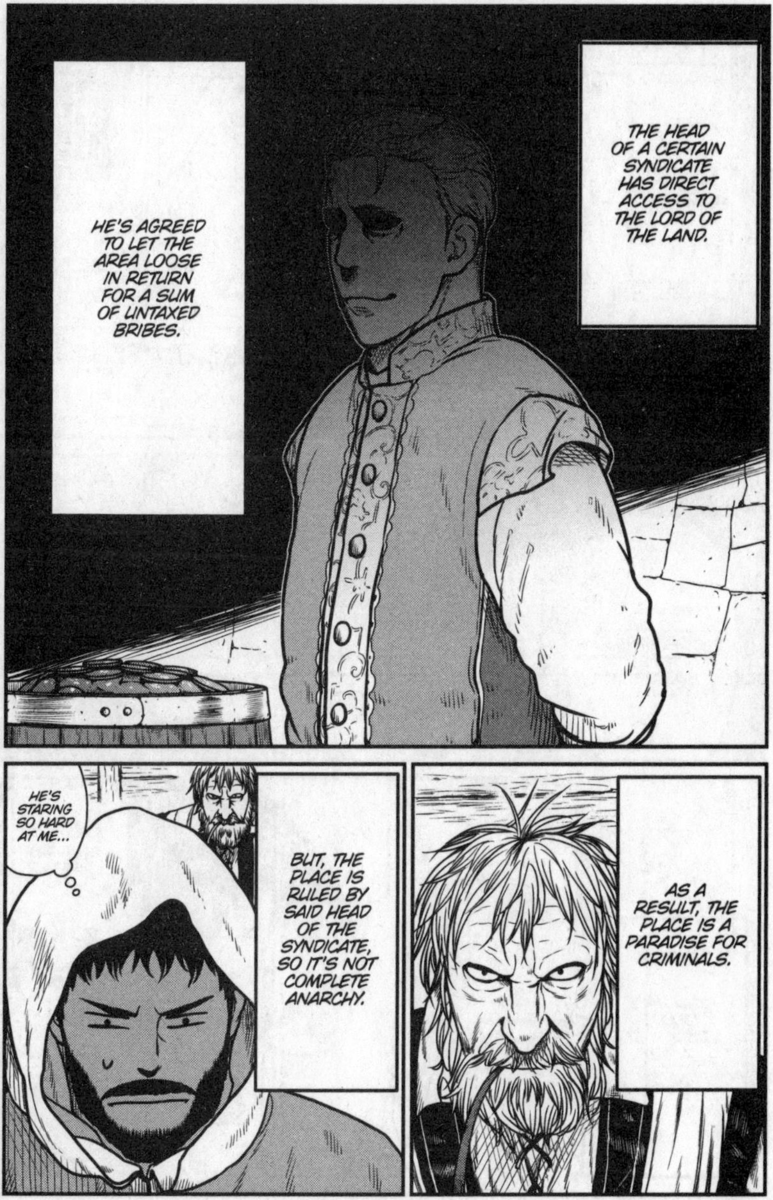
THE HEAD OF A CERTAIN SYNDICATE HAS DIRECT ACCESS TO THE LORD OF THE LAND.
HE'S AGREED TO LET THE AREA LOOSE IN RETURN FOR A SUM OF UNTAXED BRIBES.
AS A RESULT, THE PLACE IS A PARADISE FOR CRIMINALS.
BUT, THE PLACE IS RULED BY SAID HEAD OF THE SYNDICATE, SO IT'S NOT COMPLETE ANARCHY.
HE'S STARING SO HARD AT ME...

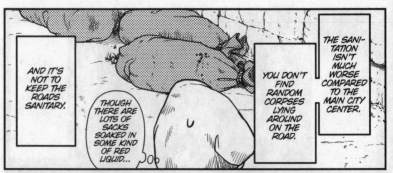

THE SANITATION ISN'T MUCH WORSE COMPARED TO THE MAIN CITY CENTER.
YOU DON'T FIND RANDOM CORPSES LYING AROUND ON THE ROAD.
THOUGH THERE ARE LOTS OF SACKS SOAKED IN SOME KIND OF RED LIQUID...
AND IT'S NOT TO KEEP THE ROADS SANITARY.
DEAD BODIES MAKE MONEY.
HAIR IS STITCHED INTO WIGS.
BONES ARE GROUND INTO POWDER FOR FERTILIZER OR ALCHEMICAL EXPERIMENTS.
AS FOR THE FLESH...
THERE'S A REASON THEY SAY NEVER TO EAT THE MEAT IN THE SLUMS.
THE SLUMS MAY SEEM QUIET...
BUT I CAN ALWAYS FEEL SOMEONE'S EYES ON ME.

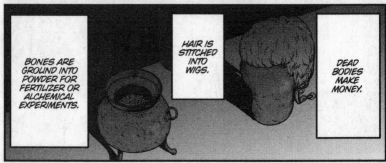

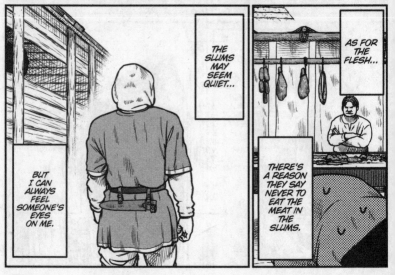

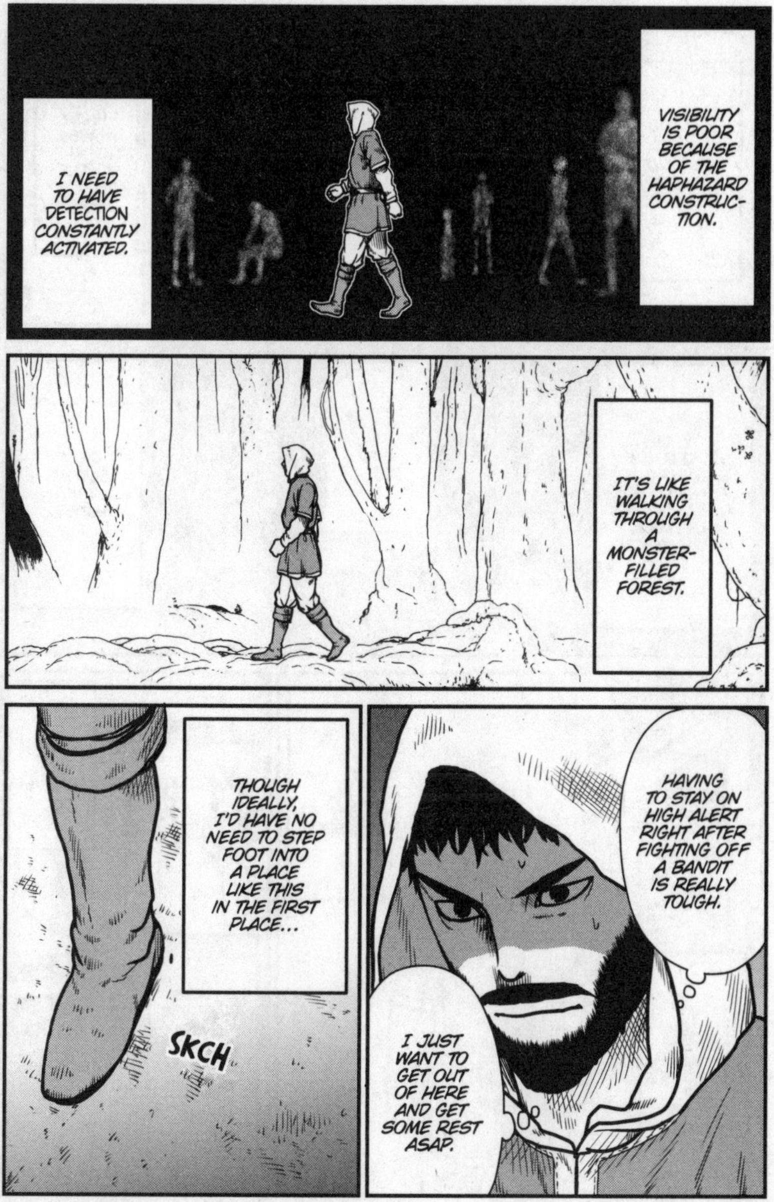
VISIBILITY IS POOR BECAUSE OF THE HAPHAZARD CONSTRUCTION.
I NEED TO HAVE DETECTION CONSTANTLY ACTIVATED.
IT'S LIKE WALKING THROUGH A MONSTER-FILLED FOREST.
HAVING TO STAY ON HIGH ALERT RIGHT AFTER FIGHTING OFF A BANDIT IS REALLY TOUGH.
I JUST WANT TO GET OUT OF HERE AND GET SOME REST ASAP.
THOUGH IDEALLY, I'D HAVE NO NEED TO STEP FOOT INTO A PLACE LIKE THIS IN THE FIRST PLACE...
SKCH

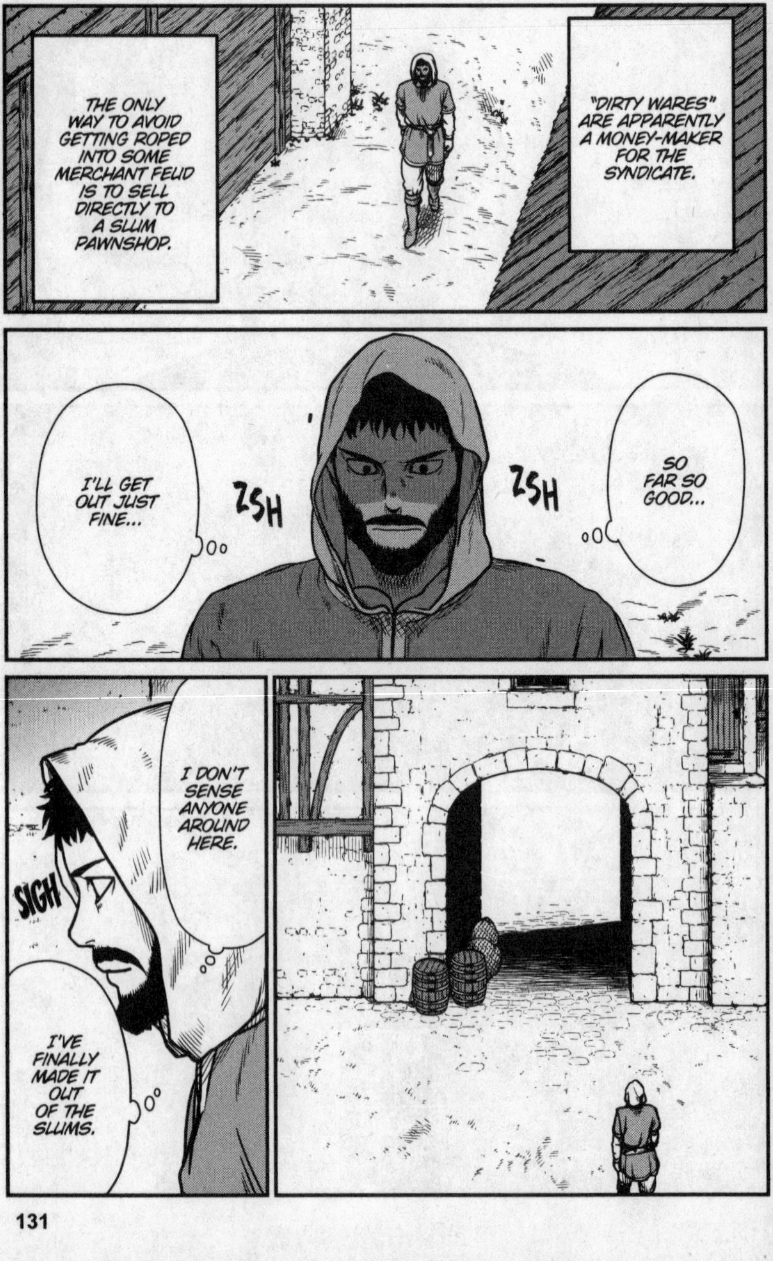
"DIRTY WARES" ARE APPARENTLY A MONEY-MAKER FOR THE SYNDICATE.
THE ONLY WAY TO AVOID GETTING ROPED INTO SOME MERCHANT FEUD IS TO SELL DIRECTLY TO A SLUM PAWNSHOP.
SO FAR SO GOOD...
ZSH
ZSH
I'LL GET OUT JUST FINE...
I DON'T SENSE ANYONE AROUND HERE.
SIGH
I'VE FINALLY MADE IT OUT OF THE SLUMS.

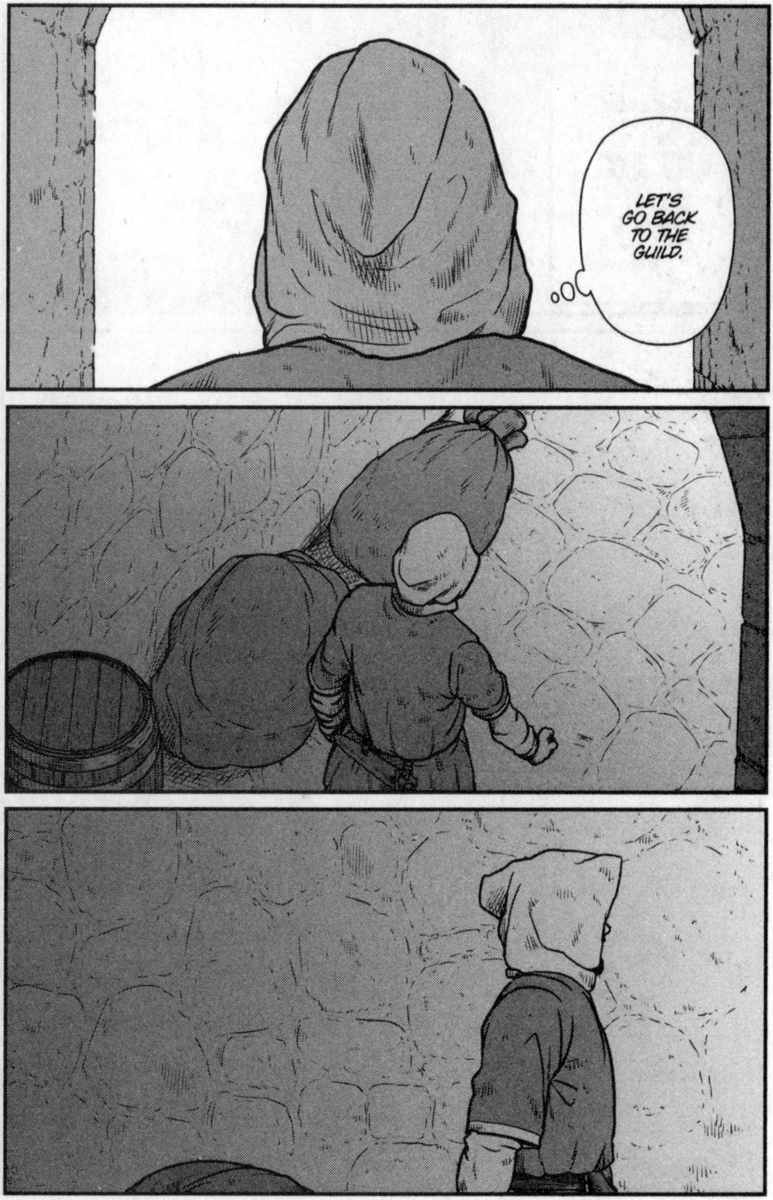
LET'S GO BACK TO THE GUILD.

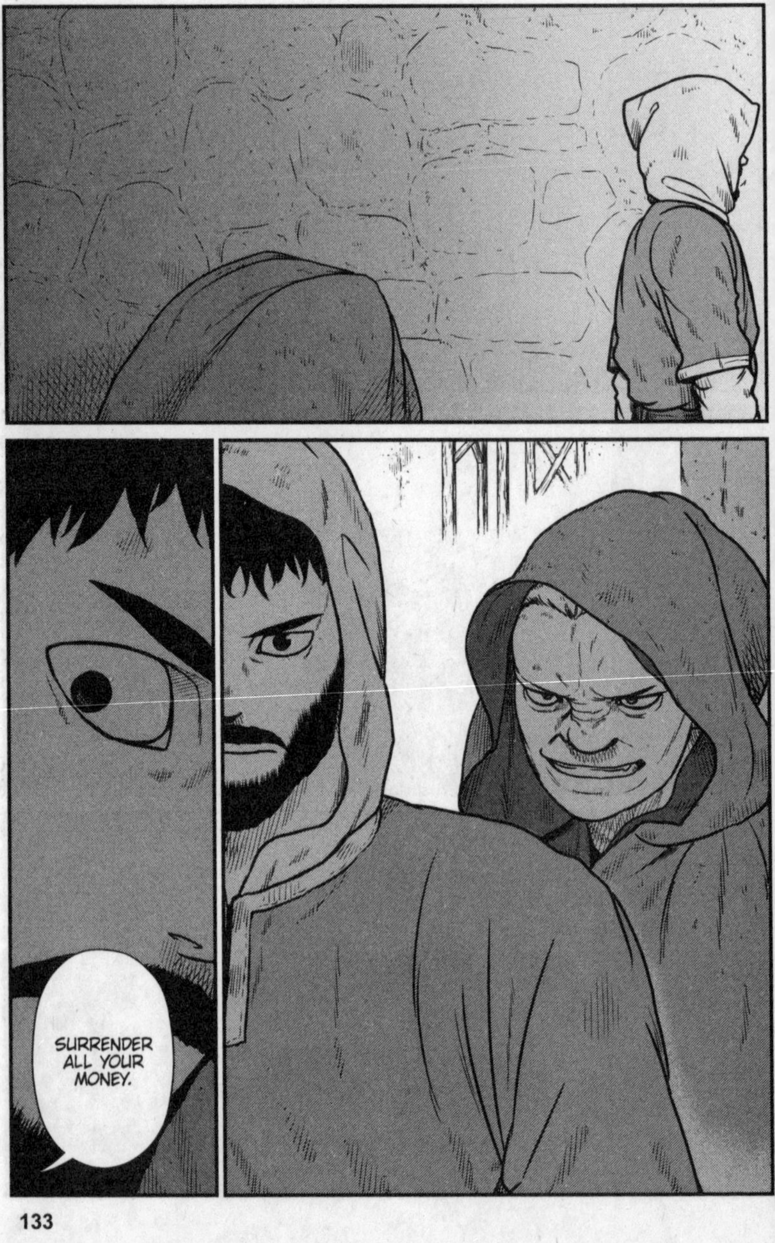
SURRENDER ALL YOUR MONEY.

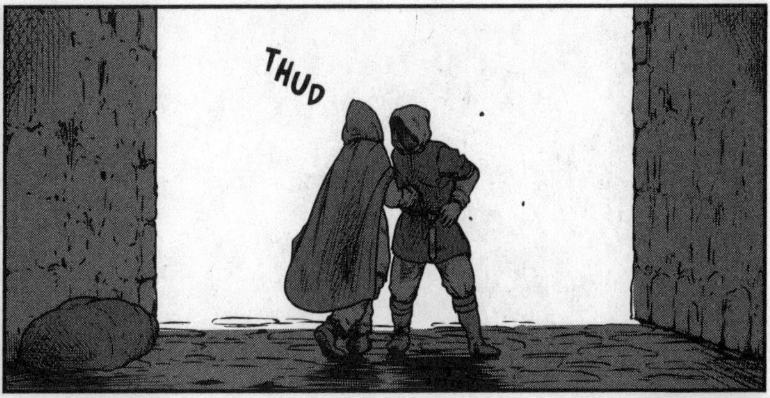
THUD

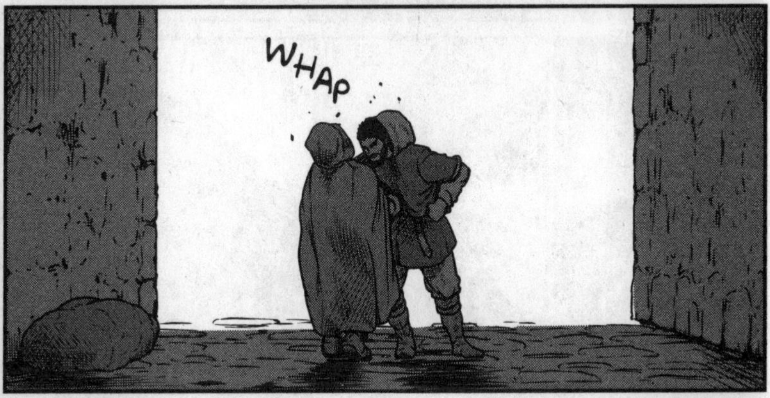
WHAP

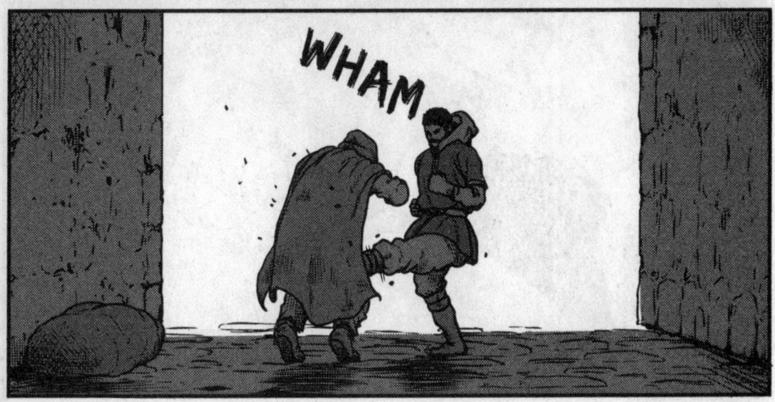
WHAM

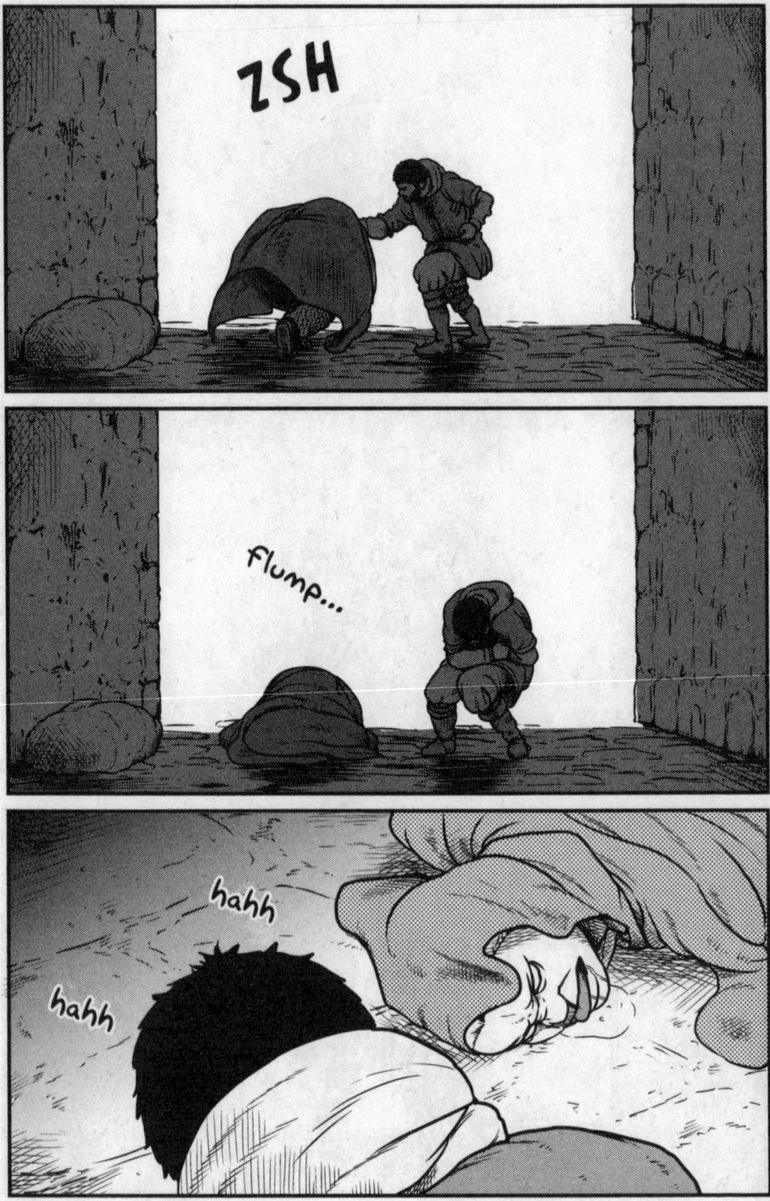
ZSH
flump...
hahh
hahh

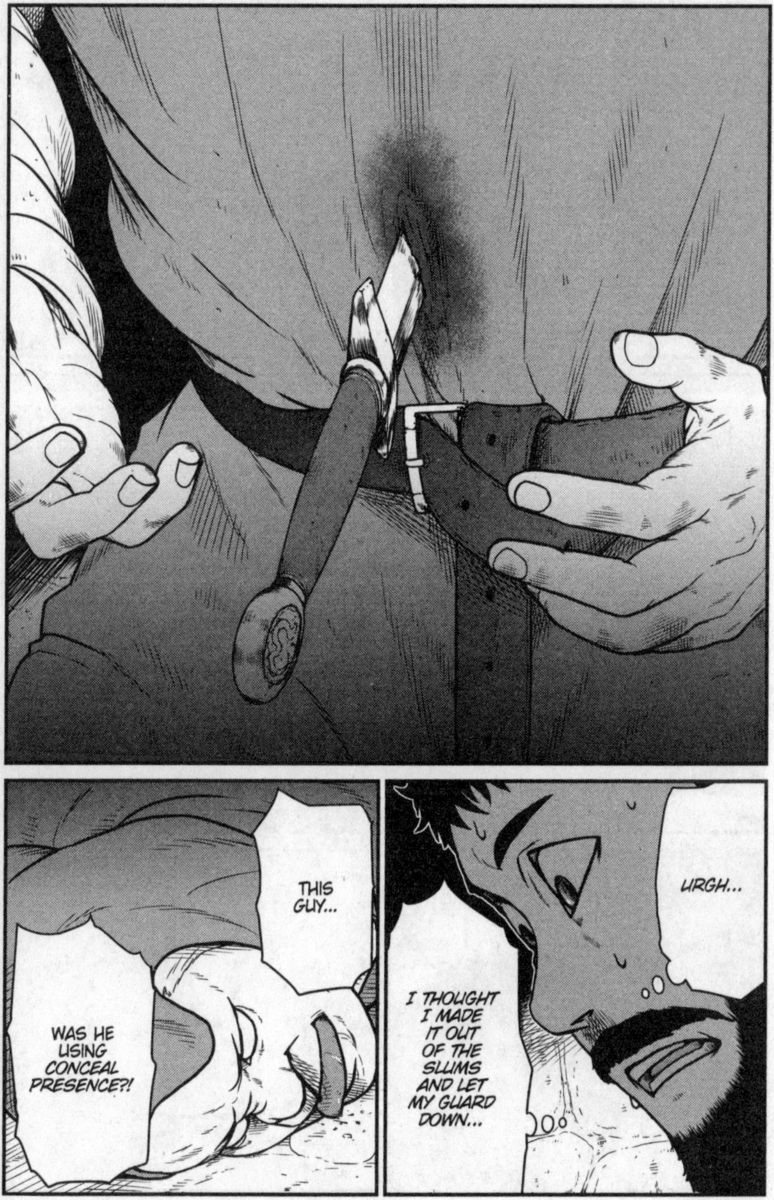
URGH...
I THOUGHT I MADE IT OUT OF THE SLUMS AND LET MY GUARD DOWN...
THIS GUY...
WAS HE USING CONCEAL PRESENCE?!

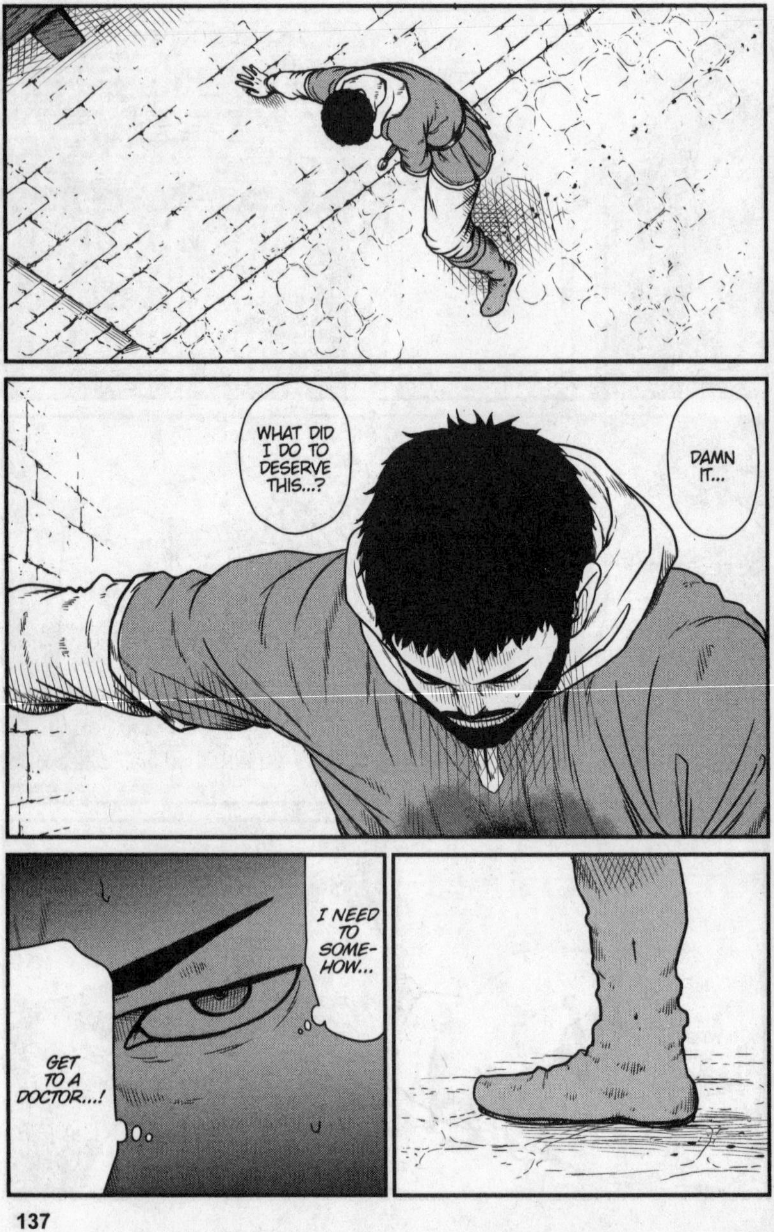
DAMN IT...
WHAT DID I DO TO DESERVE THIS...?
I NEED TO SOMEHOW...
GET TO A DOCTOR...!

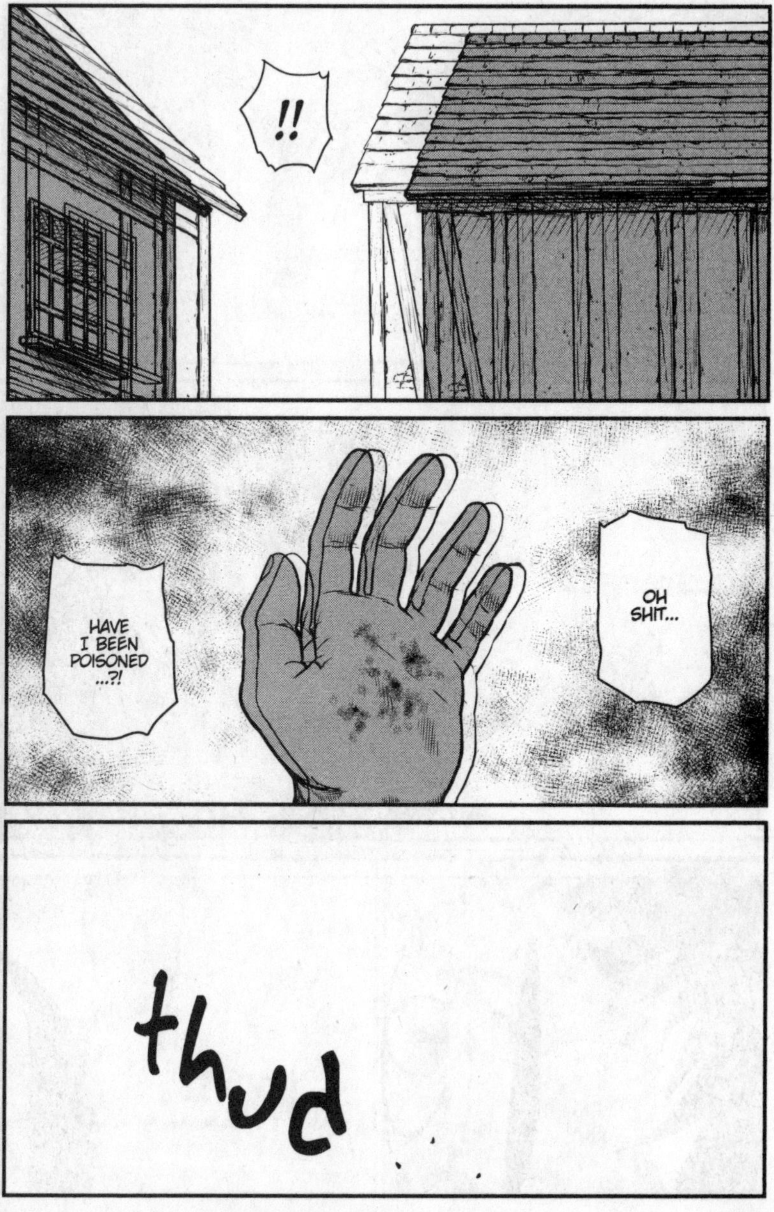
!!
OH SHIT...
HAVE I BEEN POISONED ...?!
thud

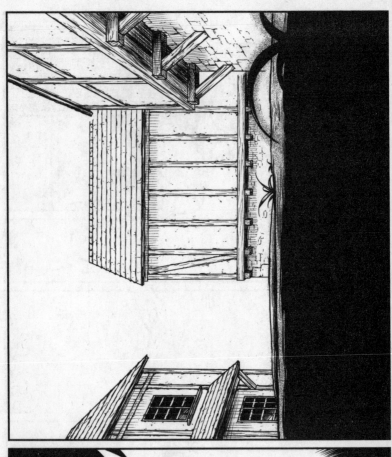

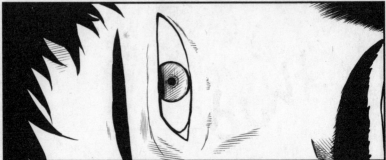

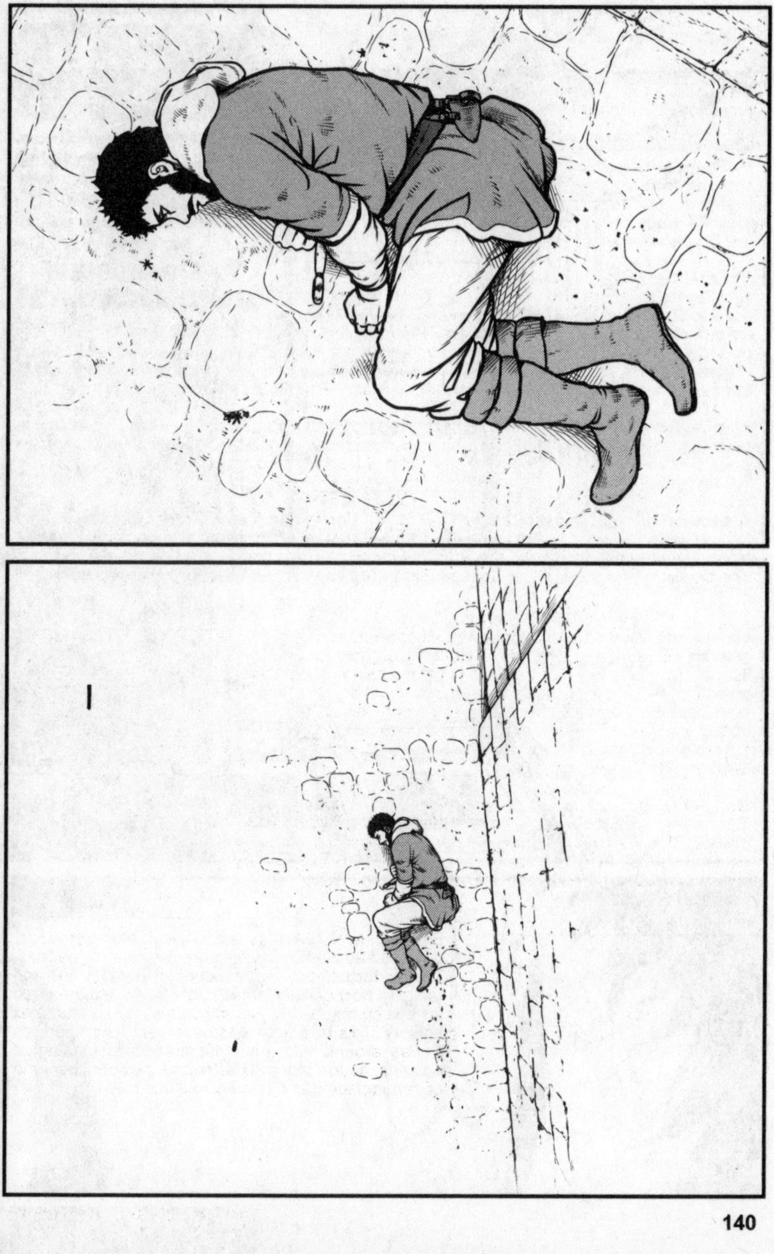

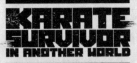

SPECIAL COLUMN BY AUTHOR, YAZIN

KARATE SURVIVOR IN ANOTHER WORLD

INTERMISSION
SAVAGE RULES 17

POISONS, THEN AND NOW

Though not obvious, poisons are all around us.

Take a stroll outside and you'll find poisonous weeds all over the place. Even pretty flowers often contain compounds poisonous to humans. The ubiquitous bacteria, *Clostridium botulinum*, produces nature's most potent toxin. There is even poison in the very food we eat. Potato sprouts and bits that have turned green are well-known for being toxic. You can overdose on ginkgo seeds if you eat too much at once. Plenty of animals are also poisonous or venomous, and they kill many people every year. To put it short, poisons are absolutely everywhere.

Since ancient times, humans have been using poisons to fight ferocious predators. Poison-dart frogs were literally used to tip blow darts with their poison. The Ainu people used wolfsbane to defeat brown bears. The indigenous people near the Amazon River use poison for fishing. They flush herbs containing paralytic agents down a stream to catch vicious piranhas. You might wonder if it's safe to use poison on the food you intend to eat. It turns out these poisons denature when heat is applied, and thus it loses potency.

Humans have been using poisons for hunting since ancient times, but they have come to use poison against other humans too. Sometimes, poisons were used to provide an advantage in a fight. In other times, they were used to assassinate an inconvenient rival. Poisons are ruthlessly efficient.

Assassination by poison ran rampant in Ancient Rome. The great Emperor Claudius is said to have been poisoned by Agrippina the Younger, mother of his eventual successor, Emperor Nero. Even the mighty ruler of the Roman Empire can lose his life to a little bit of poison. The deadliness of poison is evidenced by all the people it has killed throughout history.

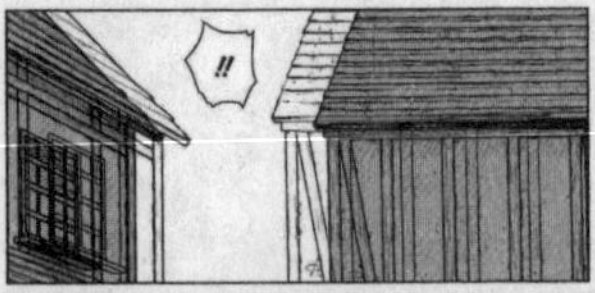
!!

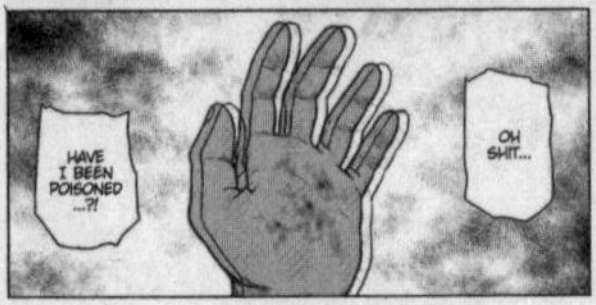
OH SHIT...
HAVE I BEEN POISONED ...?!

Martial arts have always been a part of conflict, and poisons played a role here too. The mythical "poison hands" technique involves treating a fighter's skin with poison. Special concoctions with obscure antidotes were devised. Targets were assassinated with poison-tipped needles. The art of poisoning has always stayed in the shadows, and has been passed down through generations in secrecy.

But the world has since become more peaceful. Scientific advancements have made forensic investigations more effective. Poisoning became riskier. Martial artists also no longer needed to regularly risk their lives in battle. Eventually, the art of poisons was lost to time.

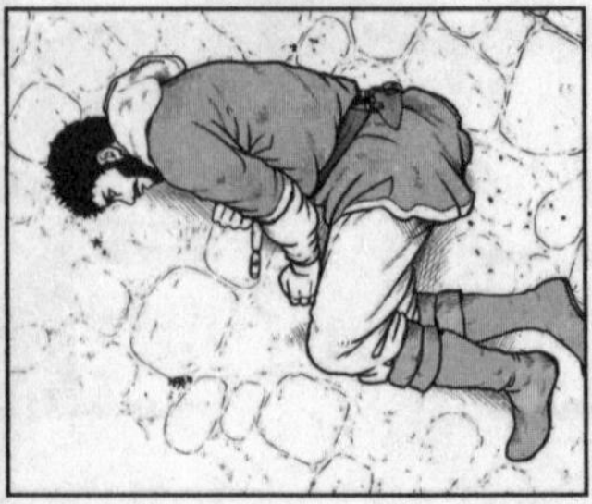

By the time Nozaki was learning karate in our world, poisons had already become irrelevant to martial arts. We had forgotten how commonplace poisons are, and the man now called Nomad might have paid the price for this complacency. Nomad was sent to a medieval society. This attack should have been expected, as it was around this time that the understanding of poisons flourished on Earth and poisons became commonplace enough to be sold in stores.

野人転生

KARATE SURVIVOR IN ANOTHER WORLD

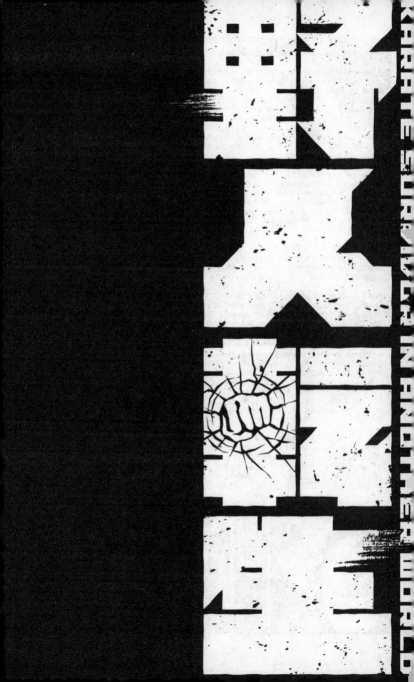

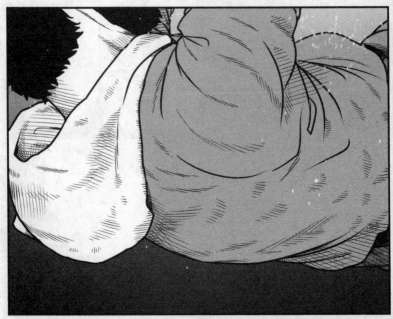

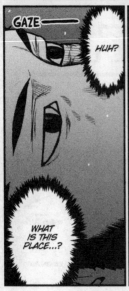

GAZE———

HUH?

WHAT IS THIS PLACE...?

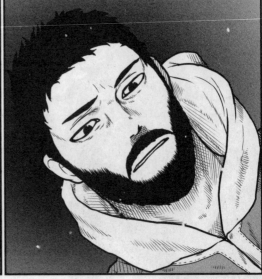

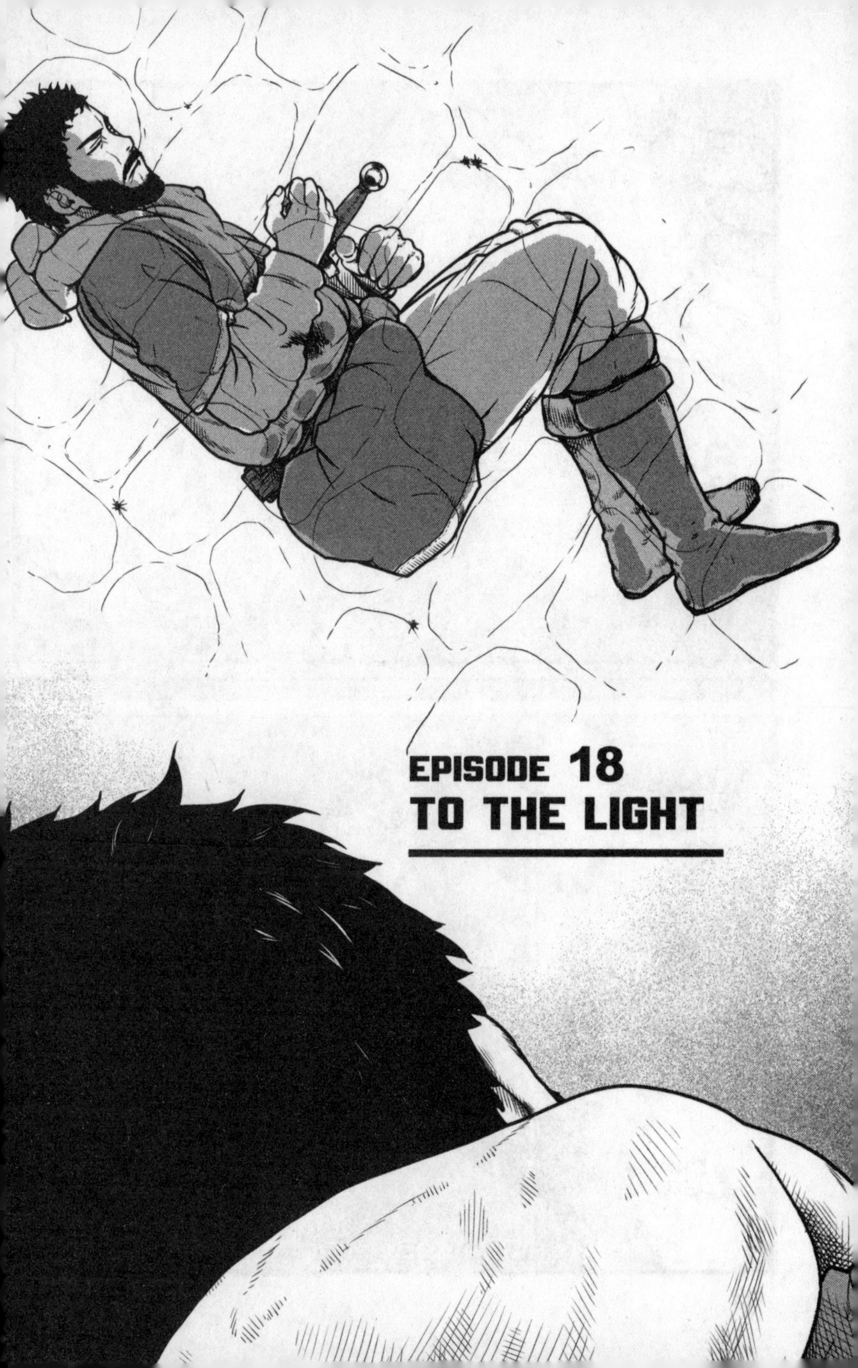
EPISODE 18
TO THE LIGHT

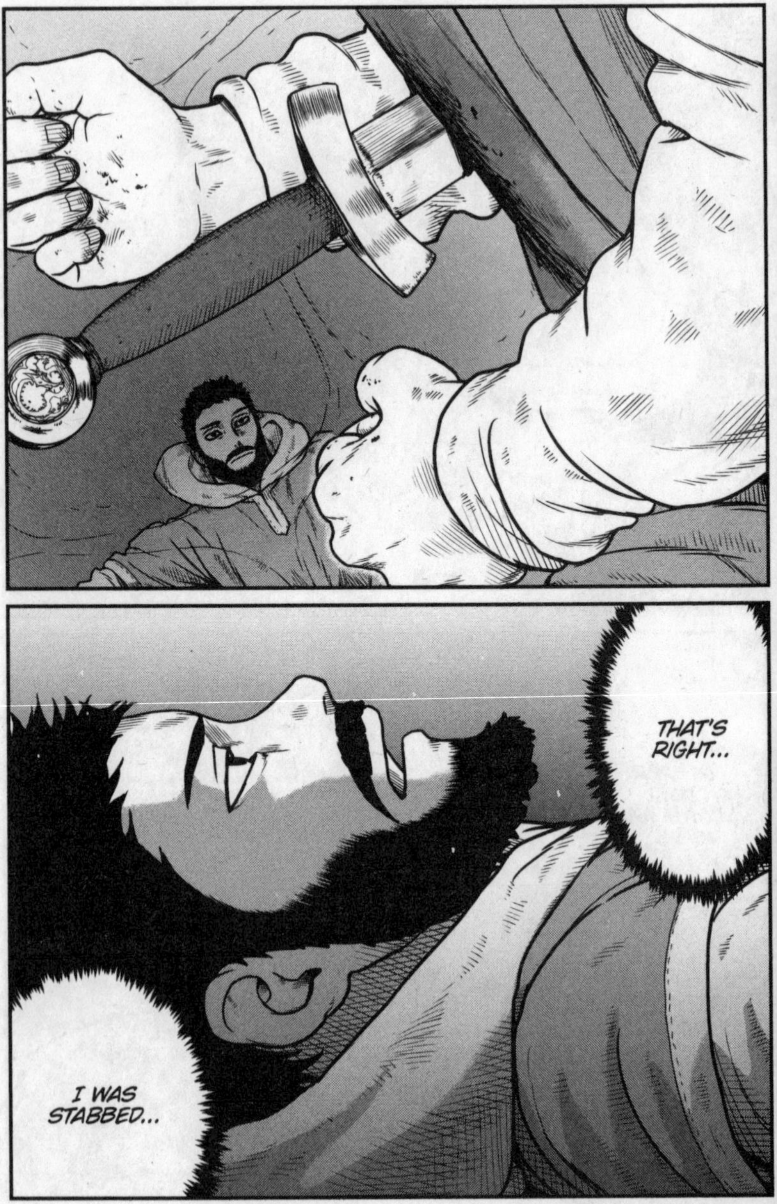
THAT'S RIGHT...
I WAS STABBED...

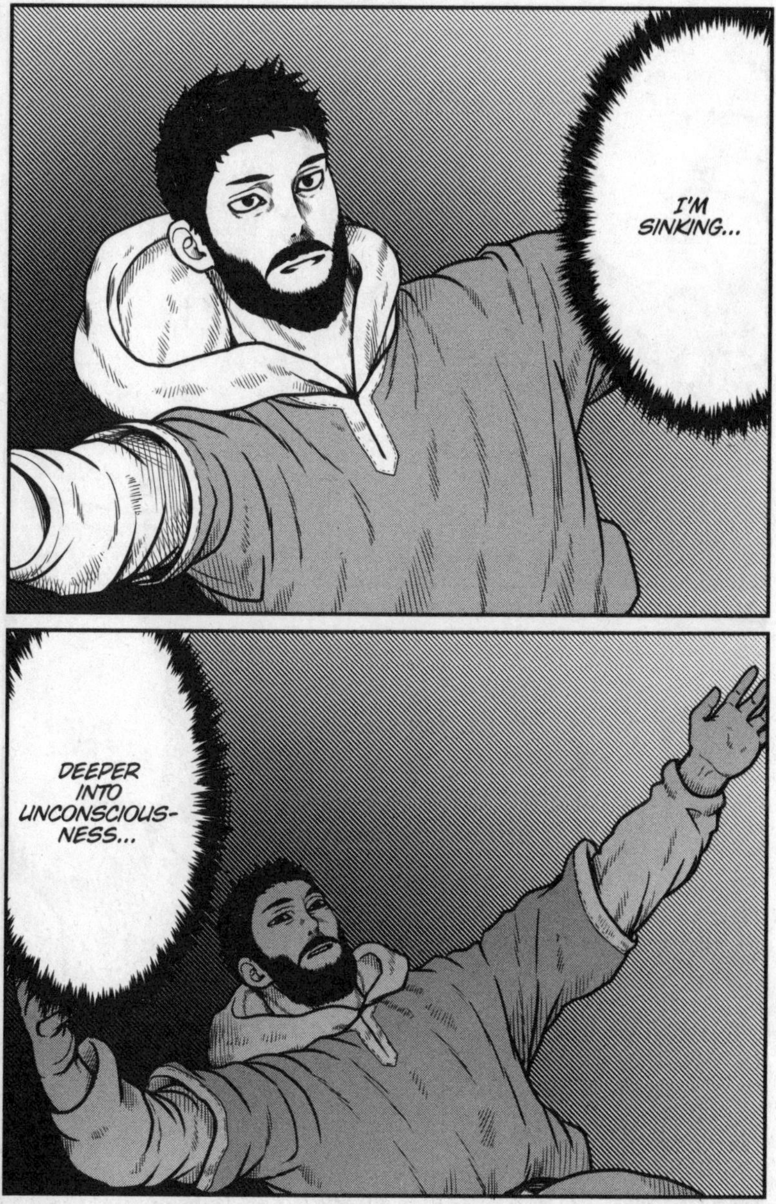
I'M SINKING...
DEEPER INTO UNCONSCIOUS-NESS...

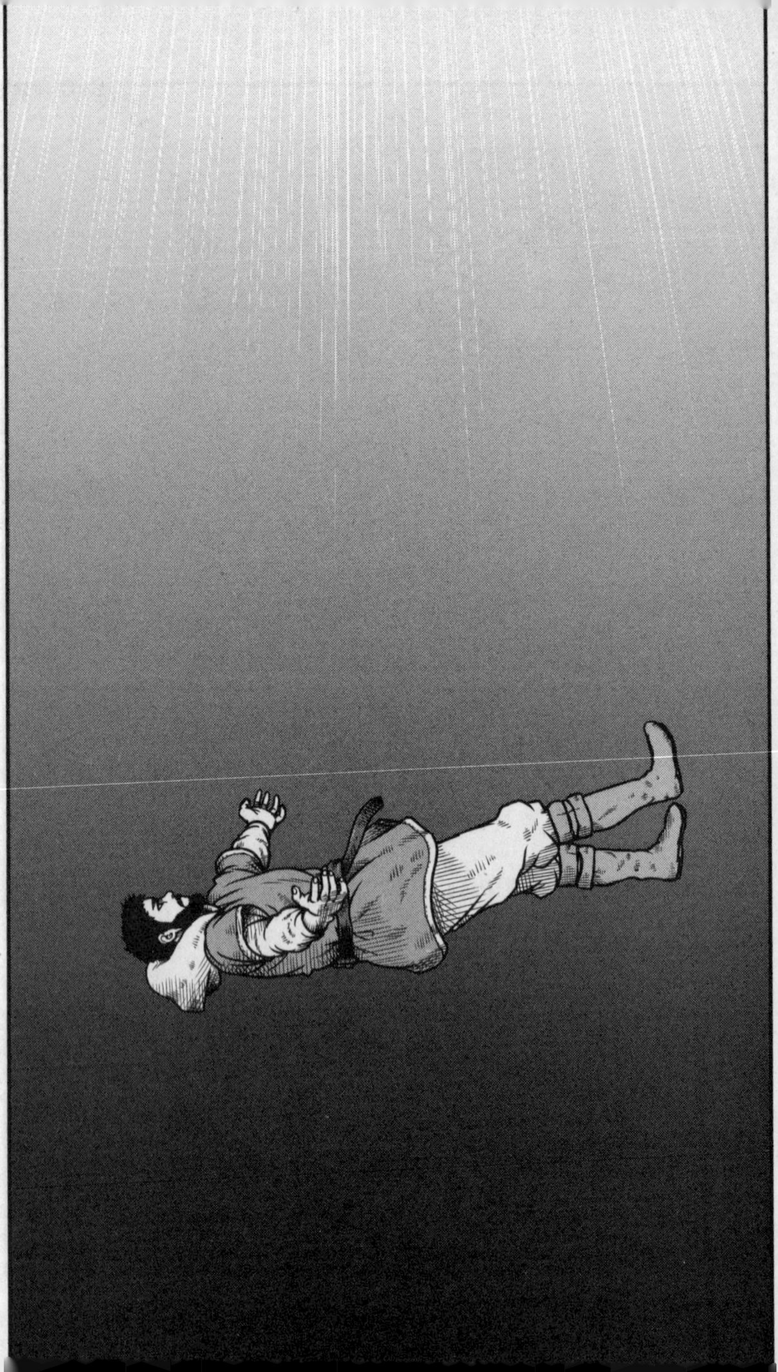

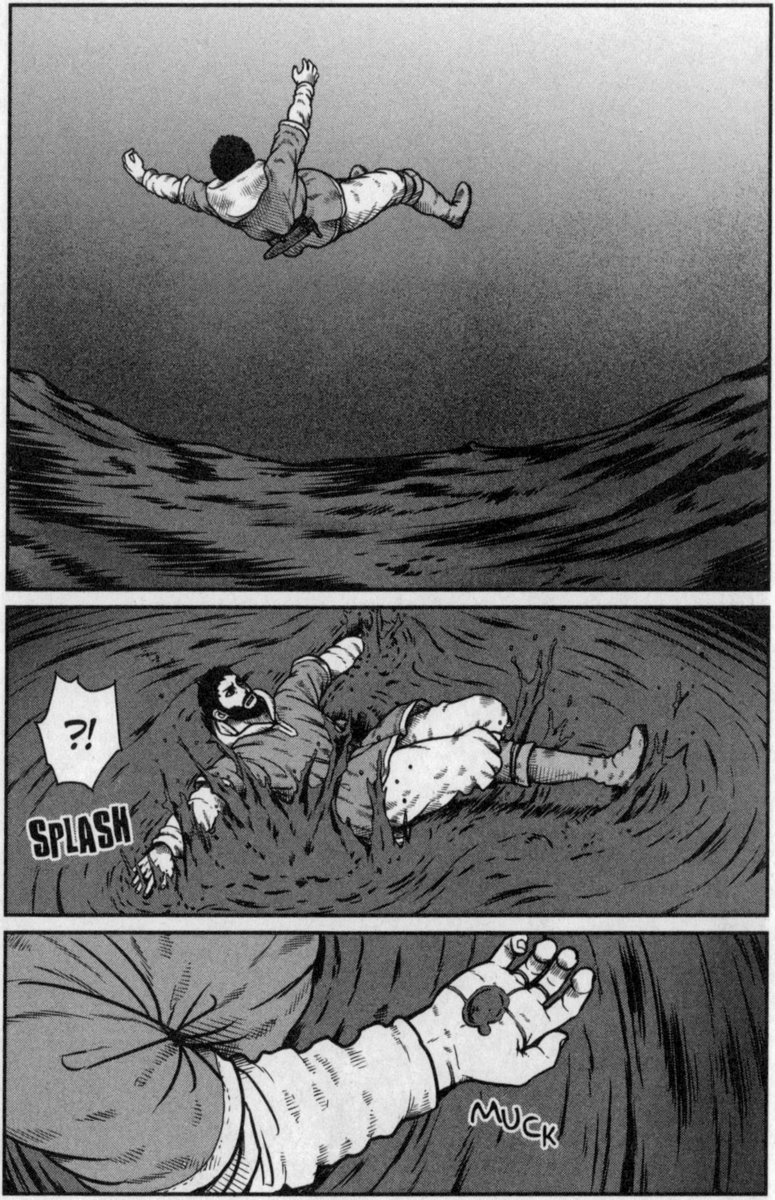
?!
SPLASH
MUCK

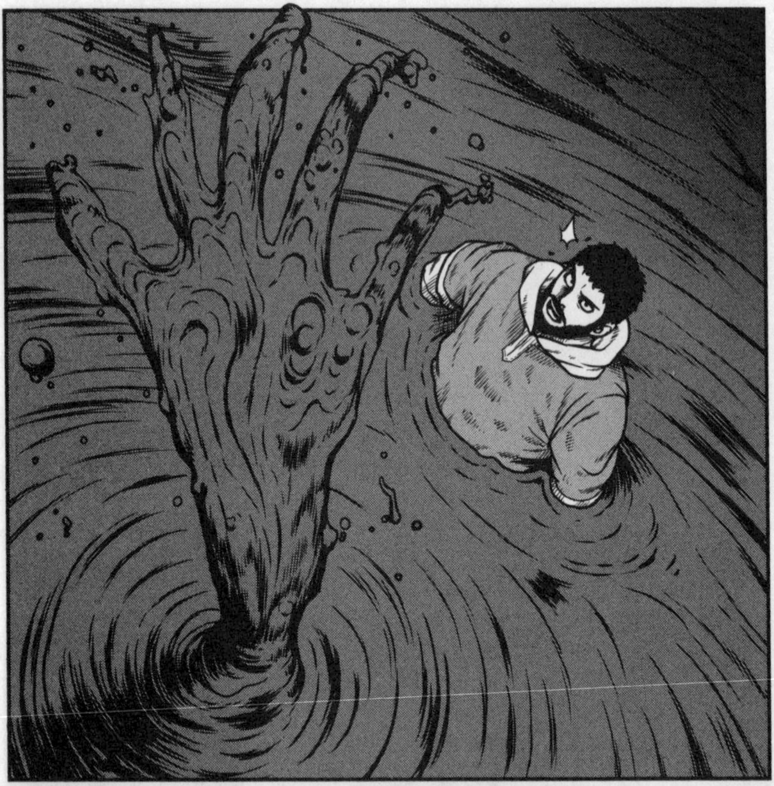

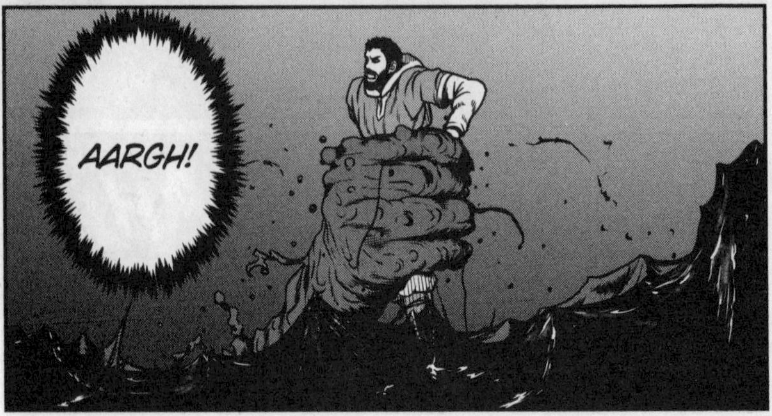

AARGH!

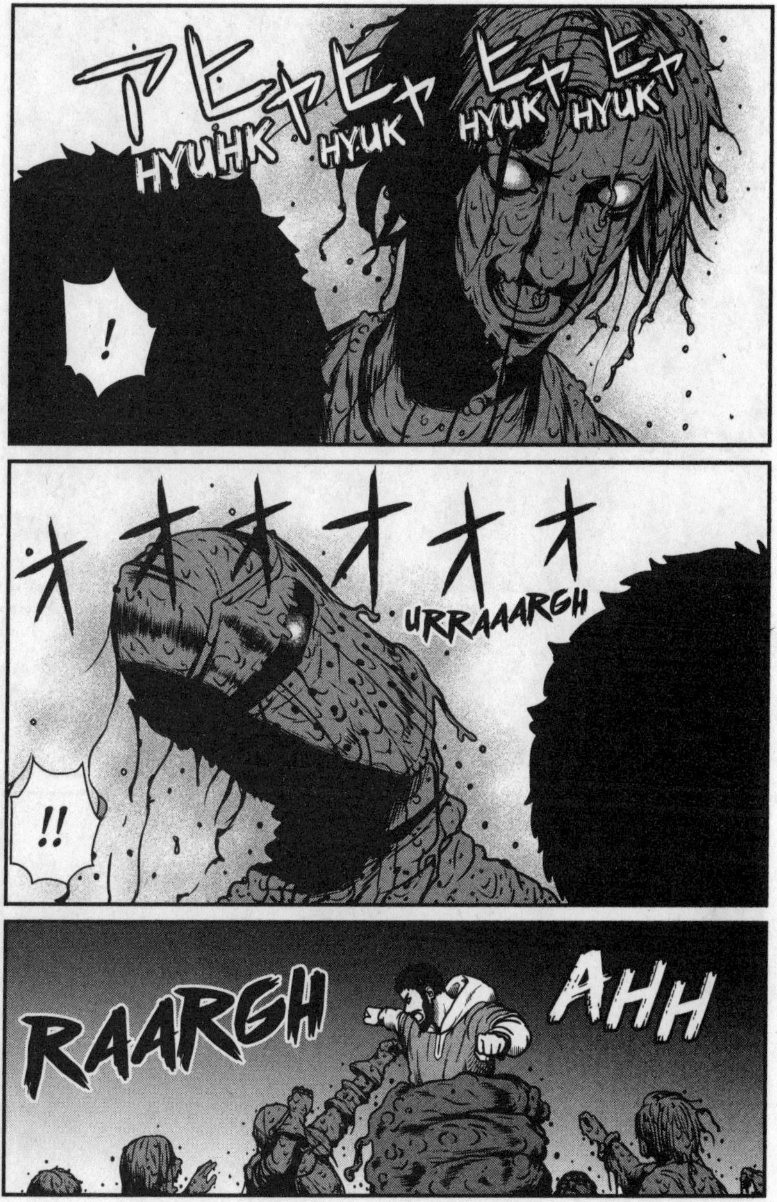
アヒャヒャヒャヒャ
HYUHK HYUK HYUK HYUK
!
オオオオオオ
URRAAARGH
!!
AHH
RAARGH

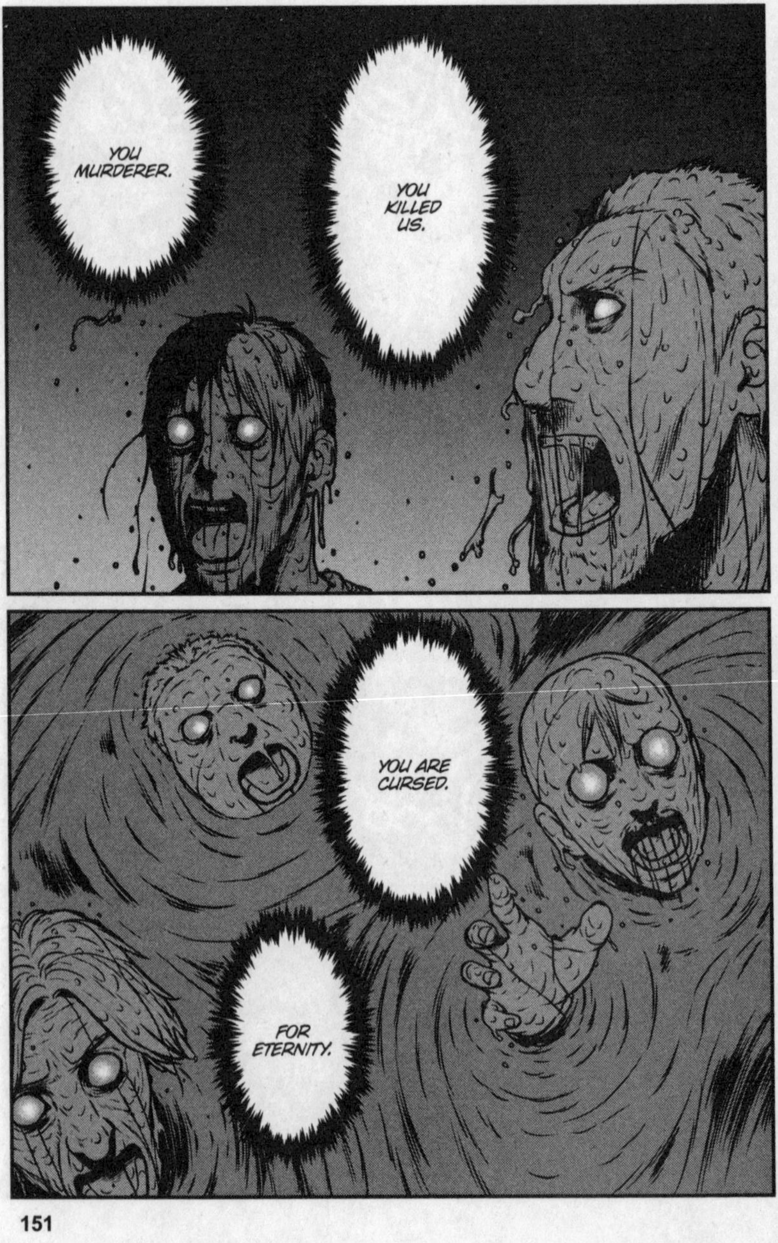
YOU KILLED US.
YOU MURDERER.
YOU ARE CURSED.
FOR ETERNITY.

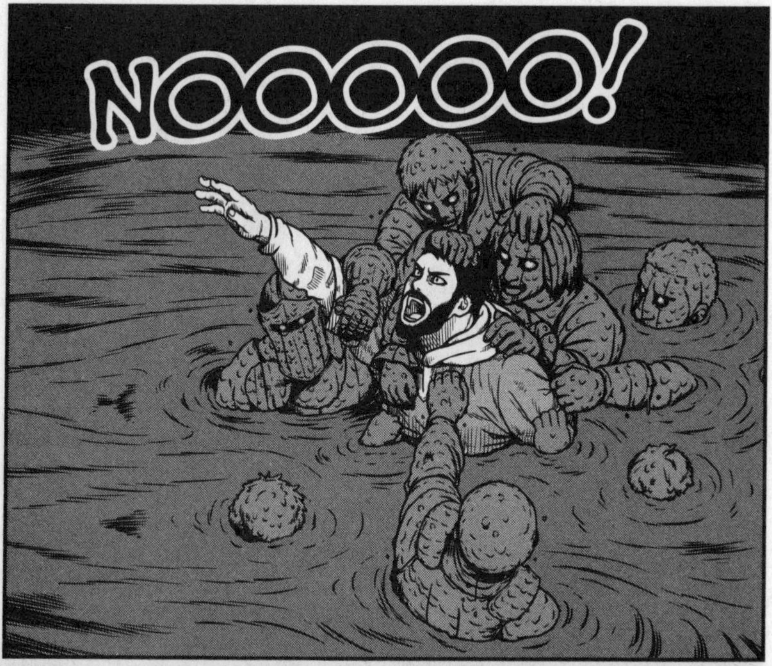
NOOOOO!

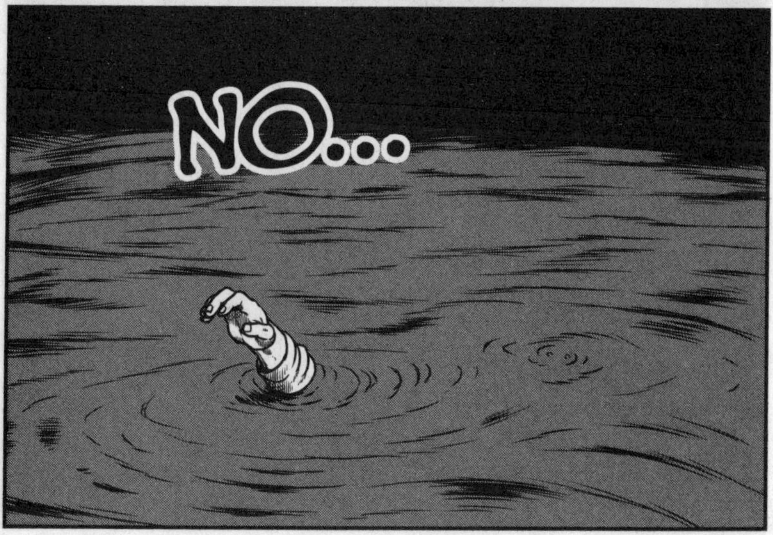
NO...

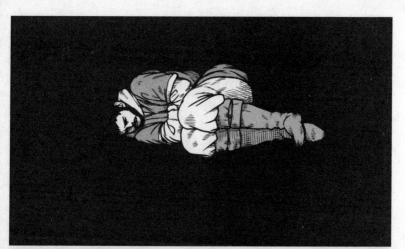

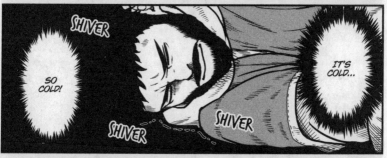

IT'S COLD...
SHIVER
SHIVER
SO COLD!
SHIVER
IS THIS HOW I DIE?
IS THIS A MURDERER'S FATE?

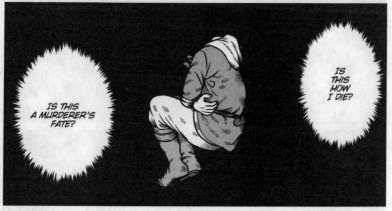

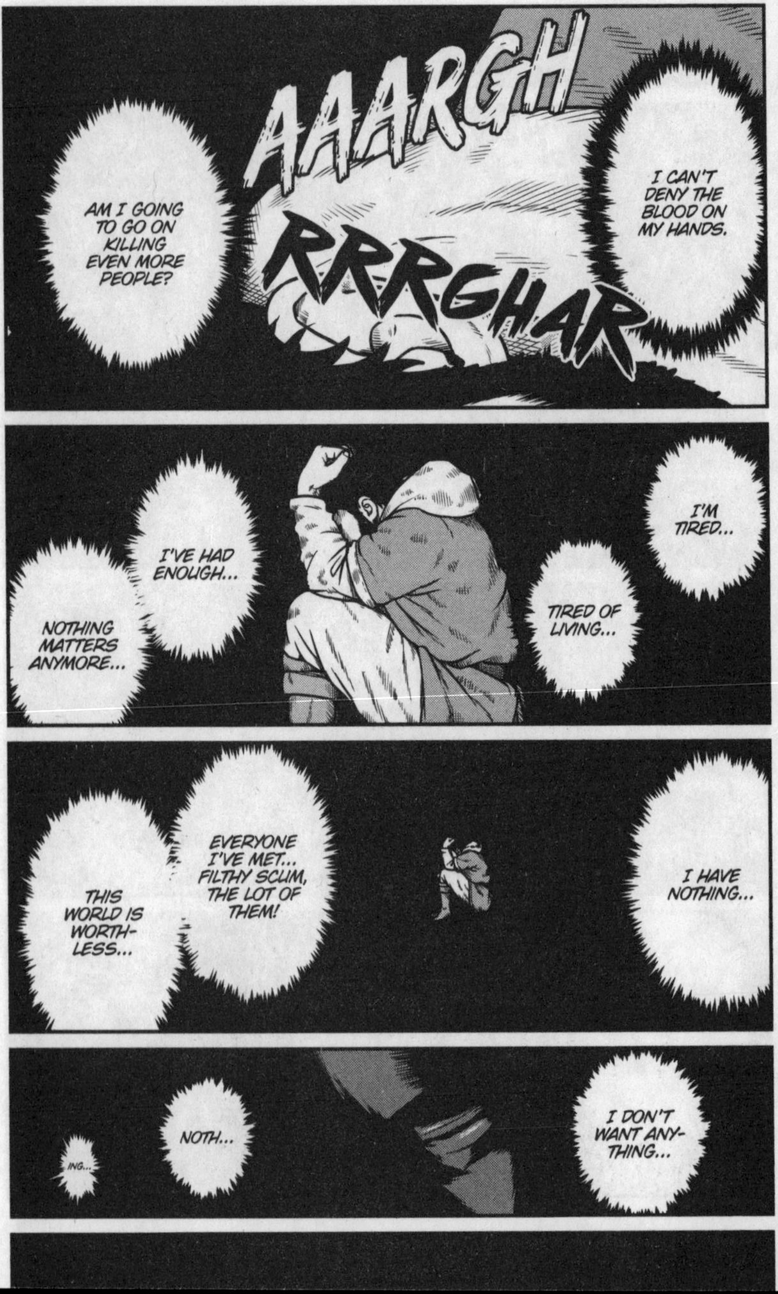
I CAN'T DENY THE BLOOD ON MY HANDS.
AAARGH
RRRGHAR
AM I GOING TO GO ON KILLING EVEN MORE PEOPLE?
I'M TIRED...
TIRED OF LIVING...
I'VE HAD ENOUGH...
NOTHING MATTERS ANYMORE...
I HAVE NOTHING...
EVERYONE I'VE MET... FILTHY SCUM, THE LOT OF THEM!
THIS WORLD IS WORTH-LESS...
I DON'T WANT ANY-THING...
NOTH...
ING...

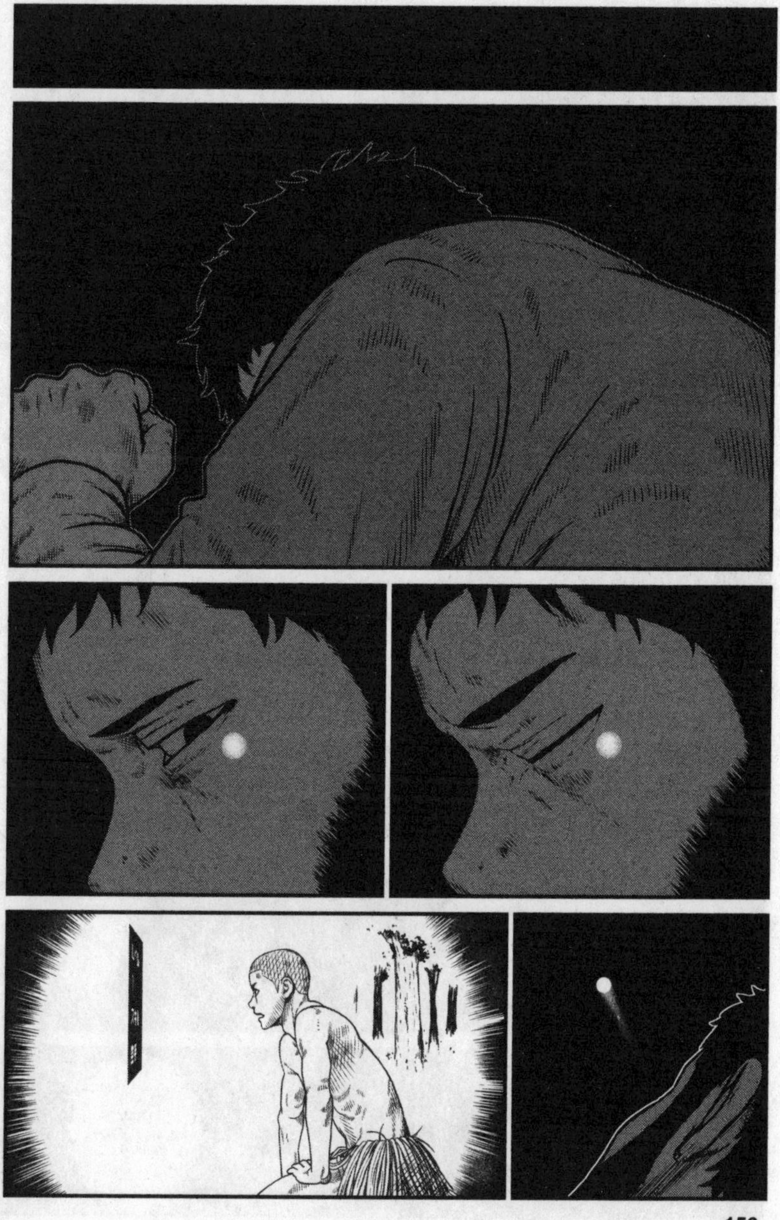

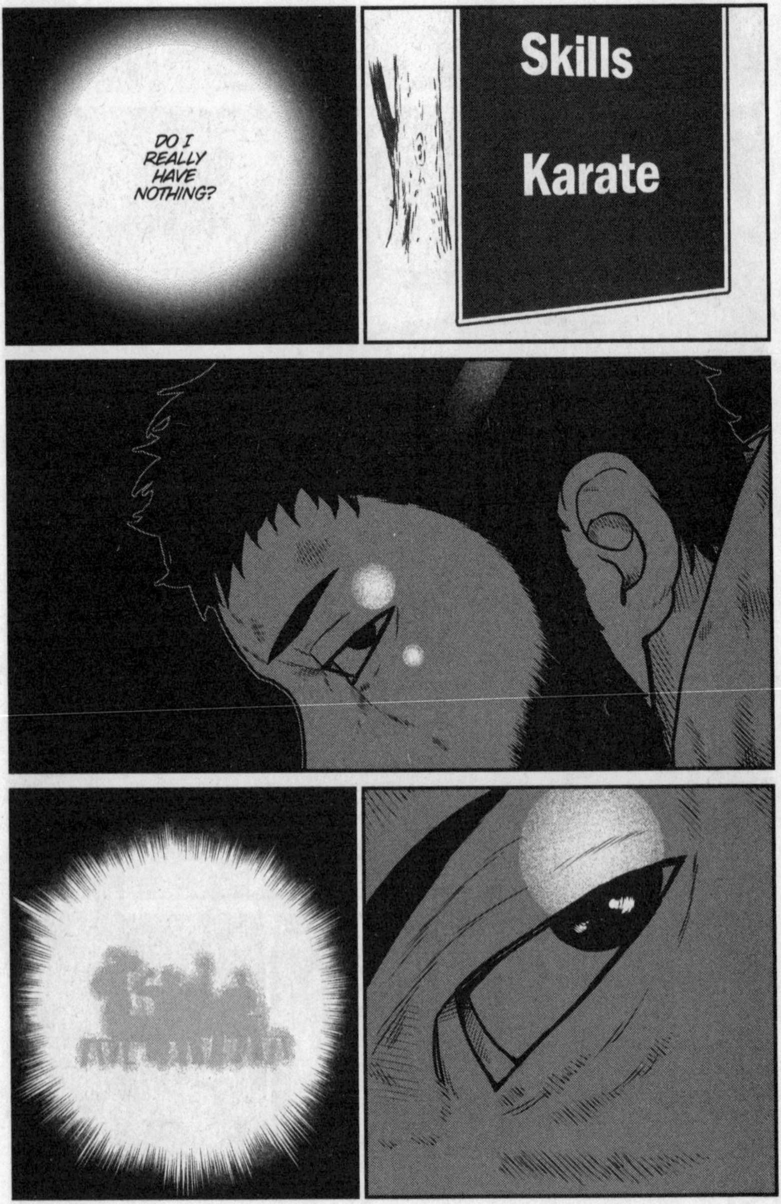
Skills
Karate
DO I REALLY HAVE NOTHING?

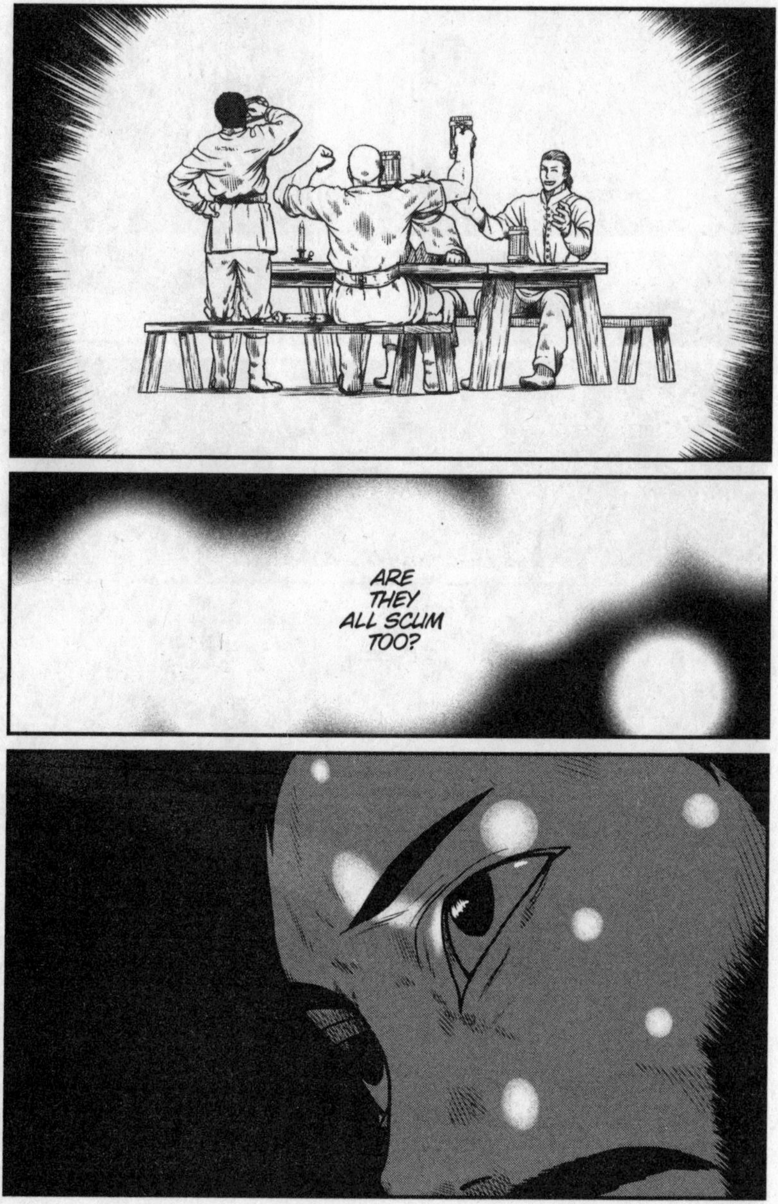
ARE THEY ALL SCUM TOO?

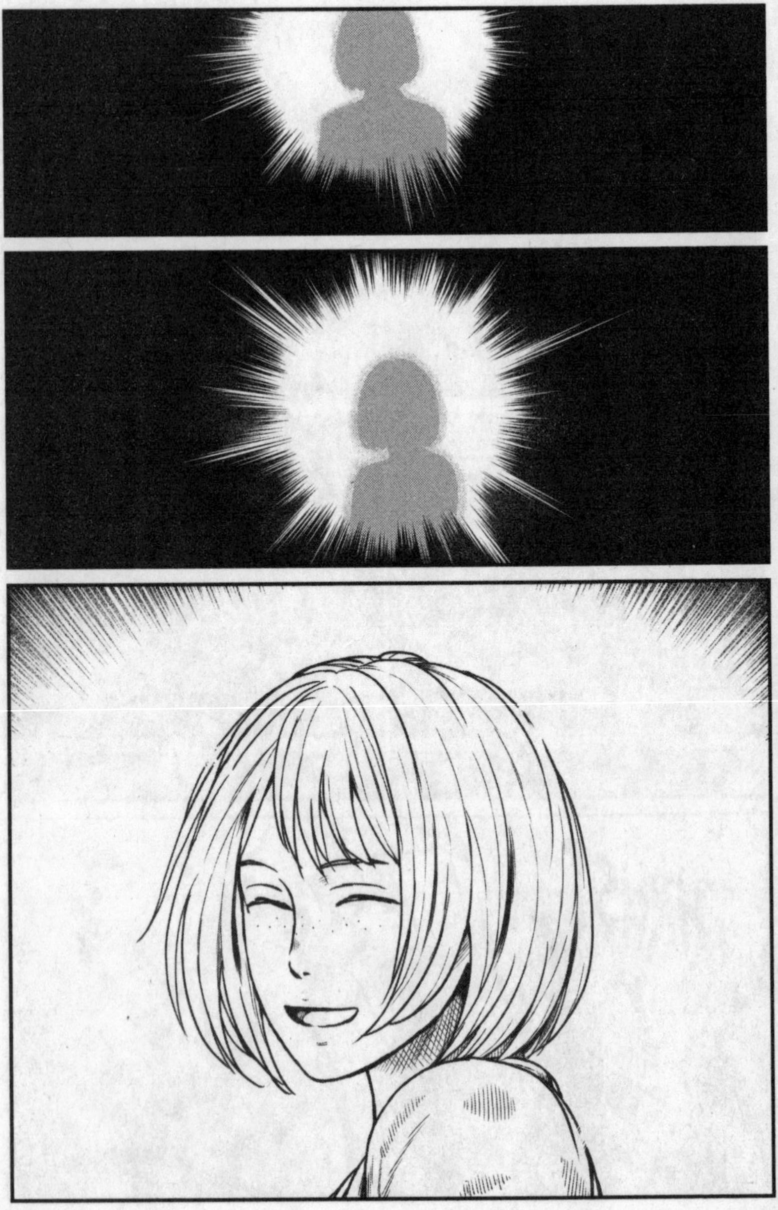

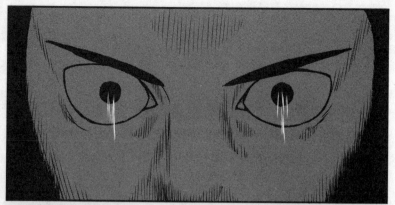

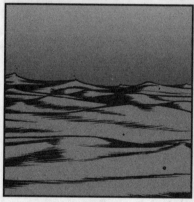
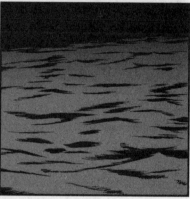

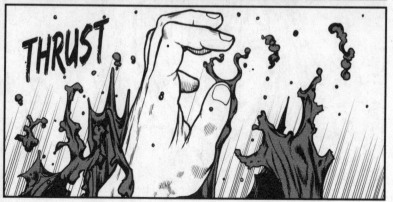

THRUST

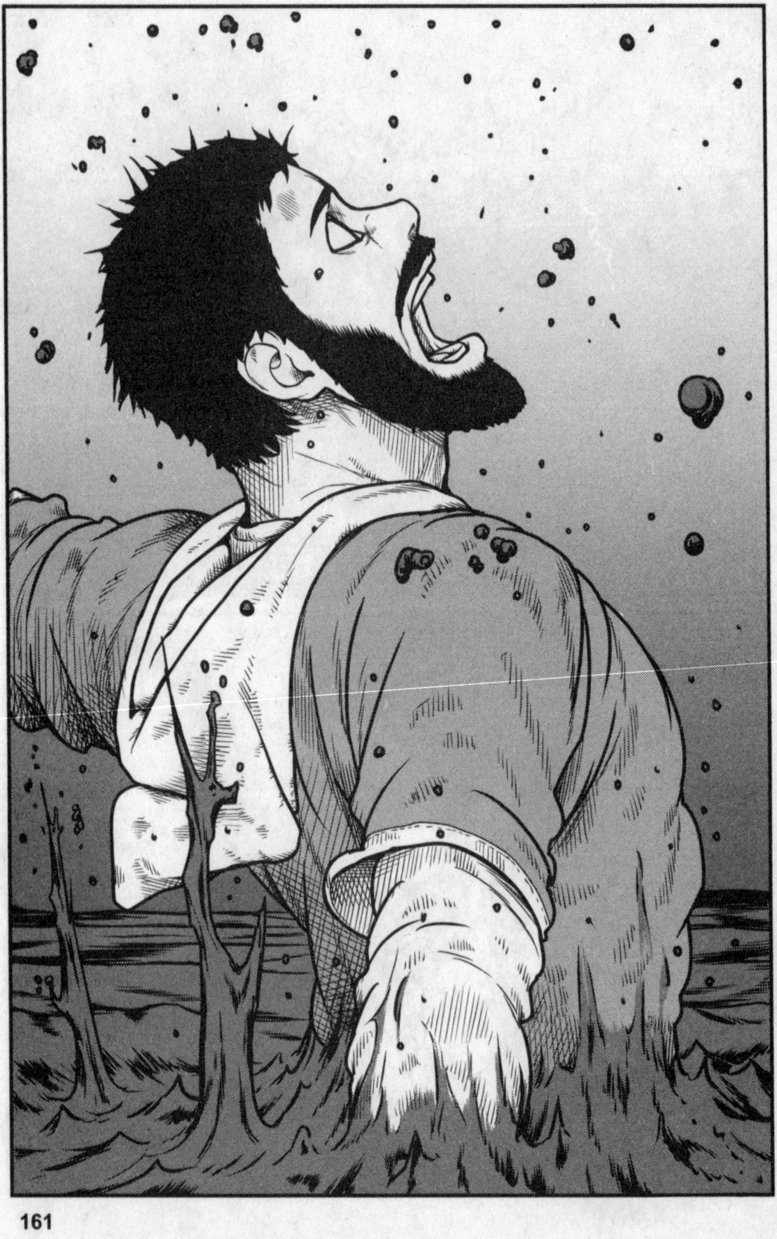

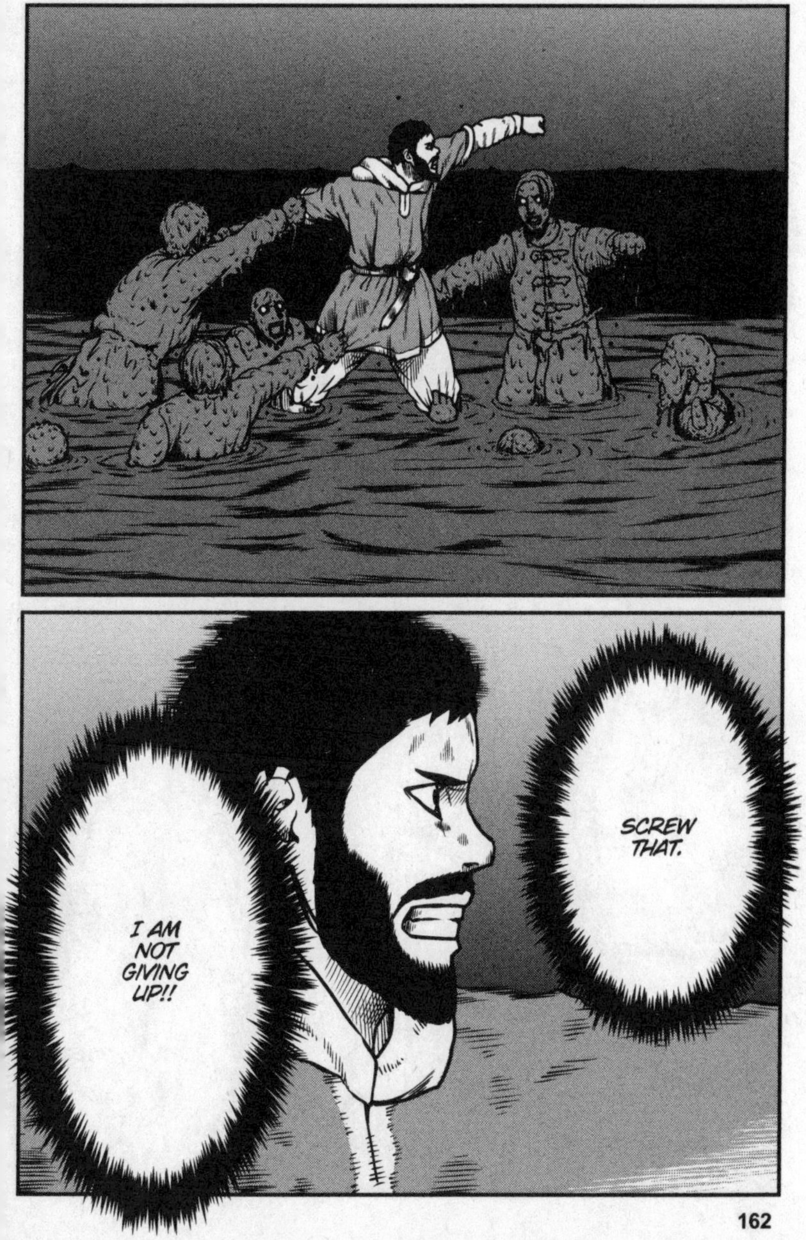
SCREW THAT.
I AM NOT GIVING UP!!

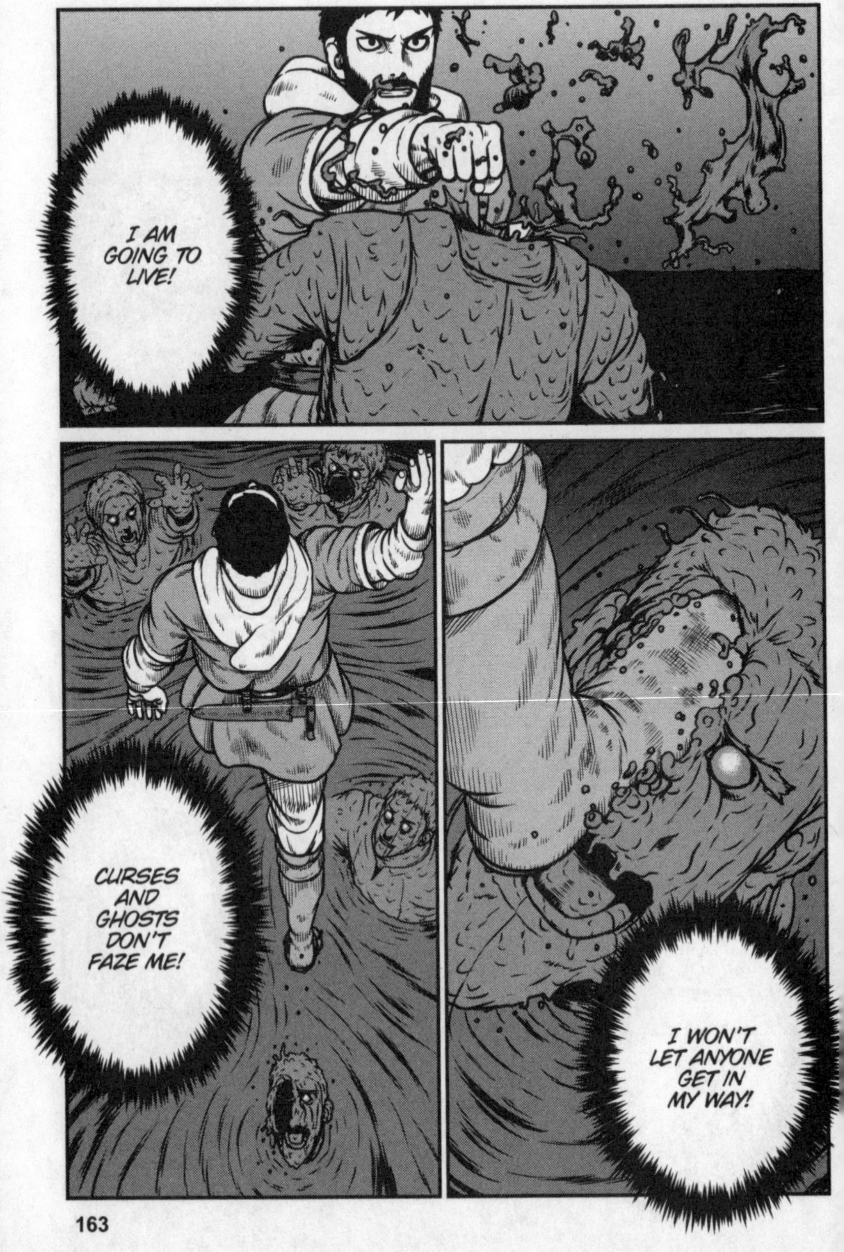
I AM GOING TO LIVE!
I WON'T LET ANYONE GET IN MY WAY!
CURSES AND GHOSTS DON'T FAZE ME!

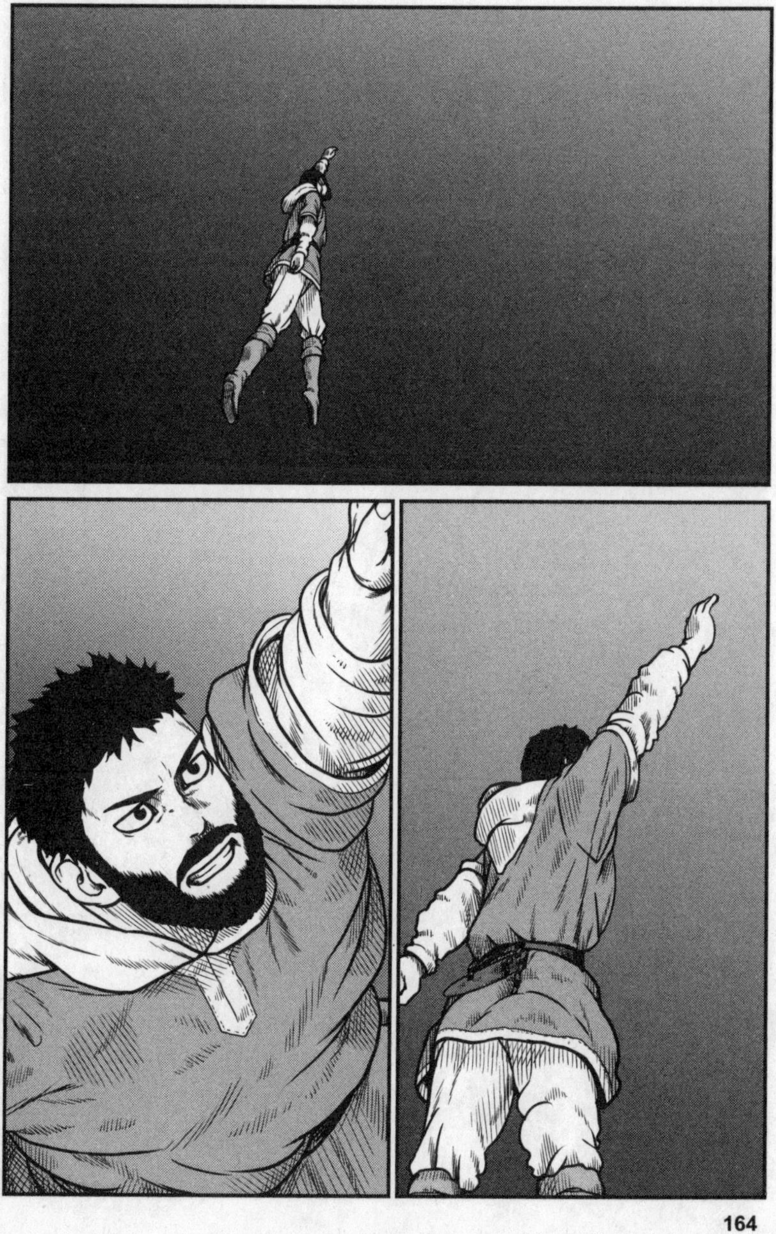

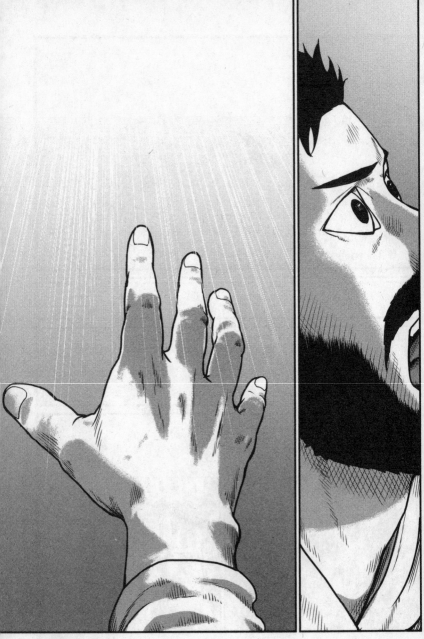

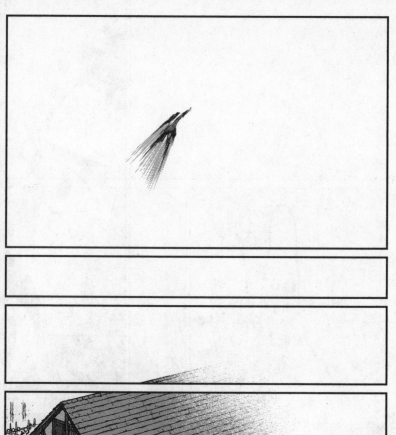

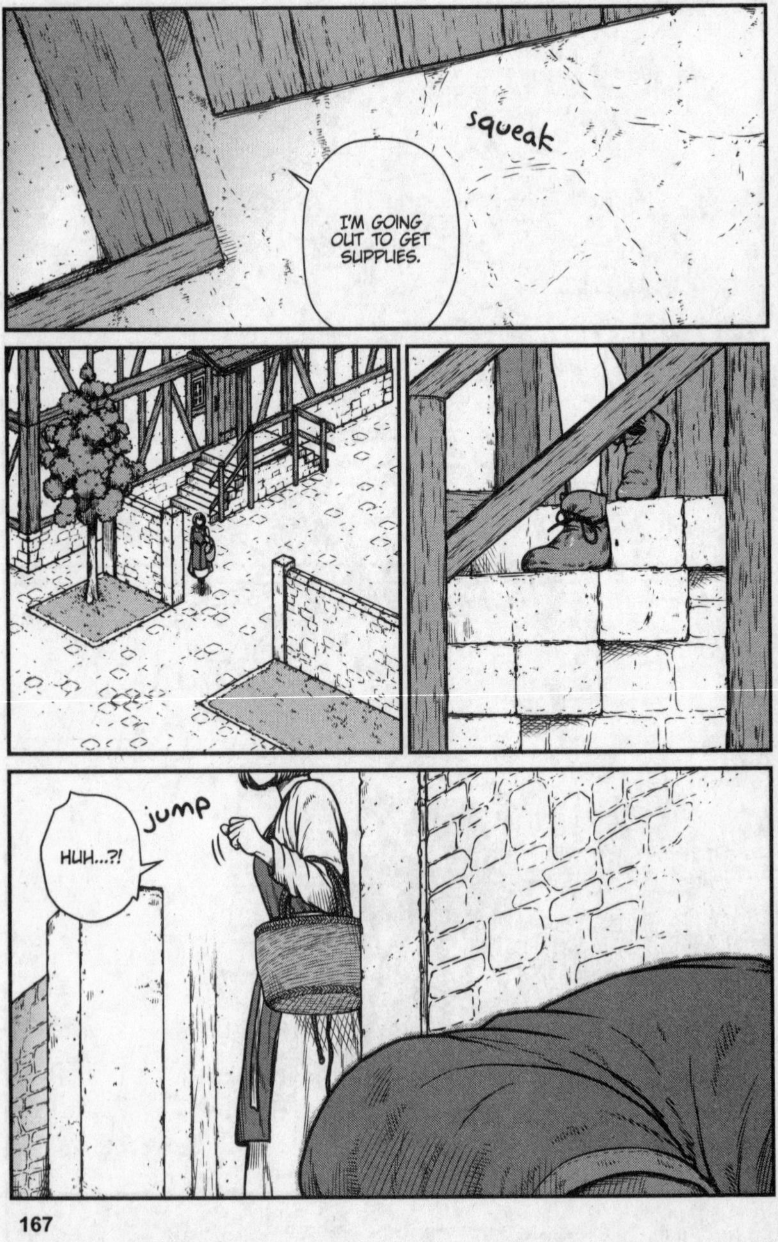
squeak
I'M GOING OUT TO GET SUPPLIES.
jump
HUH...?!

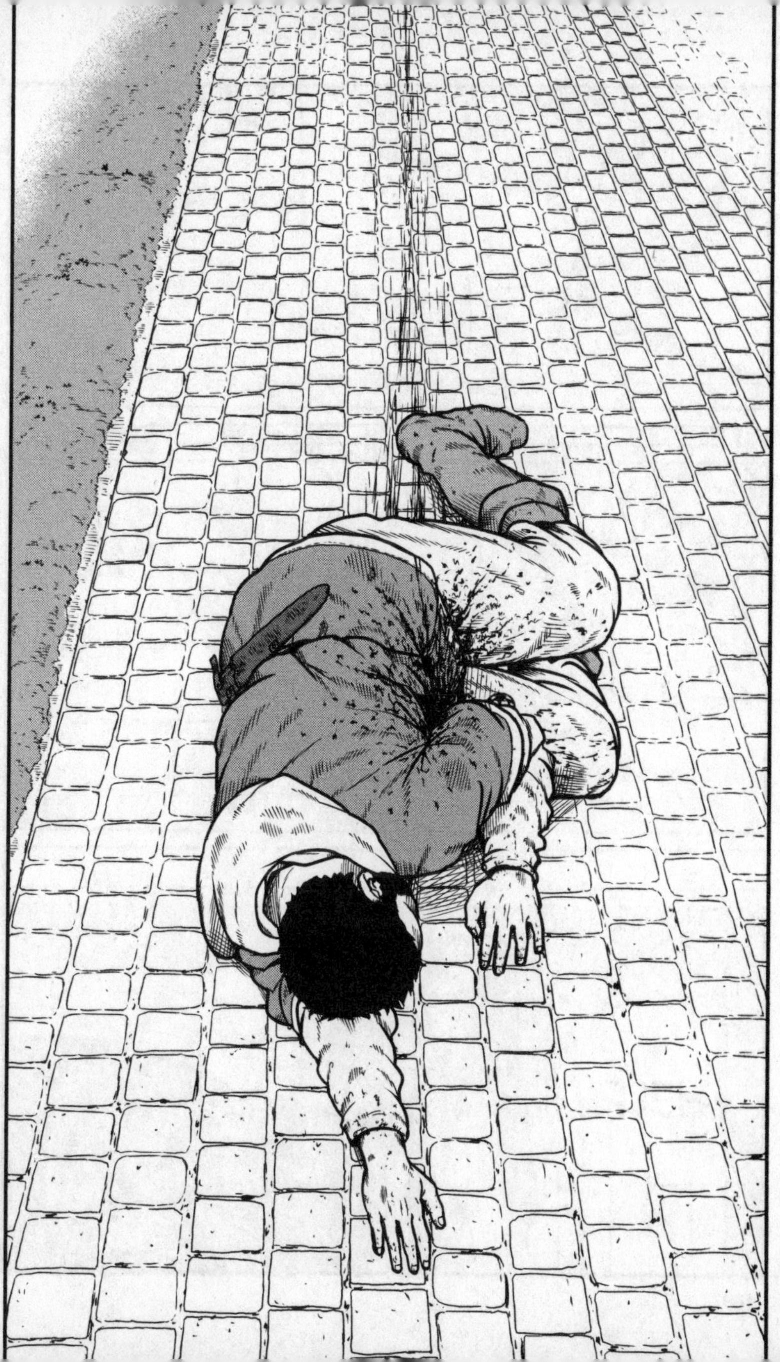

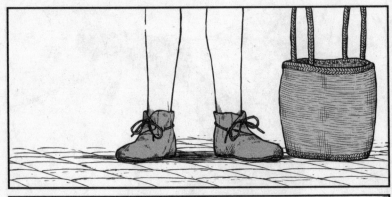

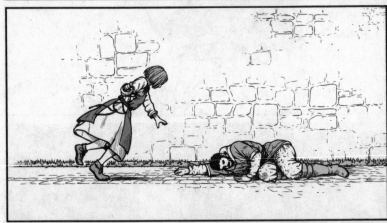

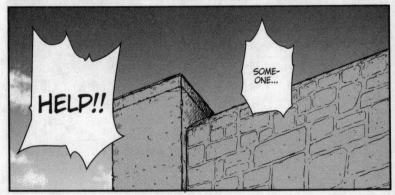

HELP!!

SOME-
ONE...

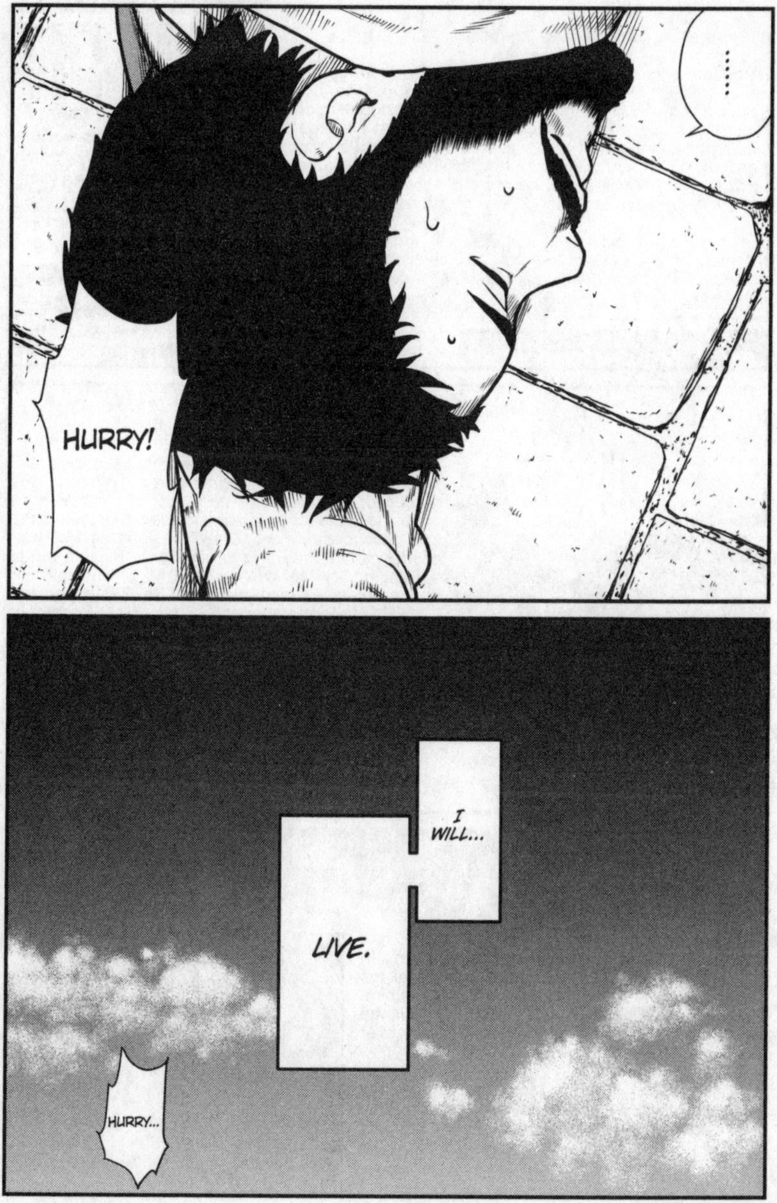
......
HURRY!
I WILL...
LIVE.
HURRY...

SPECIAL COLUMN BY AUTHOR, YAZIN

KARATE SURVIVOR IN ANOTHER WORLD

INTERMISSION SAVAGE RULES 18

TO HARM A HUMAN

Humans abhor harming other humans.

This might sound pretty ridiculous, when there are so many violent crimes and wars happening all around the world. However, no sane person would be able to randomly go up to someone and smack them in the face without a twinge of remorse. It is only when we are overcome with rage or mortal fear that we discard our concern for others and are able to harm another person. This is the result of our moral upbringing and the self-preserving instinct inscribed in our DNA.

Most people are also aware that violence and illegal activity are rarely worth the risks. There are a whole host of instinctive, intellectual, and practical factors that dissuade humans from violence.

HE KILLED HIM!
HE... HE KILLED REUBEN!!
I...
I ACTUALLY KILLED HIM...

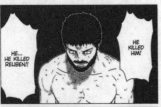

It is extremely rare to face a situation where all these deterrents are disregarded and a person resorts to violence. The psychologist Carl Jung said, "The healthy man does not torture others—generally it is the tortured who turn into torturers." Normal humans are naturally disinclined to hurt others.

The people who harm others fall into two categories: those with abnormally functioning psyches (the so-called psychopaths), or those that have been driven to violence by their situation. Excluding the rare psychopath, most people are a product of their environment. They might have had a poor moral upbringing, or they were raised in an environment where violence was normalized. The disenfranchised have little to lose and are freest to wield the power of violence.

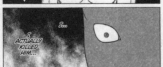

The former group can be found thriving in harsh conditions or within organized crime families. They are raised surrounded with violence and learn the most effective way to exploit it. They are born having no reservations about using violence as a means to an end.

The latter group includes people who have lost everything they ever had. With no options left for them and nowhere to go, the law no longer restrains them. The massacres these people commit is a testament to their destructive capacity.

So, what of the people of Nomad's new world? Everyone, especially adventurers, are thrown into an environment that is rife with violence. They are quick to use violence for their own gain, and have very little to lose. An adventurer's life is fast and furious, thus they have very different values to the modern person.

In order to adapt to his new environment, Nomad also had to lower his threshold for engaging in violence. However, the numerous deaths at his hands had been subconsciously weighing on him. The nightmare he saw represents the guilt he buried deep in himself, and it very nearly took over him at his weakest moment.

What saved him were the friendships and bonds he formed in this new world. It was people who tore him down, but people who built him back up.

YOU ARE CURSED.
FOR ETERNITY.

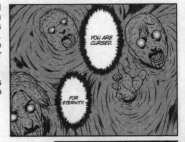

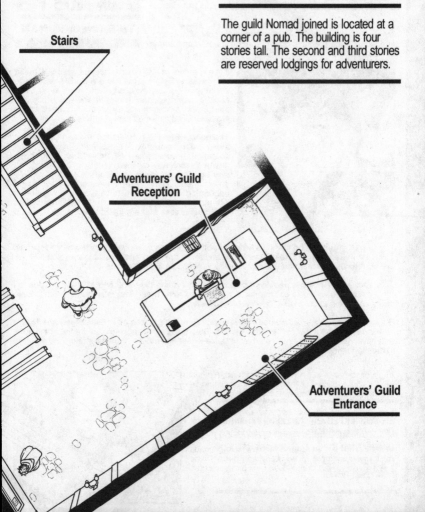

Adventurers' Guild

The guild Nomad joined is located at a corner of a pub. The building is four stories tall. The second and third stories are reserved lodgings for adventurers.

Stairs

Adventurers' Guild Reception

Adventurers' Guild Entrance

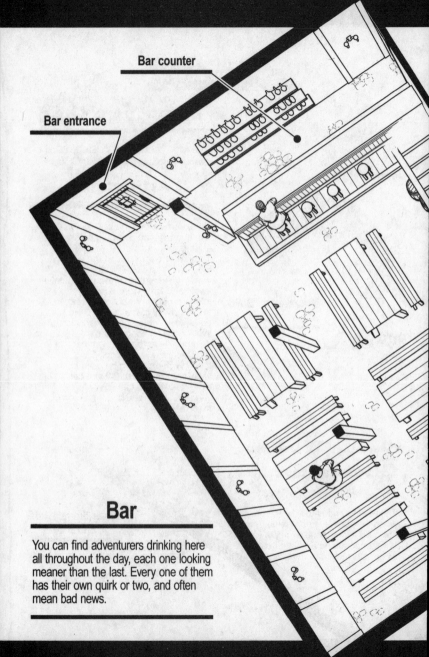

Bar counter

Bar entrance

Bar

You can find adventurers drinking here all throughout the day, each one looking meaner than the last. Every one of them has their own quirk or two, and often mean bad news.

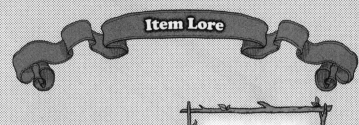

Item Lore

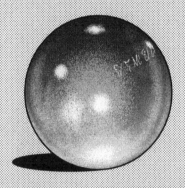

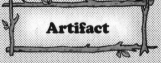

Artifact

An extremely rare magical tool that can quantify and display a person's abilities.

They were discovered in the labyrinthine city of Malibel several hundred years ago. Previously, only levels and skills were known to inform a person's abilities. However, the discovery of the five parameters—strength, constitution, intelligence, charisma, and dexterity—was a revelation that affected the whole world.

It is only permitted to be used by a very few, and it is said that it can even reveal skills that are only vaguely recognized by the person themselves.

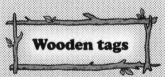

Wooden tags

These are handed to adventurers when they take a commission from the guild. Having one exempts you from a queue and an entry tax when returning back into the city.

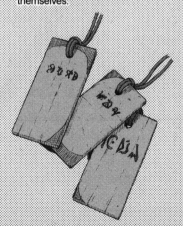

Magicite

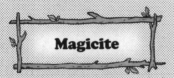

A resource used as a catalyst for alchemy and to fuel enchanted equipment.
These are formed within long-lived monsters, and often in high-level monsters, such as the Blackwolf Nomad defeated.
They are hard to obtain and extremely precious. They also form quickly in areas of high mana concentration, such as dungeons, but these tend to be of lower quality and less valuable.

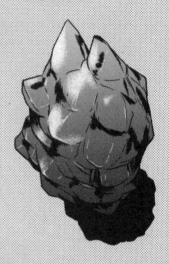

Nahl Plant

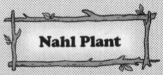

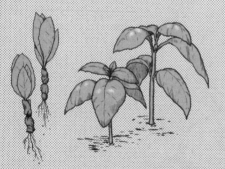

An ingredient for the healing salve. Can be found growing near bodies of water.
They are harvested with their roots intact, and must be stored with their roots wrapped in a moist cloth to avoid damaging them.

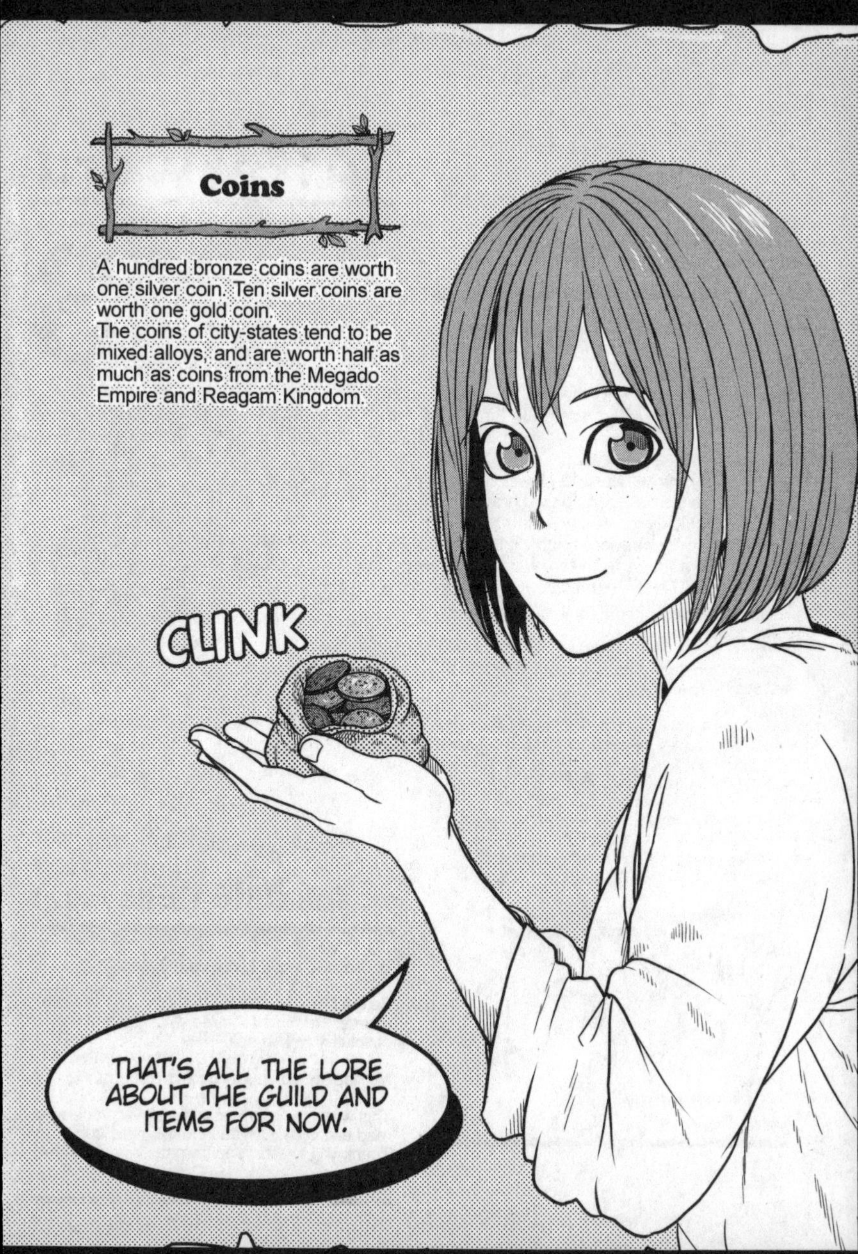
Coins
A hundred bronze coins are worth one silver coin. Ten silver coins are worth one gold coin.
The coins of city-states tend to be mixed alloys, and are worth half as much as coins from the Megado Empire and Reagam Kingdom.
CLINK
THAT'S ALL THE LORE ABOUT THE GUILD AND ITEMS FOR NOW.

Afterword

Karate Survivor in Another World

3

Story Writer
Yazin

Hello. I'm the writer of the story, Yazin.

Once again, despite the current turbulent situation, we managed to release a third volume. Thank you very much to everyone who supported us.

The story this time is focused on Nozaki's growth. He learns how skills work and rediscovers the joy of learning and growing.

But he soon finds himself attractive prey for rogues... Will he be able to survive against the greed and malice of men?

Hopefully, we will meet again in the afterword of the next volume.

Thank you to: My editor, T-sama; our artist, Kobayashi-sensei.

To everyone who read the web novel, all my writer friends who helped me, the editing team at the publisher who checked over the work, and the designer who perfected the look of this book. To the people involved in proofreading, shipping, marketing, and selling the book.

Thank you all so much.

And especially you, the reader holding this book right now. My most sincere gratitude to you all.

Manga Artist
Takahito Kobayashi

Hooray! Booyah!! It's volume three!!!

Before I started on this it was my goal to have a series continue for three volumes, so I am absolutely overjoyed!

My hope is to keep this going.

This was only made possible by everyone who read and was involved in making this book. Thank you to everyone from the bottom of my heart.

SEVEN SEAS ENTERTAINMENT PRESENTS

KARATE FIGHTER IN ANOTHER WORLD

Vol. 3

story by YAZIN

TRANSLATION
M. Fulcrum

LETTERING
Alexandra Gunawan

COVER DESIGN
Nicky Lim

LOGO DESIGN
George Panella

PROOFREADER
Kurestin Armada

COPY EDITOR
B. Lillian Martin

EDITOR
Nick Mamatas

PREPRESS TECHNICIAN
Melanie Ujimori

PRINT MANAGER
Rhiannon Rasmussen-Silverstein

PRODUCTION ASSOCIATE
Christa Miesner

PRODUCTION MANAGER
Lissa Pattillo

EDITOR-IN-CHIEF
Julie Davis

ASSOCIATE PUBLISHER
Adam Arnold

PUBLISHER
Jason DeAngelis

YAZIN TENSEI vol.3
©Yazin/Kobayashi Takahito 2021
First published in Japan in 2021 by KADOKAWA CORPORATION, Tokyo.
English translation rights arranged with KADOKAWA CORPORATION, Tokyo.

Seven Seas press and purchase enquiries can be sent to Marketing Manager Lianne Sentar at press@gomanga.com. Information regarding the distribution and purchase of digital editions is available from Digital Manager CK Russell at digital@gomanga.com.

Seven Seas and the Seven Seas logo are trademarks of Seven Seas Entertainment. All rights reserved.

ISBN: 978-1-63858-159-8
Printed in Canada
First Printing: March 2022
10 9 8 7 6 5 4 3 2 1

READING DIRECTIONS

This book reads from *right to left*, Japanese style. If this is your first time reading manga, you start reading from the top right panel on each page and take it from there. If you get lost, just follow the numbered diagram here. It may seem backwards at first, but you'll get the hang of it! Have fun!!

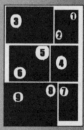

Follow us online: www.SevenSeasEntertainment.com